# LIFE'S A CATASTROPHE

# LIFE'S A CATASTROPHE

Kirstie Pelling

embla books

First published in Great Britain in 2022 by

Bonnier Books UK Limited
4th Floor, Victoria House, Bloomsbury Square, London, WC1B 4DA
Owned by Bonnier Books
Sveavägen 56, Stockholm, Sweden



A CIP catalogue record for this book is available from the British Library.

eBook ISBN: 9781471411977

This book is typeset using Atomik ePublisher

Embla Books is an imprint of Bonnier Books UK
www.bonnierbooks.co.uk

For Marilyn Dugdale (Edwards); cat lover, author and friend, who believed cats make us better humans.

# Chapter 1

The London branch of Glimmer gobbles up the clouds with its steel and glass frame. The show-stopping feature is the revolving door. Standing on the pavement opposite, I watch a stream of people gliding through it; all more groomed than my high maintenance cats. The Glimmer talent factory is even more extra than I imagined, and I poke my tongue out to see if I can catch stardust. When nothing drops, I pop in a tab of chewing gum. Wouldn't do to breathe last night's garlic over one of the UK's finest digital talent managers, right?

Glancing down at my phone before I plunge in and flirt with the traffic, I'm reassured by the screenshot of my besties. MollyCat is as friendly as ever, while MillyCat's icy stare could shatter a lens. I tug at a hair bobble while I walk; forcing my frizz into tight plaits this morning gave me a headache, while my legs itch in my rainbow tights. The Glimmer strapline that appears at the end of every email laces the panoramic windows fronting the building; 'Shooting Stars into Infinity'. Deciding to shoot myself into reception, I run slap bang into one of the worker bees revolving outwards.

'Unremarkable Instagrammer mowed down in hipster rush hour' – that'll be the headline in tonight's snoozepapers if I continue like this. I take a deep breath, counsel myself to slow down, and allow the door to move me glacially forward into a foyer staffed by women born to meet and greet.

The first receptionist captures my face on a screen while requesting my name and job title.

'Aly Meadows. Catfluencer.' Whoops – almost said care worker.

She frowns. 'I'm sorry, I didn't catch that.'

'Er . . . Instagrammer?'

'Perfect.'

Flipping the screen around, she shows me a picture where there's so much nostril I'm tempted to examine it for nose hair. Before I can ask for a retake, a second woman prints the image and pops it into a plastic case, reminding me to hand back the wallet and ribbon afterwards.

'So, I don't get to keep the trophy? You clearly don't know the street value of a collector's lanyard.' The joke doesn't land; she's already moved on. I sidestep to the next receptionist, twisting the gold ribbon around my fingers until it hurts. She tells me to report to the fourth floor five minutes before my meeting, and did I read about lift protocol in the email sent to all visitors? I assure her I did, although I'm pretty sure I didn't.

As I prepare to walk away, she taps at her tech with Samurai swords for nails. 'I see Patricia asked you send a saliva swab in advance of your meeting. If you'd like to pop across to the smart-bar over there, you can pick up your results while enjoying a treat on us.' She points across the foyer to a white counter, staffed by a man with broad shoulders who is busy polishing a mahoosive coffee machine. When he turns around, I notice his T-shirt is emblazoned with the words 'Be YOU'.

Well, I can't think of a more appropriate way of being me than accepting a free brew.

Slipping the lanyard around my neck, I wonder about changing the job title back to catfluencer. It's a lame name I know, but I'm happy to be part of social media's breakout tribe. I reckon people turned to us for comfort when hygge stopped wowing everyone with Scandi cool. According to the email I received from Glimmer agent Patricia, catfluencers are in huge demand from brands right now, although I'll believe that when I see it, as the only demands I've received lately have been from my landlord. My popcorn rent (marginally bigger than peppercorn) might be a steal for west of West London, but it's still crippling on my carer's wage, and there are rumours amongst the Oddities that it's about to rise. I suppose we couldn't expect to be subsidised forever, especially as some of our artists' collective are dabbling in dubious crafts – Karen's yak knit kit is the prime offender.

My throat is sore from running through my elevator pitch last night but I'm nervous about glitching in the meeting, especially now the stakes are gilded in gold. I whisper it to myself as I wait for the barista to serve a man in front of me. 'Catfluencers are on the up in a crowded and competitive Instaverse. I believe I am more successful than others as I also harness current affairs in a satirical way. My business is hard to copy. It isn't easy making a sleeve in a miniature cowboy or pirate outfit, squishing a paw into it, coaxing a cat into a light box, grabbing a decent image, uploading it with an inspirational quote and capturing public attention. But I do it. And I love it. And others love it too.'

I don't always love it though; Milly is basically a teenager with claws.

The man ahead of me takes his coffee and moves to one side, swiping at his smartwatch. He clearly didn't buy the gadget or his suit from a charity shop.

'The lady at reception said to claim a treat before my meeting. I assume it's a coffee and not hard cash.' I smile, attempting to get some bants going with the barista, perhaps the only guy in the building on my pay grade. 'But I do have to say I'm impressed at this firm's dedication to disease prevention.' The barista raises an eyebrow as though he lost me thirty seconds ago. 'The swab,' I clarify.

'Ah yes, the swab. Let's take a look, shall we?' He glances at my name tag and taps into a laptop on the counter. 'I've got your stats here. Why don't I make your personalised coffee and if you have time we can talk through the results, figuring out a way forward that makes the most of your genotype and gender. Unless you'd like a smoothie?'

'Coffee is my poison – I don't bother with fruit as a rule. I like my sugar hits to be dirty and processed. And preferably on the hour . . .' I tail off as London's most earnest barista goes into overdrive, picking up a tall glass jug and pushing shots into it from optics loaded with sludge. Plonking myself down onto a bar stool, I try to quell the ants in my pants caused by my evil tights. I turn to the man next to me whose legs are almost too long to fit under the pop-up counter. 'Think he might have a shot of gin under the bar for me?'

'Not unless you're genetically predisposed to AA meetings,' he mutters without looking up.

'I'm sorry?'

He looks up.

The itches disappear as I'm fixed to my seat by his gaze. This bloke's eyes are deep, so deep. Bourneville brown and framed with laughter lines, they're matched by a good set of lashes and the most perfect eyebrows I've ever seen, floating above his eyes like sideways commas. Jolting myself away from his good-looking face, I watch the barista solemnly press the coffee and add it to the sludge in the jug. He then pours it into a mug, tops it up with milk and froth and hands over my treat, the cup reaffirming the invitation to be me.

Normally, at this time, I'm 'being me' in my PJs, on a similarly high stool at my breakfast counter, eating porridge loaded with sugar before trying to drag a brush through Frizzmageddon. Sucking the end of one of my plaits, I imagine coughing up a tangle of hair and nerves onto the polished tiles of the agency floor. Then I take a sip of coffee and gag for real.

'Eurgh!' Brown liquid spatters onto the counter as I wipe my mouth to try and rid it of the taste. 'What in the name of Eru is that?'

'A genetic hug in a mug?' says Handsome, a smile tugging at his mouth, before he knocks back the liquid in his super-small cup. 'Don't you like it?'

'It's revolting!' A gleam in his eyes intensifies as my voice rises. I glance around to see if I've disturbed the beehive, then cover my embarrassment by wiping up the mess with my sleeve.

*As usual, clumsy as an elephant.*

'Elephants are not actually clumsy. They're just big,' I say under my breath, before grabbing Handsome's sleeve. 'Hey, a what kind of hug did you say?' Beneath the navy jacket, his cuff is pure white, like he took his shirt fresh out of the box this morning. I have a sudden urge to stroke his fingers and find out if he's real. You don't get men as stunning as this on the Uxbridge Road. They'd distract the bus drivers.

'A genetic hug,' he repeats, nodding at the barista who gets busy with the machine again. His sly smile widens. 'I'm curious; which ingredients turned you off so violently?'

Sipping again, more slowly, I search out the flavours with my taste buds. 'OK, I can taste salt, and more salt – I can handle that – I don't even mind oysters if they're pre-suffocated in Tabasco. Then there's something that tastes like sherbet, also creosote and I'm sure I'm picking up pea soup.'

The barista jumps in, smiling for the first time. 'Pea protein. Well spotted. This unique recipe will replace all the things you are missing naturally from your body and boost the areas where you have been handed down weaknesses or deficiencies. If you continue to drink this coffee at home, we think you will see significant improvements in your well-being within three months, and you'll hopefully inhabit the "you" your body is craving.'

'How do you know what my body might be craving?' I'm totally confused now, while still trying to process Handsome's words. *Genetic hug?*

'We got a clear picture of your DNA from the saliva sample that came back from the lab yesterday.' The barista pronounces his words as though I'm foreign or deaf. 'Analysis of fifty genetic variants have gone into creating the perfect nutritional coffee for you. If you give us your permission, we can also go back and test you for Alzheimer's as well as suggesting tweaks that may prevent osteoporosis.'

*You slouch like Auntie Sarah on your father's side. I sent her a grabber to keep her back straight when cleaning up after that terrible husband of hers.*

I straighten my shoulders and turn to back to the barista. 'It's nice of you to make me a DNA brew and it's all very innovative, but I think I'll stick with Nescafé.'

'You can use instant as your base blend; the type of coffee has no bearing on whether your body is getting the vitamins and minerals it needs. I'm recommending A-K for you as well as a collagen boost. Let's break it down some more if you've a moment: you have a high tolerance to salt but a decreasing ability to hydrate, and your metabolism may be sluggish at times. I suggest you ditch the sugars, decrease your carbs and add a tad more iron. It also appears you are genetically sensitive to caffeine. You should try and cut down.'

Handsome guffaws into his phone at the irony of the last statement. I turn to him, vaguely irritated. 'What's yours then?'

'My what?'

'Your unique recipe.' I gesture towards his teeny coffee cup.

'Are you asking if I'm your genome type?' He smirks,

making a blush rise to my cheeks. His jawline has the look of a leading man effortlessly bossing the screen while his eyebrows are still wowing me with their stage presence. There's no way on this earth we'd have compatible DNA. 'I like my coffee indecently strong and black,' he says, holding my eyes a second too long before standing and reaching for his bag. 'And preferably without creosote.'

The barista peels off a sticker from the sheet in his hands. 'I'm going to pop your recipe on your free mug so you can make your drink at home.'

I mumble thanks while scanning the foyer. I need to wash my mouth out as well as readjust my tights in case I'm tempted to scratch my butt in my meeting. But I draw a blank on the location of the ladies' toilet.

'Over there. Our toilets are all gender neutral.'

It's five minutes until my appointment, which means I'm late as I like to be five minutes early, and I still haven't sussed out the lift protocol. Looking for the button to call it, I catch sight of myself in the mirrored doors. Despite my gargantuan efforts this morning, I am as unappealing as ever – one reason I never put myself on camera. My paper-thin skin is flushed as pink as spring cherry trees. My muddy green eyes are too big for my face and make me look like a monkey, while my own eyebrows can't keep away from each other.

A plaque on the wall tells me the building was designed by rising 'starchitects' James & James. Does all Glimmer language need to be stellar related? I groan quietly as I see Handsome heading my way with a leather man-bag slung over his shoulder; probably full of products for his catwalk hair; short at the sides and groomed into spikes at the front. He's a bit older than me – in his early thirties, I guess. Are those premature silver hairs or streaks that reflect his firm's obsession with metallic colours? He doesn't look like a city boy, but there's an air of good school about him and his height means he owns the space around him without trying to dominate it. When he looks up from his phone, he meets my gaze in the reflective doors. Oh God, now I'm going to be stuck in a lift with him.

'You haven't called it. Do you know how?' he asks. What idiot doesn't know how to call a lift? 'Scan your pass on the blue light. We found limiting access to upper floors keeps out unsavouries, and anyone who supports Arsenal.'

'Bad decision, if you ask me.' Which he's not doing, admittedly.

'Are you a Gooner then?' He puts on a thin smile to go with the small talk.

'I meant the buttonless lifts. People have called lifts the same way for the last century for a reason.' Cringing at the sound of my own voice, I open a pocket of my handbag and notice him looking at it, like he's never crafted anything out of an old pair of jeans. He steps up to the doors, wafting expensive cologne as he scans his wrist against the blank wall. Boom! the lift arrives.

He gestures for me to go first. 'The blue light is faint today. Must be the sunshine.'

'Bit of a design flaw in an office block built around an atrium. Did you just call the lift with your hand?'

'My watch; smarter than Alan Turing.' His smile has

some actual warmth in it this time as laughter lines ripple around his eyes.

'Not that smart though; he's been dead for half a century.' I curse my smart mouth as he steps in behind me. There's a moment's pause as he raises those lovely eyebrows expectantly. (I'd love to get a cheeky shot of them and take it to the threader I've seen torturing people at Westfield. Tell her, 'I'll have two of these please.')

'You need to tell the lift what floor you need. Unless you'd like to come with me to mine?'

'No, you're fine!' I say. He stifles a smile. 'Er . . . floor four please?' When the lift thanks me in a voice I recognise from the TV news, I gesture towards the speaker. 'If I ask the announcer dude to order me a bacon butty will I be able to pick it up after my meeting?'

'That's not a bad idea actually.' He grins. 'You're here to see one of our talent managers I presume?' How can he tell? It's not like I've been flashing any talent around this morning. 'What do you do?'

I don't normally blurt my business out to strange peeps, but as we are in a lift, isn't this the perfect time for the elevator pitch I practised to death? 'I'm a catfluencer,' I say, hesitantly, before going for it. 'This particular section of influencers is on the up at the moment in a crowded and competitive Instaverse. I believe I'm . . .'

'What's an Instaverse?'

Is he winding me up? 'The Universe of Instagram?'

'Right. And by the way, who's Eru? You swore in his name when you spilt your coffee.'

'Spat my coffee. I can still taste it. Eru is God.'

'Old Testament?'

'Tolkien. Our barista friend failed to spot the hobbit in my DNA,' I reply, checking my wayward hair is covering the ears I've always found suspiciously small.

'Ah right. I believe you can't beat George Lucas for world building.'

'Are you kidding? Hyperspace is a black hole in comparison with Middle Earth.'

'I would never joke about the galaxy.'

The lift announces the nine o'clock headline. 'We have reached the fourth floor.'

'When you get to call the lift to the tenth floor, you'll know you've hit the jackpot. The more important people are, the better view they have of London. I expect that'll infuriate you too.' He shoots me a sideways look, as though waiting for my rise.

'Well yes, that does peck at my head,' I respond as predicted, putting my foot in the doorway to stopper the doors. 'Why shouldn't people further down the chain have a view? They work as hard don't they? And I've been thinking about the DNA coffee. It's ridiculous, trying to manipulate our nature, even with the most advanced science. We are what we are and the only thing I am genetically disposed to do is like cats – that particular trait goes back as far as Grandma Dobson who ran an orphanage for ginger toms; including the infamous Boris Big Balls. And the saliva swab? That's an invasion of my privacy and I wonder if they've thought through the implications. Whatever next, taking a pint of my blood in reception to check I'm not on the sex offenders register?'

'Are you?'

'Of course not. But actually . . .' He's smirked at me one too many times with his hot mouth and whirlpool eyes and I cast my mind about for a way to surprise him. 'I am an Arsenal fan and proud of it.'

I quickly take my foot out of the doorway as I'm not even sure which borough Arsenal is in. The mirrored doors close. And then, disaster – I catch sight of my dress, tucked into my tights, showing off a striped woolly backside.

My spirits sink further when I peer through the glass door of Patricia's office. She's the head of the hockey team. Like the receptionist, she has manicured nails, but with unexpectedly neon nail polish and something tells me she burpees a hundred times before bed. I decide to go home to my cats and reverse towards the lift, hoping she hasn't seen me. But she rises, throws back the door and beckons me in.

Thankfully, I don't need to make my elevator pitch again as she knows all about me. In fact, she has printed off a raft of my best posts and assembled them in a 'style file' with my name in a bold gold font. I didn't know I had that much style and am curious to see what posts she considers my best. With consonants that have been clipped and buffed, she starts gushing over the fat wodge of screenshots, enthusiastically pushing the file towards me as though she's trying to sell me my own brand. 'In this one AlyCat subtly criticises our carelessness of the environment while reminding us of our responsibility to avoid fast food chains.' There's nothing subtle about it;

I've basically mugged Ronald McDonald in broad daylight by dressing Molly in his trademark bright yellow jumpsuit and striped sleeves, using a bright orange wig (eBay £2) as cat litter. And I'm thinking if I did it again, I'd reconstruct it out of plastic straws and get Milly to poop all over them.

'I adore AlyCat's attitude. And how she zips into the zeitgeist so purrfectly.' She actually purrs as she says this. Can you zip into a zeitgeist? My English teachers were mad on alliteration, but I think the excessive Zs would be too much even for them. 'The butcher cat outfit on World Vegan Day was superlative. How did you get AlyCat to hold the cleaver?' Thank heavens for a question I can easily answer. If can relax and go with this then perhaps I can stop looking for an escape ladder?

'I use a special type of fixing tape that doesn't hurt her when I rip it off. Kind of like the stuff models use in fashion week. You'll have noticed she doesn't look like other cats. Sphynx cats are hairless, although they do have a peachy fuzz, and they often have sensitive skin, but AlyCat has always been happy to dress up and dress down and do anything really, as long as she has a nice bath once a week to clean her skin. And she loves wearing clothes. They keep her super-warm you see; hairless cats lose body heat just by standing still. The cleaver is from a miniature kitchen. I use an online dolls' accessories supplier who has thousands of props. That's if I can't make it myself, which I often can.'

I'm enjoying this, now I've found a cat lover who gets what I'm trying to do creatively.

'Tell me, how do you do the dual cat shots?' she asks.

What? That's a curved ball, lady. 'I'm sorry?'

'Like the time where you put her in the boxing ring dressed as the EU and the UK? Or when she popped out of the coffin on National Funeral Director and Mortician Recognition Day in the two different guises? Do you photoshop her in? Does she get irritated at having to change outfits?'

She's done her homework; I wasn't expecting this depth of questioning. Do I confess AlyCat is two cats? Perhaps she should know that if she's auditioning me for a role as one of her talent minions. But, on the other hand, it's a closely kept secret; my fans and followers would be horrified to know I've hoodwinked them.

While I flail, she deep-dives. 'I want to come to your next shoot and see how you work. In fact, I'll bring a photographer and we can profile you and AlyCat on the company blog. Lots of brands with big budgets regularly read it; we have an impressive email subscription list.'

'Actually, Patricia . . .'

'You might find yourself Glimmer's "Meteor of the Month"?'

'To be honest with you . . .'

'Rick Harvard, our CEO, chooses them personally but I'm sure I can put a word in. Your mix of quirky talent and humour would definitely appeal. Your cat has potential to be a social media treasure, as famous as Grumpy Cat or Nala. And it's interesting you mention honesty as truth is Rick's guiding principle; in fact, he based the foundations of Glimmer on it.'

I shrink a little more in my seat. The great truth-teller is not going to be impressed that AlyCat, who makes a living exposing fake news and hypocrisy, is not one genuine shiny article but two cats and a carer who lives in an old warehouse. If I signed up to this agency, I'd be the guy behind the curtain continually waiting for Dorothy to discover he's not the wizard.

I look around a cubed office, which makes me feel like I'm sitting inside a mint, and regret answering her email. I am out of my league here. Even if the rumours of a rent rise are true, maybe I can stretch my budget further instead of pimping out my pets? The cats eat tons, but I could restrict my own food shopping to the knockie-downies at Tesco on a Friday night? Or take on even more extra care shifts and hope my ailing car can cope with the additional miles. Or, worst case, dip into my precious house deposit savings? But right now, I have a more immediate problem; she seems really into this, and I don't want to be rude.

'Patricia, now I'm here, I don't think I'm right for Glimmer. Or maybe I'm just not the kind of influencer who needs an agent or a management company. I'm probably more of a one-man band really.'

'Oh, we're not agents. We are the One Stop Talent Shop. Perfect for a one-man band,' she replies, sweeping her blonde hair behind her like a vanilla mane.

Otherwise known as agents.

She rushes on, 'We are your pinprick of light in the dark, your inflatable raft in a tsunami. We will guide you through the maelstrom of life and the media and find you a place in the melee.'

Still agents. It must be difficult not to talk down to me. It's all part of the job – a talent manager is the same as a talent spotter and no one spots upwards do they? They do it from their glass tower, from a nine-to-five job and a position of security.

'Well, I already have a place in the melee. If the melee you are referring to is social media,' I venture. I am a child of social media; but one that really shouldn't have been born or allowed to grow so big. I'm grateful to Instagram for featuring me at the end of one of their global weekend challenges. It was American Independence Day and I dressed Milly up as a rapper, with a costume made out of the US flag. I found some lightweight neck bling online and she tolerated it long enough for me to get the money shot. I was over the moon when I picked up thousands of extra followers over the next twenty-four hours and my Insta-fame has never dipped. I don't know why it works, or why I strike a chord in people, but cat lovers lap it up, and those who aren't fussed about pets seem to appreciate the humour and enjoy commenting. It's probably all just a fluke and I'll be dumped by next Tuesday, but if I sign up to Patricia and am managed by an agency like Glimmer, do I risk being shoved off the bridge from a much greater height?

'Oh, it's *so* much more than social. We will make you viral on platforms that haven't even been invented yet,' she says. I'd love to see her try and market me on platforms that haven't been created yet. Perhaps CEO Rick Harvard and his crew can see around corners? Maybe that's what people pay them for? Even so, I don't think this is going to work for me.

'Have you ever made any real money?' Posh changes

tack. 'How much do you charge for a sponsored post or Insta-story?'

'It depends.'

'On average?'

I shuffle around in my seat. Truth be told, I haven't successfully monetised my channels.

'Ten or twenty?'

'Ten or twenty what?'

'Well obvs I'm talking about pounds. It's not like anyone is going to pay me in dollars.'

'We're negotiating fees of ten or twenty thousand for our top clients.' She closes my file. 'You can take it in pounds or dollars or Ukrainian hryvnia if you like. Aly, if Glimmer were to offer you representation, even with a junior member of our staff like myself, you cannot afford to turn it down. We are the stellar agency; we shoot stars into infinity.' She's actually quoting their strapline at me. 'I promise we won't interfere in your creativity, And I guarantee we will enhance your image and profile, both online and in the traditional media. People need to get to know the Aly behind the AlyCat brand. You are part of the package. We will bring you exposure in ways you've never dreamed of.'

*Whoah, lady!* I hold up my hand like a comedy policeman. Limelight to me is like sunlight to vampires. 'Look, Patricia. I do well with my Instagram channel. I get quite a few likes and loads of comments, and it seems to grow on its own. I am happy in my work, and AlyCat is totally chilled about doing it, which is more important to me. I don't need international fame.

I'm not an interesting person. In fact, I'm a great big yawn. I was curious after your call the other day and sponsorship would have brought in money I need, but I wouldn't fit in here.'

'We could make you global; you could orbit the earth with essence of Aly! We have contacts with all the household brands. Think of your products as confetti; we will scatter you liberally and see where you land.'

I've never been to a wedding and I don't like her calling my cats 'products'. I grab my jacket from behind the chair and her expression changes as she clocks I'm leaving. 'Are you sure you want to throw away an opportunity like this?'

Course I'm not! I would love to be catapulted out of my life. Forget aiming for the stars, most of the time I'm sitting in my car, waiting for my next job, and trying to figure out how to pull myself out of the gutter. I work almost 24/7. I'm either not paid properly (for the driving time), or at all (for the waiting time between appointments), and no one looks after me like I look after my old ladies. I live in a building with a concrete floor and fungus on the ceilings. Our garden is an overflow car park for a DIY chain. I shower in a drizzle of water in a shared bathroom and I'm the only one who ever cleans the toilet. I put up with the noise of my housemates' chiselling and hammering through the night while trying to quash imposter syndrome that I'm not a real artist and shouldn't be taking up a subsidised room for a creative. I am heartily sick of value beans, bread and eggs and can barely afford to keep the cats warm while I squirrel away spare pennies to try and get on the property ladder in one of the least desirable parts of London. Constantly on a treadmill trying to run uphill, I sometimes worry I'll tumble off the end. But this? This confetti-filled tower block of talent? It's not me.

'We could do takeovers for pet food commercials, magazine adverts for cat products, a book of inspirational cat quotes – for humans, not cats to read of course!' While I love how she felt she had to qualify her last statement, I need to halt this bullet train.

'Patricia, other Instagrammers would no doubt bite your hand off; most of them seem to be gagging for global fame. I thought I was ready to grab some of that pie, but I think I came in for a steak bake and you are offering a chicken and gammon pie in a crème fraîche sauce. The gap between us is too big and I'm sorry for wasting your time. And anyway, I keep all the cash I make right now. I'd have to pay you if you took me on. That's probably about ten per cent . . .'

I can tell from her silence she costs more than that. 'If you sign with Glimmer, you could go to the stars and beyond and we'd fly with you. Just think about it, Aly. You could have a percentage of infinity.'

These people can divide up infinity? With a heavy heart, I say goodbye, push her business card into the lanyard and shove the plastic case under my dress. Having exploded my future this morning, I deserve to keep a piece of the shrapnel.

There's no bacon butty waiting for me when the lift doors open.

I check my image in my phone. Released from its bondage, my hair looks like it's powered by London Electric. Slopping tea onto the table of a café trying too hard to be bohemian, I add another sugar. With my purse upside down, I count the coins that clatter onto the table, wondering whether to splurge on another coffee. Today is a rare day off and an escape from a life that should have been more. I think back to my dreams of a career in the fashion industry, which ended when I spectacularly failed to go to university. My photography ambitions didn't go any further than snapping the foxes behind the bins at Stockley Park. Today I had the chance to claw back some of that potential with an introduction to an actual talent manager. And I blew it, to protect my cats, and my reputation as an influencer. Was there another way?

I cast my mind back to the day I heard the Oddities had a spare room for rent in the old computer warehouse I've called home for six years. Having left school with not much in the way of qualifications, I'd stalled like a sailing boat in shallow water, racking up an impressively average CV of screwing extractor fans together, serving in a fabric factory outlet and answering phones at a car showroom.

I was trying to work out what to do with my life while making the more important decision of fruit shortcakes or custard creams in Kav's Kozy Korner, a local shop with new owners. In the end I took both to the counter. My shoulders must have reflected my joyless existence as the woman behind the counter commented that my handbag was too heavy.

I almost agreed with her, before frowning. 'I don't have my handbag with me.'

'It looks heavy,' she repeated, a tiara crowning black

flowing hair, the jewels matching a tiny stud in her nose. 'Can I help take some of the weight off your shoulders?'

Her kindness stripped my thin skin and I crumbled. 'You're right, my backpack is full of rocks. I am twenty years old and have no job prospects, no boyfriend and an impossibly high blood sugar level.'

Within minutes, she'd barked an order at her partner and sat me down next to her behind the counter, quizzing me on my family life, my hopes and dreams. When she found out my passions lay in textiles and photography, she put her head to one side.

'You are Mary Quant.'

'Ha, ha, I don't think . . .'

'Hear me out, my new friend. Her parents were teachers, just like your mother. They would not let her attend a fashion course, just like your mother. She had to go to night school to learn how to use patterns. She rocked the miniskirt and hot pants and invented the swinging sixties.'

'One woman cannot invent a decade of change,' said a bear of a man, emerging from the storeroom with a steaming hot cup of tea.

'Princess Diana!' she shouted, banging a box of lighters onto the counter and dislodging the tiara. They then proceeded to argue about her royal radicalism, topped off with a row about how one might eat a scone if one got an audience with the Queen. Forget the lighters, I feared the sparks might set fire to the newly delivered *Hillingdon Star*. After shooing him back into the stockroom, she pulled a pink piece of card from underneath the till.

'All right you may not be Mary Quant yet, but this might help you spread your wings.' She dialled a number on the card and started a conversation with a man named Henry, who made exotic lions.

'I'm not creative enough for an art collective,' I whispered as I listened in.

'Can you cut a pattern?' she hissed.

'Well, yes.'

'Did you make the outfit you're wearing?' We both glanced down at the polka dot cargo pants with pockets for phone and wallet which meant I no longer needed to carry an actual handbag. 'You are creative. And I noticed you eat Jaffa Cakes upside down. What could be more artistic than that?'

My phone jolts me out of my thoughts and grounds me back in the café. I'm tempted to let it to go to voicemail, but as today is already quite different, why not take a chance?

A man says he's calling on behalf of Rick Harvard, CEO of Glimmer. I think I recognise his voice from earlier, and my stomach flips. 'We don't think Patsy got you, or correctly communicated what we are all about. No matter. She's leaving us,' he says.

Patsy? Patricia didn't strike me as the kind of woman who shortened her own name. 'Don't worry, she did. And then some. I'm just not interested.'

'Well, you were interested enough to meet her,' he says with undeniable logic. 'Are you still in the building?'

'I'm . . . no I'm not.'

'Could we get you back in? Rick has a cancellation

in his diary and would like to have a quick chat. He's curious about you.' I don't want to be one of Rick Harvard's diary slops. But the voice at the other end of the telephone, and the body I suspect goes with it, makes me reconsider. Would I get to see him again? Maybe he's Rick Harvard's PA? Those eyebrows, wide bottom lip and suspected six-pack under a crisp cotton shirt draw me back. Just one more burst of delicious eye contact would surely refresh me more than another latte. And it would be free.

It seems this guy can read tea leaves and has figured out my cup is empty. 'There's a little deli around the corner that delivers fantastic mini croissants and pastries. We can send out for decent drinks to go with them as the stuff in the office kitchen is a bit generic, and I'm guessing you don't want another DNA coffee.'

I blush with embarrassment as I remember spattering my unique recipe all over the pop-up bar. But I do adore doll-sized pastries, and if rumours about a rent rise are true, I won't be able to afford luxuries like that unless I start working triple care shifts, monetise my Instagram channel or dip into some of the boxes cluttering my flat. And much as I want to say no, I'm still basking in the attention this guy gave me.

I quietly sigh, which he takes as a yes. 'How do you like your coffee?' he asks.

'Massive!' It slips out but he laughs.

'A massive coffee it is. Milk and sugar?'

'Just milk.' I pocket three sugars to sneak into the cup. My sweet tooth brings out the dentist in everyone.

'Tell the lift to take you to the tenth floor. We'll try and correct any misconceptions you have of us.'

The tenth floor? It seems I have hit the jackpot.

A receptionist sitting equidistant between two offices shows me into a room where the panoramic windows are laced with the company logo. I walk over to the other side of the office, entranced as I gaze down to the street below. This firm must have super-efficient window cleaners; there's not a smudge of dirt on the glass. I lick a finger to see if I can put my print on the top of a landmark building.

'It's like Lego, isn't it? A big Lego mess created by a toddler on crack.' Snatching back my hand, I spin round. Handsome rests on the edge of a large glass desk, his hands in his pockets. And he's got even more unnerving in the last couple of hours.

'So, Rick Harvard. He's head of all this . . .' I gesture to the view like his boss is CEO of the sky.

'Are you here to complain about the firm's interior design choices?'

'No. Honestly!' I try to work out if he is serious, praying he hasn't already passed my remarks up the chain, or my meeting could get awks. He crosses his feet, as relaxed as I am tense. I've never seen brown shoes so shiny; if he looks down, can he see his face? No socks?

Picking up a folder that looks like the one Patricia showed me earlier, he flicks through it, his watch flashing notifications. It dawns on me he's had a lot of these in the short time I've spent with him, like someone who is important.

Oh, you're kidding me.

'Ummm, so you are . . .' I spit into the void.

'Rick Harvard. Good to meet you again, Aly. Short for Alison or Alice?'

'Neither.' He raises an eyebrow, so perfect I could lick it. 'Alyssa,' I answer after a pause. A name from another life.

*An alley is a street filled with litter. I bothered to give you a decent name, so the least you could do is use it.*

I, not we. Could my mother and father not even agree on their daughter's name?

His confident grip envelops my fingers without crushing them. I feel him like a static shock and not just in my hand; I don't know where he ends and I begin. I'm floating; the kind of floating where you pop out of your seat at the top of a funfair ride before tumbling downhill at a hundred miles an hour.

A knock on the door makes me feel like I've been caught doing something naughty. The woman who showed me in hands her boss an envelope. 'Any sign of those pastries? Can you chase them up along with the two massive coffees?' he asks, winking at me. When she leaves, he continues, 'I'm not into cats myself but Patsy was keen and I'm not too busy to listen to my staff when they unearth someone they think is special.' Special? I shiver, without knowing why. He holds the envelope out. 'Take it. It won't bite.'

Oh Lord. I always like to have advance warning of what might be inside a present. I grasp it and hold it up to the light. As I examine it, I pick up another faint whiff of his cologne. I'm guessing the scent probably cost more than my monthly rent, but then such a gob-stopping jawline must require some serious upkeep. Resembling a security guard looking for anthrax, I rip the envelope and pull out two glossy tickets for an Arsenal match.

'Sorry. I can't accept a gift of this size. Presents bring me out in hives and big ones like this give me palpitations.'

'It's not a gift. It's an opportunity. For you to relax, courtesy of us. See the kind of lifestyle you could aspire to. Of course, if you want to Instagram from there – take AlyCat, dress her up a bit, and use the Glimmer hashtag, we certainly wouldn't stop you. It's a pet friendly box.' For a minute I allow myself to daydream I'm in that VIP enclosure, holding a glass of champagne. Handsome is next to me and I imagine his hand creeping under my skimpy pinafore, to the top of my thigh, stroking the lace around my . . . Stop it! '. . . or you're welcome to take a friend,' he finishes.

Oh.

*Why would a man like him choose to spend time with you? Unless you are giving it away.*

The words creep in before I can stop them, prompting me to rush in and decline his offer. 'Look, it's really nice of you but I can't accept a gift of this size.'

He taps at his phone and looks up. Not at me but an older man who is standing in the space between the two offices. Rick Harvard grimaces and bashes out another message. He notices me following his line of sight and nods irritably. 'It's "Take Your Father to Work Day".'

'Really?' I usually notice national days – they're an easy win on the Insta front.

'Nope. William H. Harvard owns most of the company.

I just make it profitable.' I make a mental note to google how profitable and then remember I don't care.

He pulls out a leather chair and sits down, opening a silver laptop and surfing around.

'You and the cat are Liverpool supporters, not Arsenal after all? I'll get my PA to phone around again.'

'Please don't. In the spirit of full disclosure, I don't like football. I'm a tennis fan.' I'm not that either but I figure it's a cool sport to be on my fictional hobbies list. 'I admit I dressed AlyCat up as the Liverpool mascot a few weeks ago to promote new footie tours but that's because I was offered hard cash.' A rubbish fifty pounds but he doesn't need to know that.

'Now *that* I approve of, as your future talent manager.' I thought he was the guy on top? I briefly wonder if he's a cleaner and a fantasist. But whatever position he holds, this firm is not for me.

'I'm sorry but I don't want an agent.'

'We're not . . .'

'Yep, I know. Patricia wanted to be my "rescuer in the typhoon of life" after she had her marketing muesli for breakfast.'

'Patsy was . . .'

'I don't need to be rescued,' I rush on, trying not to smell the promised warm croissants. 'And before you send them by courier, I'm not interested in tickets for Wimbledon either.'

He starts to laugh.

'What?'

'Nothing.'

'Then why are you laughing?'

He hesitates. 'You've reminded me of that classic Athena poster. You know the one?' What's a Greek goddess got to do with anything?

'Google it,' he says, with a grin.

The lift makes the smoothest of landings and I prepare to re-enter an orbit where things are not quite so shiny or marketable. As I make my way past a gold Dale Chihuly sculpture, I google 'Athena poster'.

My screen is filled with an image of a girl in a white tennis dress, lifted up to show a bare bottom. I clearly wasn't the only one who caught a flash of my tights as the lift doors shut.

O.M.G.

# Chapter 2

The Turtle Dove Care app directs me to 'Flat 19, Almond House'. There are no further instructions. Typical. I press random buttons on the touch pad at the front entrance before ringing the contact number on the app. No answer. It's just past seven, the sky is blue and there's a delicious breeze. Saturday mornings should be for chilling in bed with a coffee and Instastories, not running around the perimeter of a sheltered accommodation block like school sports day. Our training specified we should always have an introduction to a new client by one of their regular carers, but like so much with Turtle Dove, it never happens. What they say and what we do in the home care industry are oceans apart.

I scan the quadrangle for anyone who might be able to help me locate flat nineteen, or even better, break me into it. As there's no one nearby, I turn my attention back to the keypad. Then I punch in the code in the client's medication plan, hoping it might be the same – I'm not Alex Rider or anything but people are lazy with their passcodes.

A gnarled man limps up behind me. 'You a carer?'

I always put on my gloves and apron as I sprint for the front door as it saves precious time during appointments, and now I brandish my blue latex fingers like I've seen surgeons do on telly. 'Actually, I've come to operate on the woman in flat nineteen.'

He presses a code into the keypad, breaking out into a slow smile. I know that look, although I'm never sure if it's the latex, or the nurse fantasy that turns them on. Most men I care for get over it when I make them beans on toast, empty their commode and complain about the last carer clogging up the sink with yesterday's spaghetti.

After taking the lift to the second floor, I run the corridor looking for the flat before navigating the stairs back down. I'm now ten minutes late for a 45-minute appointment which will make me increasingly late for the next, and the next. My care shifts are a forest with no fire break and the match is always lit and lobbed at the first call.

I knock loudly on a door I think might be the right one. 'It's Aly from Turtle Dove Care.'

No answer. I try the same code as before on the keypad and then rap harder when it doesn't open. A woman flings open the door opposite wearing only her knickers and a smile. Her small dog yaps and sniffs at my ankles. At the same time, her neighbour appears in a full winceyette, poised to pounce like a Dobermann because I've got her out of bed at this ungodly hour.

'I'll put the kettle on, shall I?'

'Is there anything else you'd like me to do for you?' This is my cue to leave. I say it at the end of every appointment, and most of them understand and wave me away with a cheery 'no thanks'. I wait patiently in front of the QR code by the door, all set to scan out. My employer docks pay if I cut the appointment short, even by a minute. I don't know why she doesn't go the whole hog and electronic tag us.

I have done well to complete about forty tasks in three-quarters of an hour, helped by the client's cheerful instructions. I panicked when I took her pet out into the garden and he refused to do his doggy-do, thinking I might have to wait till his bowels opened, but she gestured for me to bring him back in. 'Sometimes he just enjoys the thought of going outside. I know how he feels.'

'Don't you ever get out?'

'Never.'

'You would if you were one of my regulars. I wrestle people into wheelchairs and march them around the block until their lungs are recharged with carbon monoxide.'

'Be nice if you came again.'

'I'd like that too.' I cross my fingers behind my back. Lovely as she is, it's an extra twenty minutes to this part of the Uxbridge Road, the traffic is always unforgiving, and I hardly get paid anything for the driving. The less time I spend in physical contact with my oldies, the less I'm earning.

Time's up and I scan out. 'Oh, yes, there is one more thing I'd like you to do. Can you make me a quick cappuccino?' What? An artisan coffee was not in the plan. I sprint back into her kitchen and search for a cup. Grabbing a carton of milk from the fridge, I tip some in and bang open the microwave to heat it up, cursing under my breath when it spills.

'You'll find the box on the top shelf, next to the cereal.' Huh? Following her new instructions, I fling open the cupboard and pick out a pack of cappuccino sachets. Then

I kick into reverse, opening the microwave, dumping the milk in the sink, flicking the kettle on, and ripping the packet open with my teeth, while the dog nips at the lace of my trainers. 'You can't want to go out again!' I whisper loudly.

Popping the mug down beside my client, I smell eucalyptus oil and notice the de-humidifier I filled earlier has leaked all over the table. Sighing, I take the machine back into the kitchen, where the dog has left me a present. I really do hate unexpected gifts.

My next client is an octogenarian who makes me a coffee, sits me at her patio table and gives me career advice. The old ladies are the reason I stay. I've been enjoying their company for two years and can recite many of their life stories by heart. I could earn more money behind a bar for sure, but I doubt it would bring me such regular bursts of gratitude.

Once a month I call into the office for a chat, and today I park in a zone with a twenty-minute restriction, so I'm not tempted to stay all day and gossip. When I push open the door, two young women look up and smile. The twins have worked here since I started at the agency, scheduling appointments, paying expenses and reassuring clients not to panic when we don't turn up on time. They act as a barrier between us and the boss, who doesn't like to get her hands dirty with staff or client interaction. Making me a coffee, they immediately fill me in on her entrepreneurial adventures. 'She's opened offices in Cambridge, Oxford and Wigan this month.'

'. . . and a new dementia centre in Ealing Broadway. We haven't seen her since February, but she gave me a written warning the other day about using too many Post-its . . .'

'You do eat Post-its though. And I got told off for letting the carers cherry-pick their clients . . .'

'We're allowed to cherry-pick our clients?'

'. . . most of them want jobs close to their home because of the driving . . .'

'. . . and not getting paid for that.'

'We do get something for the driving though.' For some reason I defend a boss I've never met.

'Well, that's about to be cut. She reckons she can save loads by paying the carers for petrol only. She told us to make it clear you are all freelance and not actually employees of this company. And she's introducing fines for being late.'

'We asked for a coffee maker, and she sent us a kettle . . .'

'. . . and someone put a padlock on the stationery cupboard over the weekend,' they power on, winding each other up with their complaints.

'Oh, and you know you took Eileen to the doctor's surgery in your own time? She rang up one day last week to praise you, but the boss said she'd bill her an extra hour because you are freelance not free.'

Since I've last seen them, the schedulers have dyed their blonde bobs the same shade of blue. 'What made you go for the blue rinse?' I laugh. 'All that time spent on the phone with the oldies or trying to blend in with the Turtle Dove uniform?' All the carers hate the tunic we have to wear, with the watch attached to the pocket that always ends up in the wash.

'No, we copy our fave celeb, Katy Perry!' says one, while the other shouts, 'Kylie Jenner!'

'You look like Thing One and Thing Two,' I joke, before wondering if that'll upset them.

'That's what our mum said! Super cool! Want to come back to ours for a takeaway and a glass of vino? We've found a Prosecco where you can screw the lid back on, although we've never managed to do that obviously.' I smile at two colleagues who could possibly grow into friends. Right now, there's nothing I'd rather do than sleep, shower, and get drunk with someone under the age of seventy. But I can't accept their hospitality without inviting them back to mine. And that will come with the inevitable questions about the boxes. Over the years they've piled so high I can barely get through my front door.

'I'm busy tonight. Another time?' They don't answer as they've picked up calls through their headsets; one discusses a house move and the other answers an SOS from a newbie. 'You've basically superglued her teeth to the roof of her mouth? Best advice – rip them out quickly and hope you don't permanently massacre her gums.'

Back home I spend ages on a pic of Milly sending up the transport minister's latest crisis. Making the costume is tricky work and a nightmare to get the stitching right. Lacing Milly into the corset isn't easy either, although she does happily climb onto the toy bus for just about long enough for me to take her picture. Out of the corner of my eye I see a spider running across the ceiling and scurrying into a crack in the wall. Molly has also seen it; she darts from floor to coffee table, onto the small stack of boxes, then takes the bigger crates like stairs until she's balanced on the top box. Her athleticism always delights me. Molly's sleek grey body, stripped of the fluff of other cats, looks almost human when she's moving fast.

Like a flash of clippers in the hands of a Turkish barber, she streaks from the top box to the next stack and makes a leap for the sofa, where Milly joins her in a play fight; Milly's long ears always prick up when Molly calls. And then both of them are chittering at me, and I know what they want, and they know I know it, and they rub against my legs until I make my way over to the fridge and divvy up the rest of last night's poached fish. I might not buy decent food for myself all the time, but the cats eat a lot and eat well, or as well as I can afford.

'There you go, sweet kitcats . . .' I pop two bowls on the floor for Milly and Molly; two cats who combine to form one virtual AlyCat. As they noisily neck back the food, I remember the transport minister is still an unpublished kitty meme on my phone. While I upload it, Milly finishes her food and hops onto my knee with a low growl and a sharp claw.

'What's your problem, MillyCat? If you carry on like this, I'll make you do cat-wailing videos for YouTube.' I stroke her backside affectionately as the likes start to pile up in seconds; a hundred and growing. Although she has no fur, her skin is soft to the touch, like suede, and she is always warm. Especially since she loves to wear a little knitted sweater. I have no intention of switching to YouTube, our success on Instagram went beyond my wildest dreams last month when we tipped over 100,000 followers and it seems to be on an exponential rise.

I answer a comment asking what kind of toys AlyCat likes to play with, and then click away as I could spend all day interacting and answering questions. When I check my emails I notice an Evite to a conference hosted by Glimmer. The swag event will be filled with 'the best of the nation's influencers; all so hot and aspirational you could burn your hand on them'. So why send it to me?

A second email answers my question. 'Pinged you an invite to our first annual influencer bash. Can I tempt you to come to GlimmerCon? I'm convinced we can change your mind.' Rick Harvard is all about the arrogance.

As I click away, I notice an envelope on the mat. I open it and want to weep. The rent isn't going up after all.

The landlord is selling the building.

# Chapter 3

Hallelujah – pink wafers in the bargain bucket. I pick out a pack and tear into it. Manolis is giving me the evil eye over the top of his script but I'm confident he'll indulge me. I buy so much from Kav's Kozy Korner these days he's recently given me a tab.

'New role?' He swipes the biccies with a scanner he argued about buying for a year. Manolis looks tired and I'm increasingly convinced the man never sleeps. He sorts the papers at dawn, accepts deliveries, runs backwards and forwards to the cash and carry, works in the shop till 11 p.m., and still finds time to squeeze in rehearsals for amateur operatics. Apparently he invites favourite customers to his performances on a rota system and it's my turn this time around. I'm secretly delighted, although I've never been a fan of musicals.

'I am going for a Pirate, obviously,' he says.

'He will get it.' His wife pops out of the stock cupboard with three jars of Marmite in her hands. 'They are short of competent men and have made the dubious decision for *The Pirates of Penzance* to have an all-male cast. My husband can sing like Pavarotti, even if he does go a little flat in the shower sometimes.' I hope she isn't referring to their sex life again. They have a habit of oversharing about their downtime, especially when the shop is full of customers. 'You will see he is also an unsettling combination of Pavarotti and a pirate when viewed from the side,' Kavita continues. Manolis turns sideways, putting a hand over his eye so I can assess the likeness. He does kind of resemble a young Pavarotti, with smiling eyes, a generous brown moustache and beard, and a barrel of a chest widening into middle-aged spread.

I cram half a wafer into my mouth, hoping they'll put the kettle on before I choke on vanilla dust. My visits to their mini market have become one of my favourite parts of the day, especially when Kav plies me with refreshments from their new food bar. This morning, as I fill my basket, she hangs out at the till expressing her anger at dogs fouling the footpaths while Manolis stands with her, trying to identify a type of cloud he saw while filling in for one of his paper boys.

'I should walk around and squat on their doorstep, let them know how it feels. Would you like to try our new coffee?' she asks, pushing back a purple sari that's fallen over her shoulder to reveal a pink T-shirt saying 'Bite Me'. As Kav heads into her forties, her style is an unapologetic mixture of Western teenage sass and traditional Indian sequin. With the same arm, she flicks the shiniest hair outside of a TV advert out of her eyes. Long and thick, without a hint of a curl, it taunts me daily.

Manolis continues to describe the cloud he saw this morning while ambling down the aisle to make us all a brew. 'It looked like an alien spaceship, literally like the craft in *Close Encounters*. Kavita, you cannot offer hospitality to everyone who comes in. We need to have a discussion about this.'

'We have a licence to serve food and have just invested in a good coffee machine and two brand-new tables outside. The whole point is to offer hospitality to everyone who comes in. Or do you think our food is there to feed the birds, you unnecessary man? The only thing we need to be discussing is how slow you are at sorting it out.'

'Aly is a social call.' He raises his voice and if it were anyone else, I'd flinch and back out of the shop. But they fight so exaggeratedly and with such good humour, it's all part of the service. Some customers even join in apparently.

'Rubbish. She is our number one, tip-top, top of the corner shop customer and friend and we need to keep her happy. In fact, I have a badge for you, Aly.' Kav pulls a sticker from a page like a primary school teacher, then slaps it onto the pocket of the denim dungarees I've customised with an image of the cats, also wearing dungarees, which I thought was suitably meta. I'm touched by the badge but even more grateful she thinks of me as a friend. I've been thinking of her that way too but wondered if bonding with your local shopkeeper might be a gastro-mutation of Stockholm syndrome.

'What kind of coffee would you like?'

'Can you knock me up a latte?'

Manolis sighs loudly and his partner grins, the diamond in her nose twitching like she's about to put a spell on him. 'Manolis, please bring our top customer her beverage in the sunshine.'

'Do you have a few minutes to sit with me?' I ask her, never taking her limited time for granted.

'Well, I'm not staying to play stockroom bingo with this incompetent fool. And what's the point of having your own café if you can't stop and sample the goods?' Kav winks, as she pushes me outside.

'Café' is an overstatement. Two tiny wrought iron tables sit on the uneven pavement, along with four chairs purpose built to trip up passers-by. My friend pulls her notepad from her jeans pocket, slips it under a wonky table leg, pulls her long black hair into a tight ponytail and ties it with an elastic band she sweeps up from the ground. 'The postman leaves them lying around. I clear up the planet while channelling IU.'

I raise an eyebrow; enough to make her sigh.

'KPop?' she says. 'How old are you, Aly – seventy-five?'

'Full disclosure? At just over a quarter of a century I am in grave danger of turning into an old woman with cats, as a client rightly pointed out yesterday. My life sucks even more than normal, Kav; I'm about to be evicted.'

There's surprise mixed in with her sympathy but we both know property around here has shot up in price and the warehouse car park alone must be worth a fortune. Kav and Manolis are themselves trying to pay back their loan on the shop and they live above it in a space hardly big enough to swing Milly 'It's a disaster, although it's spurred me on to try and get out of that semi-squat ASAP. You know I've been working towards that for a while anyway.'

Kav takes my hand. 'My advice? Do the lottery every

Saturday night. Luck feeds on luck and even if you only win ten pounds, it will open you up to good fortune. Use Craigslist to house hunt as it's not all about sex. You must immediately increase your intake of apples, celery, carrots and baking soda . . .'

'Why?'

'They make your teeth look whiter. One of the quickest ways of achieving your dream might be hooking yourself a successful man. When I first hooked up with Manolis, he collapsed inside like one of those Belgian chocolate bombs we sold on Valentine's Day.'

Manolis plonks two cardboard cups onto the table. 'The bombs everyone brought back when they exploded in their microwaves? I did not collapse, woman. My heart is strong as an ox, the doctor said.'

'He said it was strong for a forty-nine-year-old man with high cholesterol, not a creature of the nativity. Please take those coffees inside and bring them out in proper china. And then price up the borlotti beans and stop hanging around us like the smell of fried cabbage.'

'I cannot price those beans because we are not going to sell them. I informed you of this news half an hour before you went to the cash and carry.'

My friend raises her voice. 'You cannot bar all foods that you do not personally like, you lumpfish.'

'I am the owner of the shop therefore I can sell or ban whatever I choose.' Manolis stamps off, leaving our cups where they are.

Kav sips delicately at her coffee, her piercing glinting in the sunlight. 'He is *co-owner* of this shop and I think he forgets that sometimes. However, he is my barometer and I could not do without him. Aly, you need a man who has surface sex appeal and hidden depths, although sometimes they're both so hidden with Manolis you need a shovel. What am I to buy him for his fiftieth birthday? The man who has a bucket list of things he can't tolerate.'

As I cross the warehouse car park, one of the Oddities is talking to a guy in a suit. She snaps a bubble into her own face, and I sigh at the times I've scraped sticky gum from the communal shower. I try to remember what she called herself when we were first introduced; I want to say Tonya but maybe that's because I'm worried she's about to kneecap our visitor.

Drawing closer, I notice he has a scanner in one hand and a clipboard in the other. 'If you have a parcel it'll probably be for Joy, our luxury hutch-maker. She has so many deliveries I've wondered if she might have Amazon on speed dial,' I inform him.

My neighbour raises a Trumpian fist. 'Not a delivery guy. Estate agent. He's not coming in though. We will not be assisting the acquisition of our property by greedy venture capitalists today, tomorrow or any time next week.' She blocks the doorway and stabs at his upper body with her finger as she speaks.

'I need to measure up. The current landlord suggested it might be better to drop in and speak with all of you individually, as I believe there is no communal phone,' the brave man says, continuing to face off with her, even when she pops a bubble so close to his face he'd surely feel the blowback.

'The only way you'll be able to drop in is by helicoptering onto the roof from a chopper. Think of this as our French Revolution; this door is the barricade, and we will grab every last broom handle to fight you off. You'll have to set fire to me to make me move.' She crosses her arms. I'm guessing she saw the *Half-Hour Les Mis* the Middlesex Players performed last summer; Manolis dragged several customers along to witness his interpretation of Monsieur Thénardier as a little-nuanced villain with a Greek accent.

The visitor swings around. And I realise I know him.

'Greg?'

'The very same. Hello, Alyssa.'

Not quite the same. Although my teenage romance seems hardly to have aged, he has filled out significantly. Tall and blond, with skin so fair he could give Snow White some moisturising tips, his arms are practically bursting out of his short-sleeved shirt. His light blond fringe lazily flops across the lightest of blue eyes. Back at school I remember wondering if his irises were flecked with sky as he moved in for a snog. He is missing the knitted jumpers he always used to wear even in summer, but his trousers are as skintight as ever. Greg's family never felt the cold: their house was heated from the floor up and then ventilated from the ceiling down; no one seemed to have any idea you could close windows. If a barista was to create them a DNA coffee, it would undoubtedly be an iced one.

'How are you, Alyssa?' Greg asks, holding out his hands like Jesus in a picture book.

'It's Aly now. And I'm doing great, thanks. What are you doing on my doorstep? It's been a while.'

'A long while,' he agrees. 'I've come to measure up, Aly.' To be fair, the shortened name sounds wrong coming from his lips.

'Maybe you should come back some other time. We're not geared up for estate agents. If you give me a few days, I can rally the troops for you.'

'As fascinating as this *High School Musical* is, I have to get on now,' says my neighbour, letting the front door go. I grab it and prepare to follow her inside.

My teen crush sweeps his hair from his brow, before appealing to my good nature. 'I can't return empty handed; it's taken me half an hour to get here, and I need measurements for five flats plus the hall areas and the garage at the back.'

'The garage is Henry's apartment. He'll probably let you in although Joy won't. Not without a search warrant,' I tell him. 'And even if she does, she may tie you up and foot-whip you.'

'Can I nip into your flat quickly, so I at least have something in the bag? It'll take minutes, I promise.' I shiver when he touches my arm, it's been a while since a man has held any body part if you don't count my GP. And then I shudder at the idea of anyone seeing my home.

'I'm really sorry but my flat is a disaster zone. I'm still as messy as ever.' Or at least not as compulsively tidy as the man standing in front of me. 'If you phone and let us know when you are coming next time, I can make you a cuppa and we can catch up.' I nod a goodbye, letting the steel door swing shut and hear the familiar clang of the lock as I reach the doorway to my flat. Nudging the door open, I hear a sharp intake of breath. Greg has followed me in and is looking at the flat with his baby blue eyes.

I can't hide my irritation. 'Which part of "I'm sorry but you need to come back another time," wasn't clear?'

'Why's it full of boxes?'

I want to dismiss his question but there are so many the door doesn't even open properly. I assess my living room afresh through Greg's eyes. The uneven floor is covered with a jumble of brown and white. Stacks of cardboard boxes are piled high to the ceiling. The corners are filled with plastic crates stuffed with packages threatening to escape from beneath the lids. Three of the larger boxes form a makeshift coffee table. Several are neatly packed in themes like 'kitchen' and 'bathroom', while others are as random as a charity shop haul.

He looks at me quizzically.

'I'm storing some stuff for the Amazon depot. Helping them out.' My joke is weak; taken by surprise like this I'm unable to summon a rapid response. 'You'd better come in then,' I sigh, 'as you already have.'

I feel a rush of shame at the shambles in front of me. Some of the boxes are stained with food and many are damaged. Some of the packages are open, with their contents spilling out, while others look like they're ready for a trip to the post office. Molly lounges on a high stack she's clawed and battered for months, while her sibling is playing with a pretend mouse in the far corner of the room, drowning out its imaginary squeak with the recognisable yowl of the Sphynx. One of these cats alone is rackety, but mine egg each other on. Greg winces. I always suspected if cats came with a remote control, my ex would switch the whole species off.

'You still have a cat, then. And I'm guessing you've either just moved in . . .' he scrunches his eyes as though still trying to work out the answer to a pub quiz question '. . . or you've developed a fetish for cardboard.'

His sense of humour has sharpened since we dated; Greg's cool Icelandic manner didn't make him master of the jokes as a teen. I guide him towards the breakfast bar and the cats follow, mewing and winding around my ankles. They don't approach my ex, which is understandable as he's looking at them like they might detonate an explosion.

'Need to eBay some stuff for sure. Meet my flatmates. The fantasmagorical Molly and the no-frills Milly.' Milly hisses like a panto villain in front of an unappreciative audience, the tip of her tail twitching. Molly's ears flatten, but she stays close, rubbing her back firmly on my legs. Odd; they normally love a bit of company. I ask Greg if he wants a cuppa. I might as well pump him for info on the house while he's here and find out how long I've got to re-engineer my life.

'You still talk to cats?'

'Of course. I do. Yes, yes, I talk to you all the time, don't I, lickle-lickety-spit?' I tickle Milly behind the ears as I fill the kettle.

'Well, I suppose people talk to plants . . .'

'Not like plants though. Cats are alive, responsive, engaged.'

'Plants are alive. Remember strawberry plants from biology?'

'Er nope.'

I remember he was very keen on biology, particularly at his house after school. 'They can reproduce sexually or asexually. Only sex produces fruit. You need to select the hermaphrodites for the best chance of growing a decent crop.' He picks up one of the mugs I've popped down by the kettle and examines it. Thank heavens it is clean. The way my mother lived, combined with some of the habits of my old ladies, has driven me to do the washing up immediately after every meal.

Molly jumps onto the counter, runs her tongue along the back of my hand, and holds her chin up as though waiting for a kiss. I nuzzle her whiskerless face. But she isn't impressed; it's the pink wafer's she's after. 'Not that. They will make you sick, pretty thing.' She turns her tail on me, vocalising her gripe. Milly quickly finds her way into the space her sister vacated; her chatter softer now she's up close to me.

Greg sneezes before pulling out a gadget and holding it up to the walls. I briefly wonder if he's checking for damp. If he's allergic to that he'll be in convulsions by the time he leaves.

'I only have Tetley. Hope that's OK,' I say, glad this month's tea bags have a recognisable name. 'Who'd want to buy this place? You should see the communal shower. It's worse than the facilities at internment camps.'

'The average selling price for a decent-sized house round here is £475,000. Office property is premium. It'll sell quickly.' He sneezes again.

'Don't scare me please. I've got nowhere else to go. Do you take sugar?'

'I do not.' It must be a decade since Greg's family relocated, but the faint Icelandic accent is definitely still there. Initially he told me he came from a long line of impoverished fishermen. In reality, his family farmed salmon and were worth enough to cash buy a detached house when they arrived in the UK and still had budget left over for some action-packed visits home where they marched around ice-covered volcanoes.

'Could you help me find a cheap place to rent? Or even better an affordable place to buy? I've some money saved for a deposit but haven't seen anything even remotely possible yet. Needs to be pet friendly obvs.'

'What's your budget?'

'Zero. Or thereabouts.'

Smiling at my flippancy, he watches me load sugar into my brew, blinking when I put the teaspoon back into the paper bag and sugar coagulates around it. He glances to the doorway as if his delicate blue eyes cannot take the slobbery, but maybe he's assessing how many bedrooms I have for a quick sale.

I pop his tea on the boxes that form my coffee table, and he momentarily covers his cup. 'Don't panic, I wasn't planning to stealth bomb your drink.' I sit down on the sofa, and he sips on his drink as he wanders around. Greg was always quite fastidious about clothes and instinct tells me my former boyfriend sweats over (and into) his work trousers and shirts every morning. I look down at his shoes. Brown loafers and dark socks. Why didn't Rick Harvard wear socks to the office? It was odd. I glance at my noticeboard with three solitary socks pegged onto it waiting for a match, including an elf sock left over from Christmas. Sometimes it's so jammed with lonely soles I should put them on Tinder. I suddenly have a recollection of Greg re-pegging the washing I put on the line and Mum thanking him as though he'd personally taken the clothes to the river and beaten them with a stick.

Mum approved of Greg. He was the kind of boy she knew and understood in her role of pastoral carer at the fee-paying school we both went to. Posh kids with posh kids' problems. What she didn't understand were the misfits. The teenagers whose parents scraped together enough money to get them into the school. The scholarship kids who said inappropriate things in loud voices, in normal London accents peppered with swear words. Most kids were there because their parents deserved it. Greg was there because his parents were kings of a fish empire. I was there because my mother had a massive staff discount and was too embarrassed to have a comprehensive kid in her home. I was the bargain basement child, who wore second-hand uniform recycled at the school summer fairs. The other pupils played spot the difference every day, perhaps every moment of my school life, and my mother joined them. Unaware perhaps at first, and then later deliberately cruel, she picked away at my faults, publicly and in private. At home my hair bore a lot of her fury; she would rip chunks out with a comb in the morning to try and 'normalise it' and then blame me for making her late. She hated the way I customised my skirts by shortening the hem. I wasn't academic enough, athletic enough, thin enough or tidy enough. I just wasn't 'enough' in any way.

She was paid to care for everyone in the school and she just about managed to achieve that. But she didn't care for me.

'Are you hungry? I have a thousand pink wafers.' I rip open the second packet I bought from the Kozy Korner.

'What is it with the boxes, Alyssa?' Greg asks again, slowly, as though afraid of the answer. Maybe he has guessed. I try to remember how often and blatant the guilt gifts were, when she went too far with her tongue.

'It's my childhood,' I reply, rubbing the back of my neck as if to alleviate an invisible pain. 'And I'm not rushing to unpack it.' What did he see back then? An abandoned child? A disappointed parent? A victim and a bully circling each other like cage fighters?

*A complaining tongue reveals an ungrateful heart. If you despised it so much, then why did you stay?*

Because I had nowhere else to go. And now history is repeating itself.

Greg looks as if he's trying to read me, then says, 'Remember the dunking game?'

'The last finger standing?'

'Winner gets to keep the whole pack.'

'But you never won because scoffing biscuits is my superpower.'

'Is that a challenge? Maybe I spent the last few years practising.'

'Did you?'

'I might have.' His smile is cheeky, reminding me why I once fancied him. I dole out one brightly coloured biscuit each and we giggle as they quickly disintegrate. But when he brushes my chest to point out where I've spilled mush onto my front, I straighten my back, flick my chin up, and our eyes meet. A spark of something from the past passes between our bodies. Faint but still there. He breaks the mood by sneezing four times.

'Eight of those in a row have the same energy as an orgasm.' I regret this statement as an awkward silence falls.

'Well, I'd better get going,' he says.

'Oh. I was waiting for you to pull out a tape measure or take some snaps.'

He taps his little black scanner. 'We've moved on from that. This little gadget is a game changer.'

'Can it see into the future? I need some lottery numbers.'

Wiping non-existent crumbs off his trousers with neatly trimmed nails, he moves towards the door. 'Things move quickly with email lists and online advertising. I'll call you if a suitable property comes up that I think you may be able to afford. Or feel free to call me if you fancy going for a drink or something.' He pops his business card in my hand, and lightly brushes his lips against my cheek, before earnestly telling me he's enjoyed our surprise reunion. His eyes seem bluer than ever, and I wonder if he still wears chunky knits. I glance at the card. 'Greg Johannesson, Property Broker. Executive Estates. Ask me about your dream home.'

I snort a laugh. My dream home? I'd be happy with one of the guinea pig hutches made by Joy upstairs if it came with a car parking space.

# Chapter 4

Ruislip high street is packed with people shopping and having coffee. As usual I have a gap in my morning schedule the size of the Atlantic Rift. As Greg hasn't called with a bargain property, I decide to pop into an estate agent's after my appointment with Carrie. This client is different from my others; she isn't suffering from the savagery of old age or the onset of dementia. Before she'd even hit forty, with a chain of businesses to manage, the poor girl burned out. One day her legs gave up. Just like that. Although the rest of her body remains fully charged, particularly her nerves.

Before I even cross the welcome mat, she asks me to re-park away from her drive as her next-door neighbour, a nurse on a permanent night shift, has been complaining about the encroachment of carer cars. I circle around looking for a space that isn't residents' parking only and when I don't find one, I park in her driveway. It's a small car, I'm only here for another hour and her neighbour always seems quite friendly.

I quickly assess the jobs that need tackling, ticking the task boxes on the app as I move around the small flat. There are clothes piled high on the sofa and coffee cups crowding her bedside table, and the huge bag of meds and lotions looks like a burglar rifled through it.

Last night's carer clearly had no time for more than the basics; could Carrie be spiralling again? I log my worries into the app.

My client needs washing and dressing before we even start on the hoist that'll lift her out of bed and into a wheelchair. She's irritable as I prepare the machine and accuses me of being trigger happy with the remote. There should be another carer here to help me with the hoist, but I've given up complaining when I'm left to go solo, and I can handle Carrie. My notes tell me she hasn't been out of bed since Friday as she fell out with the weekend carers and refused to let them touch her. She wants me to do some gardening for her, so we race through medication, coffee and scrambled eggs. I schedule a community nurse appointment as I bung her clothes in the washing machine. She once told me her skimpy thongs are two fingers up to her illness and I admire her for not giving up as I peg some out on the line. Then I gently brush her long dark hair, easing out the tangles.

She winces. 'Yours must be a nightmare.'

'I have hairless cats. It all balances out.'

Flinging open the back door, I return to the living room to collect Carrie and wheel her out to the kitchen, where her anxiety levels rise. 'You already opened the door? I wanted to open it. I wanted to hold the handle in my hands and feel the rush of the air and surprise myself at how my garden has grown. I've been looking forward to it all night.'

'I'll close it now.'

'Too late, the moment is spoilt.' To others she may sound like a toddler, to me she's a woman clinging on to the edge of a cliff, and if I can help her dig her fingernails into the rock then I will do everything I can to facilitate that. We agree to close the door and go through the process again and this time she is in charge. I feel mean when I have to push her back inside, but she understands my time is dictated by the app. When I vacate her house, ten minutes late, I gulp the fresh air. Leaving my car where it is to avoid the parking meters on the high street, I wander past the usual suspects of charity shops and Turkish barbers, scanning the road for estate agents. I accidentally walk past one twice as it resembles a coffee shop with big comfy sofas and cappuccinos to order.

'Can I ask you about my dream home?' I ask a man who appears to be hanging around in the doorway waiting for customers.

'Absolutely,' he replies. He is wearing a thin knitted tank top over a white shirt and grey tie. I flashback to Rick Harvard's shirt with two buttons undone and try to banish it from my mind. 'Ask away.'

'I need something cheap as chips. With parking. Maybe near the underground as my car's been sounding off lately. Don't care about a garden.' I fold my arms. 'I know it doesn't sound like anyone's idea of a dream home, but I don't have a lot of money and it would be a property fantasy sorted just to have a bathroom of my own. I've been living in a kind of artists' squat you see, but the landlord is forcing us out.'

'Absolutely,' he says again, with more force than my landlord could ever summon. 'We sell a wide range of property for all budgets and lifestyles. Houses by the Tube station cost upwards of £750, 000 but we do have a range of cheaper options. Are you happy to consider a studio flat? I have a couple that may interest you. Can I email you the details? We are trying to move towards a paperless office.'

'How about I sit here with a coffee while you ping them over? I assume the sofas are for surfing property porn?'

'Absolutely.' He peels off to his computer while I check my Instagram feed. This is better than the library, I bet there's free Wi-Fi too; I should ask for loads of properties and chill out for the afternoon.

'Anything you like?' he enquires after about ten minutes.

'The garibaldis are nice.'

'I meant the flats.'

I sigh. 'Actually, I can't afford to buy anything round here. Not even that one where the bed is in a cubbyhole in the kitchen. Do you have anything to let while I do double shifts and turbo save?'

I expect him to get ticked off, but he holds his palms together like he's about to bless me not brain me. 'Absolutely.' In minutes he's found me a selection of ridiculously overpriced rental flats. 'All of these properties are available immediately. You will need to provide a month's rent and a deposit up front. Let me know which appeal and we can sort a viewing.'

'Absolutely,' I echo, with a lot less conviction.

After running three streets, I retrieve my car from Carrie's drive. If I move quickly, I might be on time for my next appointment. I attempt to put it into gear. Nothing. I slam the clutch down as hard as it will go and try again. Double nothing. The curtain twitches and Carrie looks out while her next-door neighbour pulls back a blind and glares at me. I rev the engine and hold down the clutch, trying to force the gears. Still nothing. Mouthing an apology to both Carrie and the scary nurse, I ring the mechanic who's more familiar with my car than he is his own. It flips to voicemail. I punch in another number.

'Hello, Turtle Dove Care, how can we make you happy today?' asks Thing One, or it could be Thing Two. Right at this moment it could be the Messiah and I wouldn't care unless he had a vehicle with a tow bar.

'I have good news and bad news. The good first. I'm currently running on time.'

'That's awesome.'

'And unheard of, I know. But my car has broken down on Carrie's drive.'

'Not awesome.'

'Not awesome at all,' her twin repeats. What's this, a conference call? 'We will need to give your next appointment away.'

'And issue a fine you because you are late.'

'So sorry.' They say this part in tandem, with a smile, as they can't help being nice.

'You can't fine me for lateness if I'm not doing the appointment.'

'New rules. And if you don't get to your next appointment after that, the fine will increase.'

'That's mad. Where's your boss? Can I speak to her?'

'. . . She's in the Caribbean.'

'. . . She's in Hull.'

'Can you let us know when you get sorted?' says the Greek chorus.

'The thing is . . .' The Things don't really want to hear what the thing is, which is quite ironic really. They disengage together while sending oodles of love.

Kav is on her own in the shop and tries Manolis at the cash and carry but he doesn't pick up. I reluctantly take Greg's card out of my pocket. 'Hello, it's Aly, your blast from the past,' I say, when he picks up on the first ring. 'You gave me your card. The one that says to ask about my dream home?'

'Morning, Alyssa. Or if you wait one and a half minutes it will be afternoon.'

'It's Aly. I use the name Aly now. I'm in Ruislip and my car is dead. I'm stuck on a driveway I can't really afford to be on, as Annie Wilkes lives in the house next door.'

'Annie Wilkes?'

'Oh, sorry, I borrow a lot of Stephen King from the library. She's the . . .'

'I know who she is. I still enjoy a nice horror film.'

I shift uncomfortably in the driver's seat. Greg and I saw a run of scary movies when we were dating, in cinema stalls that smelt of popcorn and wee. At the beginning it was terrifying. Not the exorcisms or the zombies or the men with knives and a grudge, but the fear of being underage in a certificate eighteen film after just having changed out of my school uniform. Then there was the anxiety of doing the kissing right, and not puking because his breath smelt of fish. And then the consequences of doing the kissing right with a boy who was fast becoming a man. While the heroes on screen had to contend with slashing, I was more worried about groping and grinding, and whatever else he had in mind. And months later, once we'd got over all that, I worried about the risks of going all the way. I couldn't imagine how my mother would react to news of a grandchild.

Cursing not renewing my breakdown cover last month because I was sure I could find something cheaper, I explain to Greg I'm stranded on one of Ruislip's aspirational driveways.

'You need a tow to a garage?'

Relief washes through me that he offered before I had to ask. Then I feel guilty about going off-piste with an estate agent and confess all. 'I was in Ruislip with some time to spare. A man in a tank top at Wright and Wright bombarded me with details for an impressive selection of houses I can't afford. I think I'll stick with you and your firm.'

'Give me half an hour to rearrange an appointment. And stay away from that shark. You do not want to buy your dream home from him.'

'You're so right. In fact, from his knitted tank top to his belief in the Absolute, I worried he might be the leader of a religious cult.'

We drop the car at my garage and on the ride home Greg is upbeat, chatting away about sales. 'Our bosses have forecast that next year one and a half million people will buy and sell a house in the UK. Prices may go up between twenty and twenty-five per cent in the next five years. And that's before you take into account there may be as many as a hundred and seventy thousand new homes built this year.'

'Let's hope they make some of them affordable. Price rises like that aren't good for anyone. What about the bubble popping?'

'What do you know about bubbles? Oh, I forgot, you are an Instagrammer,' he says.

'And you've turned into a comedian since we last met.' I'm surprised by the banter between us now. It wasn't there back then. We got together because no one else wanted us. Greg was a foreigner. He bored on about facts and figures, and he joined the school late which gave him less chance of making friends. We met at the place where all misfits hang out; games club. He turned up on the first day with a board game he'd found in a strange Icelandic junk shop which he claimed was a battle map for trolls. Greg believed in elves. I was rereading *Lord of the Rings* for the hundred and third time. On paper we were made for each other.

Next morning, with both cats on my lap, purring happily, I look at a selection of the rental property details and whistle at the prices. 'I think we will need to abandon plans for a studio flat and live in a mousehole, AlyCats. I wonder how much Joy would actually charge for one of her guinea pig hutches?'

A sponsored post enquiry drops into my inbox. I usually ignore the spammers as they want access to my followers in return for pennies, or even worse, exposure. But the product seems genuine, and the fee is appropriate for the work involved. Apparently the gold cat toothbrush can harness ultrasound to produce more than thirty thousand strokes a minute. Impressed, I write back and accept the job, asking for a sample of the product to photograph.

Lifting Milly's head to look at her teeth, I notice her ears are gunky again. Pushing her off me, I fetch cotton wool balls, a bowl of warm water and solution. Sphynx cats need regular ear care as well as baths. They even need regular screening for heart issues.

Milly doesn't like the cleaning ritual, but she puts up with it. Molly sees what's going on, yowls and hides under a stool, believing she's invisible.

'Oh, I'm coming for you next,' I say, putting down the bowl for now after giving Milly a good going-over.

As I scroll through my Instagram feed I trigger a video that interests me as it's a cat's head on a woman's body. Even though I recognise it as a filter, it's still bizarre. Even weirder, the woman is chatting batty about Winston Churchill.

'The former British prime minister declared "Cats look down to you while dogs look up to you and pigs look you in the eye." But have you looked at your cat in the eye lately? Your pet is not afraid to hold your gaze. This may be the precursor to aggression, or they may be sizing you up as prey. One thing is for sure; they are unlikely to blink first. And in their soul you can find the secret to being a better human. Don't believe me? Look into their eyes today. And find out more on my course at Power Towers, online or in person. Follow the web link in the profile for more details.'

As she speaks, she fondles the long dark curls that sit on her shoulders, like she's one of those whisperers who bore you to sleep by stroking fake hair on YouTube. With freshly cleaned ears Milly starts madly chasing a pretend squirrel around the living room. She is one of my two most precious friends, but honestly, who in their right minds would want to be like their cat?

Later in the morning, the company couriers over the toothbrush and the post is done and dusted within another hour. The day continues to go well; against all the odds I discover home caring can be done on the bus, with a bit of sprinting in between. Turtle Dove Care's sloppy scheduling helps. And thank goodness London buses are so cheap and plentiful. However, as I share a seat with a woman who looks older than my oldest client, I work out the fines I will receive for two of the jobs plus the time between appointments without payment will average out my earnings to about eight pounds an hour. 'When I grow up, I'd like a job that earns the minimum wage,' was not a statement I ever told a career officer. How will I ever manage a deposit, let alone shell out for higher rent in the meantime?

Standing at the bus stop, bone tired after being asked to scrub my final client's floor using a sponge, followed by an extended struggle pushing her broken arm into a shrunken jumper, I check Instagram. My new post hasn't gone down very well. My followers are damning of the cat toothbrush, its price tag and suitability for a cat's jaw. Ultrasound is for pregnant women and not pets apparently. Their outrage is interrupted by my garage mechanic, who phones to tell me the gearstick is fine. I almost cheer before he informs me the clutch was to blame.

'Mr Clutch is not fine. You've been keeping your foot on him again. Has he been grumbling? You need to listen to him more.' When the mechanic first started referring to my car in human terms I was creeped out, but I soon played along when I realised he was cheaper than other garages.

'He did squeak when I put my foot down, for a while. For more than a while. Maybe a month,' I admit.

'He's going to set you back three hundred pounds.'

'Ouch!' Like Mr Clutch, I'm prone to squealing when depressed.

'I can fix it tomorrow.'

'No. I need to think about whether he's worth it. I've spent too much on car repairs lately.'

'Fair enough. We'll leave him in our car park for now while you decide,' the mechanic says cheerfully as he puts down the phone.

As I get off the bus and drag myself the last few hundred yards to my home, I notice 'For Sale' signs outside our building and at the entrance to the car park.

'So he did it. Sold us out,' says the neighbour whose name I still can't remember, tending to a grow bag she's installed outside the front door.

'Yes, we're officially almost homeless. Don't suppose you have a hammer and a ladder, and we can bash the nails out and nick the signs?'

'Just a minute, yeah.'

'Hey, I was joking.' I put my hand on her arm. 'I'm exhausted and it's probably illegal.'

'I love illegal.' She rifles in her bag and pulls out a canister of paint. 'We could change the message. They can't arrest us for doodling. Well, they can, but they have to catch us first!'

Poor Greg. I owe him one for the tow but the chance to change the signs and put off potential buyers is irresistible. I hold the ladder and my neighbour goes to work with her spray cans, whiting out the original letters and turning 'For Sale' into 'Sold'. The artist scrawls TCP on the right-hand corner of both in fat green letters. Not so great for avoiding detection, but at least now I know her name.

Back in my flat, I imitate a human fruit machine by holding up a pack of apple pies, some defrosted raspberry ripple ice cream, and a carton of orange drink that's cheaper because someone extracted the bits to put into proper orange juice. Milly comes forward, turns her nose up at my shopping and holds her paw out for a massage. She is living her best life while I am further than ever from mine. We sit together on my baggy sofa, and I look around my flat. The cat toothbrush post is getting no traction at all, and for the first time in ages, the likes and comments across the week have dipped. The raft of cat-related hashtags I add to each post don't seem to be working as hard for me and a new generation of catfluencers is nipping at my heels. I think back to my meeting with Glimmer, and everything Patricia promised me. Whilst I don't want to be shot into infinity, maybe I wouldn't mind being raised up a little. But didn't the CEO say Patricia was leaving? I search up his invitation to the conference in my inbox and read it again. It sounds super-glam and fun. I press reply. Maybe I can get on the Glimmer train after all? My talent manager wouldn't need to know AlyCat is two cats. I can barely tell them apart myself in dim light. Cracking open the apple pies, I feed a crumb to Milly. At least I can guarantee she'll be cleaning her teeth tonight. Then I type out a note to Rick Harvard, telling him I'm reconsidering his offer of representation.

# Chapter 5

There's no DNA coffee bar at Glimmer today and I skip the chance of flailing around on one of the white helter-skelters trying to pass themselves off as seats in reception. Scanning my pass on the blue light, I issue a command to the newsreader, and whizz silently upwards. On my second visit, I'm feeling like a pro.

Wandering the corridors of the fifth floor, looking for a meeting room called Chicago, I pass meetings occurring in just about every other American city. The final door is slightly ajar. Rick Harvard is speaking to another man, and I take a moment to reacquaint myself with him. Almost accent-less and rich in tone, his voice is made for a microphone. Hovering in the corridor, I hop from foot to foot wondering whether to crash their chat. I'm ten minutes early. I was hoping a PA might show me in so the occupants of the room would look at her instead of me. Now all eyes will be on me.

Rick Harvard doesn't give me space to interrupt so I'm left standing on the periphery. 'If my ass caught fire this week, I wouldn't have had time to put it out. I barely touched down in New York before I had to be on a flight back again. But we do have a new Head of Strategy; Juliet Rae. She was as formidable as my father said. Sharp and focused with a contact book most people can only dream of.'

'If William Harvard finds her a handful, there's no hope for the rest of us,' says the other voice. 'I know her by reputation only, as the killer whale of online marketing.'

'I wouldn't say that to her face if you value your job. Mind you, she does seem to eat a lot of sushi.' I can hear the smile in Rick's words. 'I'm hoping her move to London will encourage more clients across the Atlantic to match up with our content creators. It's a good example of the revolving door that I bang on about; the agent hooks up with the brand, the influencer joins them, and round and round they go together until a better match steps in, and then round and round they go as well. If we match the right company with the right influencer no one ends up out in the cold. It's a golden circle.'

'I'm glad to be a part of it. As you know I've had two new signings in the last few days, both high-profile blisters and I'm looking forward to my appraisal.' This guy sounds like he really wants an appraisal. And even weirder, a blister. He should try cramming his feet into my red wellies.

I premiere a sound that blends a cough, a snort and a footballer gobbing onto the pitch as I take a step into the room.

Rick swings round and raises an eyebrow. 'Good morning, Aly, are you having a stroke?' I throw him a surprised look. Aren't CEOs supposed to have pokers up their butts? 'Let me introduce you to Sam. He's one of our up-and-coming account managers and he's fully up to speed with your work.'

For a moment I'm disappointed. But of course he's going

to pass me on to a junior manager. A skinny guy with a shaved head steps forward to shake my hand. 'Thanks for making yourself available today, Aly.'

'S'OK. The only thing I had on was creating a cat costume out of the bottle tops in my recycling bin. Sewing foil is tricky so I'm happy to procrastinate.' When they look intrigued I continue, 'There was something on the radio this morning about the government's proposed milk tax, so . . .' I tail off. They don't want to hear about my boring life.

'A typical example of how topical AlyCat is with her feed,' Rick says to his colleague, pulling out a chair and inviting me to join them around the long, stripped wood table.

While basking in his praise, I can't help jumping into their earlier conversation. 'What if the revolving door spins out of control?' I ask him, praying he won't laugh at my question. Rick sits down opposite me, resting his chin in his palm before gesturing for me to continue. So much for flying under the radar. 'What you were saying earlier about the revolving door; say an influencer looks perfect for the brand on paper but the followers don't buy it, as they can see it's not authentic? The brand loses money, the influencer loses credibility.' I pause, hoping I'm making any sense at all. Their attention tells me I am. 'So the brand pushes harder, the door keeps spinning and the influencer can't keep up with the pace. And suddenly, bang, the influencer's face is up against the glass, and it smashes and there's blood all over the marble tiles, but the door is still spinning and before you know it you have a pile-up; multiple sudden and unexplained deaths by social media, linked to your firm. Not the best PR.' I wonder if he's noticed I've sneaked in a quote from one of his own blog posts.

He lifts his hand and runs it through the gelled ends of his hair. 'I think there may be some projection going on here. Are you worried we might sell you out to the wrong type of brand?'

'I'm speaking hypothetically.'

Our eyes meet. Rick holds mine with ease, but I struggle to cope with the intensity of those brown, almost black features. 'Well, I'd like to reassure you that our hypothetical door is well oiled, and you get to choose how fast it spins. Brands and influencers are guided by excellent managers like Sam here. Should you find yourself with your face up against the glass and a partner that's either pushing too fast or dragging its feet, he'll be there with you, pushing back or pulling them on. That'll be his job, if you take the plunge and sign with us today. I'd like to clarify what the sticking points are so I can work out how to change your mind about us.'

In the centre of the pale wooden desk is a large, polished bean I recognise from TV programmes about the city. I'd love to go to America. In the silver curve, my face looks distorted, like cookie dough carelessly rolled out. Allowing me a moment to think, Rick pours water for us all and asks me if I'd like a coffee. A new haircut is neatly clipped to a line just above a collarless white shirt, which he's teamed with dark green chinos and a belt. He comfortably stretches out his long legs under the table as he phones for refreshments, remembering how I like my coffee.

'What's a blister?' I ask.

They freeze, like I just announced I had one on my ass.

'You shouldn't have heard that.' Rick throws Sam a look as he decides whether to give any more away. Then he shrugs. 'Blisters are our shorthand for B-listers.'

'And then there's their social climbing siblings the C-listers – which the newbies sometimes nickname Clisters,' Sam interrupts, smiling at his own joke. Rick nods, giving him permission to tell me more. 'The Blisters are what we come to work for. They've already proved themselves to be standout in their field and we help them with the next stage of their commercial journey. Sure, we manage their social media and public appearances, but most of all we manage them. We transform them gradually, from someone with potential to someone with worldwide appeal, and we ensure they cope with their fame, make the best decisions and hold up under the pressure. We understand they're human and catch them before they fall. We don't go after the celebrities living on the edge, with a drink problem, shopping habit, sex drive or ego. We sign up the hard workers and successful entrepreneurs and try and help them manage the trolls, the money and the press. There's no such thing as an overnight success, but we make their journey easier with our full package of support, in return for a fixed percentage of their Blister earnings.' He is trying his hardest to impress me. He clearly doesn't realise his former colleague already offered me a percentage of infinity. 'And if we can't fill the stable with enough Blisters, then Clisters fill the gaps, eh boss?'

'I must be a Zlister. Sounds like a herpes cream.'

Rick chokes slightly. Maybe I should ask if he's having a heart attack. 'Did you order a bacon roll?' he asks, quickly recovering. 'We're offering all staff and visitors the chance to claim a hot breakfast sandwich from the vintage Airstream in the square. You should have been given a voucher when you signed in.' I nod, hoping they'll offer me another on my way out. 'Soon you'll be able to order a comped bacon butty by asking for it in the lift, if the engineers get onto it before the century's out.' Rick seems unnaturally excited about all this. Is this some kind of sorting hat trick? If I say yes to a bacon roll does that elevate me to the Y list?

I frame my reply carefully. 'I don't think it would be very appropriate to drip bacon juice on my lap during a job interview.' The men look down at my lap. I customised my crimson velvet trousers with silver lightning strikes, which kinda work. My lip gloss matches them, and I put on a tiny bit of mascara. As my hair is having a tameable day, I've made a stab at gathering it in. I think I'm pulling off a version of normal.

'This isn't a job interview, Aly,' Rick gently explains, as though he's talking to one of my elderly ladies. 'We are a family. We look out for our clients; look after them well. I'm happy you called us, and quite surprised given your aversion to us earlier in the month. If you sign a contract with us we can start representing you in a completely tailored way. Sam will make you heard above the noise of the Net and, most importantly, he will make you a living. Other team members may advise on your image or social media and I will take a keen interest in your career path.

You and your cat are quite unique; I think you know that. I firmly believe you will do well for us, and I'm sure we will do well for you.'

A family.

He sits back in his chair and waits for my response. Sam is doodling diamond shapes on a branded notepad. He'll probably get a disciplinary for not drawing stars. I sip on some water and am relieved when the coffee arrives. My thoughts are all over the shop as I load four sugar lumps into my drink and then pretend it was a mistake. I excuse myself to go to the loo and get lost relocating Chicago afterwards. Throughout the faffing, my brain churns through the reasons I should sign, and the reasons to take a hike. Somehow I come to a decision.

I start slowly. 'I will sign your contract. But I think we might disagree about some aspects of my career. I am not the story. I don't go in front of the camera. I am probably never going to make it to the heady heights of a Blister, and . . .' Am I brave enough? I need the money too much to bottle it. 'I'd like a bigger cut of the fee. I googled other agencies . . .'

'The fee is non-negot—' Sam is quickly interrupted by his boss.

'Other agencies don't deliver like we do. Let's see how we go. I think you'll be surprised at the contracts we can negotiate that you couldn't on your own. Their fees will far outweigh ours. Let's do a six-month initial contract, with the option to elongate. You can get a feel for the agency and how we'll work together. If you push your way into being our next Blister then we'll get the full-term contract back on the table. If you become an Alister, I'll sack Sam and represent you myself,' says Rick, making my heart beat faster.

'Hey boss!' Sam laughs.

Out of the corner of my eye, I see Rick brush a lip with his thumb and it makes my mouth dry. I root around for a pack of chewing gum from my pocket. As they quietly chat about pros and cons of creating a pop-up roof garden for the office Christmas party in winter, I twirl my pen around my finger and accidentally send it flying off down the table. Retrieving it, I settle down to flick through a contract written in Egyptian hieroglyphs. Sam tells me I can take it home to sign later or get it checked out by a lawyer. But I steel myself, knock back my coffee and sign on the dotted line, realising I trust Rick to see me right on this.

He unfolds his arms. 'Welcome to the family, Aly. And by the way, the bacon butties aren't the only change I've made since your first visit. I will be giving up my spectacular view on the tenth floor for any desk that's free, as our whole firm will be moving to a hot-desking model from now on.'

My new talent manager's look of surprise is distorted in the shiny Chicago bean into a resemblance of Munch's painting, *The Scream*.

As he accompanies me to reception Sam asks me if I received an invitation to GlimmerCon. 'It's a cool way of bringing influencers together and celebrating their work. If you're free at the weekend I think you'll enjoy it. Rick is the star of the show.'

'I did thanks. Haven't replied yet but I'm looking forward to it.' If I looked in the coffee bean right now, I'd see my own face silently registering my surprise.

# Chapter 6

From hashtags to goodie bags, the GlimmerCon conference does what it says on the tin. Everyone seems colour saturated, and my sunshine-yellow chiffon dress goes with the glow. My mood is also sunny; I may find a new tribe this afternoon at this exciting sounding event, and I've just missed a rain shower. I check my Insta account quickly; I'm totally rocking the #GreatBritain hashtag this month, dressing the cats up as iconic Brits through the ages. Yesterday's was a beaut. Celebrating Vivienne Westwood, I gave my cat full-on attitude, with tartan pants and a 'God Save the Queen' T-shirt, all studded with safety pins. Molly was typically patient about me shaping a doll's tiara to her head and my follower count jumped by thousands after a teen vaguely connected to royalty reposted it on her stratospheric account.

A woman with purple hair is signing in the talent. She is being her most efficient self, ticking a VIP sheet, spotting badge names to go in the lanyards and placing gold ribbons around people's necks like they've won the Olympics. She sorts me out and seconds later she's on to the next influencer, while I'm left to find my own way into a dark, packed hall. Apparently, most of the nation's favourite YouTubers are here, including the twin makeup artists who've made a killing out of buffalo hairbrushes, and the schoolkid who swallows mobile phones and has loud, cringe-making conversations with his stomach.

Teenagers clutching fizzy drinks, wearing halter necks and hot pants, push through the crowd as skateboarding girls weave around them, selling Glimmer glow sticks and phone cases branded with ironic hashtags. It's hot and crowded and I'm slightly worried about Molly, cuddled up in a backpack on my shoulders. While I wouldn't normally take my cats out of the house, I was offered a hundred pounds yonks ago by a company who specialises in upmarket carriers. Their marketing department challenged me to take her adventuring in their most high-tech backpack, for a fun post on Insta. And what could be more fun than a social media convention? The snug, soundproof rucksack has a plastic bubble at the front so kitty can see out, and filters so she can breathe. And as Molly climbed in and settled herself in its luxury interior without a fuss and seemed to enjoy the journey, I was OK with my decision. Until I entered this over-amplified bat cave. Honestly? I pictured the Liberal Democrats conference or a TEDx Talk. But this event is hyper-teen and rock concert crowded, with microphones popping like corn in a pan. I transfer Molly from my back to my front, weaving the straps around my arms and peering down to check on her. Her blue eyes stare back at me and she blinks to tell me she's fine. Taking a pic of her in the bag to honour the Instagram deal, I then cover the bubble with my hands. I can lift her out for a proper photo shoot later if the crowds disperse.

I stand at the edge and take it all in; the assault of cheerful bants, the whooping applause and the silver lasers.

The MC explains that everyone has a five-minute slot to do their thing on stage, with a siren booting them off when their time is up. According to the rolling Twitter feed, broadcast on giant screens around the room, this is a beginners' carousel; the heavy hitters and viral sensations will apparently be up later. A screen tells me I can order a drink using my phone and a 'skategel' will bring it. No thanks, I'm not mad about necking back overpriced soda, delivered by a skateboarder with wings.

Loud music booms to signal the end of the carousel and roadies logoed up in Glimmer T-shirts reset the stage. A smell of nachos with over-processed cheese fills my nostrils from a rip-off concession stand and I realise I'm hungry. The hall is crammed, and people are still coming in, many soaked to the skin. I shiver in my thin dress. I haven't brought a coat and I'm not convinced the backpack is as waterproof as it said on the label.

Joining the edge of the crowd, I curse my lack of height as I absorb the drum and bass anthem of the next act to come on stage. Through a gap I can make out a woman who looks like a manga cartoon with her tiny waist and ski-slope nose as she leaps onto the platform and begins chucking around the contents of a box of metallic blue glitter. Soon the whole room is reflecting like a giant glitter ball and one or two people at the front of the stage are sneezing. When she's finished with blue, she moves onto 'biodegradable seaweed glitter in a muted green'; a blatant sales pitch for her online shop. We learn through her high-pitched yapping that she's unboxed glitter on YouTube for a living since preschool and is now killing it on TikTok. Maybe

I should embrace my mother's gifts and unbox my past in a series of live posts, with a Childline number stripped across the footage?

The MC, little more than an embryo himself, shuffles glitter girl off, announcing they're sticking with the sparkle for the next wannabe. He introduces a guy with a shaved head who makes glitter putty for YouTube videos. That's a job? He wheels on a gold workstation for a live demo of his craft. I'm surprised to find he's actually quite mesmerising. Next to me a young girl announces she has made his putty in a hundred shades. She and a friend each have a squidgy ball and they quickly mould characters before obliterating them again with a single squash. They could easily make some of my props. It's all very interactive and young and sparkly. Maybe GlimmerCon does have something special here?

The girl nudges her friend.

'AlyCat?' she whispers. I wonder if they've seen the cat in my bag but they're looking at my face.

'AlyCat is sooooooooo cute. How do you get her to wear the clothes? Do you make all the costumes? Did you make your own dress too? I like the daisies on your arms.' The last comment makes my heart sing; I feel the sleeves are the unsung heroes of a dress and I always customise mine. But I don't want to answer their questions. My fans know there's a woman behind the camera and that she's called Aly, but that's it. I'm not the kind of girl who stands in front of the Taj Mahal in a wide-brimmed hat for Instagram. 'How did you recognise me?'

The girl holds up a glossy programme. 'You're in here.'

'Where do I get one?' The DJ neatly segues into an even more insistent track as the girl points to a vendor a few hundred yards away. 'How much was it?' I mouth. She holds up five fingers. Maybe I will find a discarded one in a bin. She offers me a marker pen and her programme and when she meets a blank look she gestures like she's asking for the bill in a restaurant. Why would she want my autograph in a room full of social media stars?

I don't have time to question her as more glitter whirls and the stage lighting flashes silver, indicating someone fabulous is about to appear. I put a squiggle on her programme without looking at it, as a zap of thunder and lightning plunges us all into darkness. Twinkly music filters through, and the roof of the domed expo hall ignites as a constellation appears. I find myself directly under the Plough as the music swells and meteorites plummet to the floor, scattering against feet like ball bearings. We all shuffle to avoid them, before realising they're a trick of the light.

Amidst clapping and cheering, I take my eyes from the sky and focus on the stage, along with everyone else.

'Ladies and gentlemen, please welcome the CEO of Glimmer and the number one fan of all Glimmer Instagrammers, TikTokers and YouTubers . . .' The announcer's final words are swallowed by the cheering, but no one needs to hear them. Least of all me. I know who he is.

Rick Harvard bounds onto the stage, dressed in a white linen shirt, black jeans and red baseball boots. His shirt is untucked, with the top button undone and the ends of his jeans pool where they meet his shoes. He looks like a

Premier League footballer on a night out as he adjusts the small black mic placed at the corner of his million-megawatt smile. The mums who have accompanied the younger kids surge forward to grab a piece of him and even the dads whoop and yell. More meteors fall on us from all angles as a full moon drops from the ceiling and Rick appears to catch it before chucking it out into the crowd. A bunch of people lunge for it, but it's gone. Neat trick.

Rick addresses the room with his rich, amped-up voice, thanking them for attending the very first GlimmerCon. He effortlessly absorbs the spotlight before shining it back, making everyone feel like he is talking only to them.

With solid upper arms rippling inside the casual creases of his shirt, he hauls a woman in the front row onto the stage. In her early twenties, she's a perfect size six and forgot to put her clothes on for the event; the most substantial thing she's wearing is her sunglasses, which take up most of her face. The crowd cheers as she snaps a selfie with Rick, and then swings round to capture the room. In the process, her ridiculously long hair gets tangled in the button of his shirt. Her face is close to his chest as he unhooks it to free her. I can almost smell the mix of cologne and testosterone radiating from him as my eye wanders from his broad shoulders to the firm ridge of the abs you can just see. The woman onstage doesn't notice his stacked body, she's too busy talking about herself, filling him in on her hair extensions channel, her online shop, and her half a million followers. He quizzes her about which celebs have reposted her locks and we all laugh as the account of a famously bald pop singer pops onto the screens around the dome.

When she is led offstage, Rik fastens the rogue button on his shirt and accepts a GlimmerCon programme from the stage crew. I catch the word 'newcomers', shortly before he casually throws out some names. At the end of them I hear my own and I stop breathing.

'The AlyCat lanyard was claimed an hour ago from reception, so we know you are here, Aly. Please come and join me so I can introduce you to the Glimmer family.'

Searchlights sweep the hall like a bad prison movie. People blink and squint. I am not going up there. I shrink into the crowd and try to back out, but the bodies become a wall.

And Rick is determined to flush me out. 'Aly is something very rare these days; a shy influencer. Let's all put our hands together and offer her some encouragement.'

The girl next to me waves and calls out, jumping up and down to attract attention. The searchlight finds her. 'Snitches get stitches,' I mutter as people push me forward. Covering the bag on my front with my right hand so Molly isn't dazzled by the lights, I'm swept in a sea of goodwill towards the stage. I hold my left hand out for help as I try to escape the crush at the front. Above me, Rick crouches, reaches out, and his palm touches mine in that reassuring hug-shake. For a moment I am back in his office, looking into the deep well of his eyes. There's only me and him, and glitter dust swirling between us as he hauls me up.

'Welcome to GlimmerCon, AlyCat.'

The ripple of applause reminds me there's a huge crowd out there. Looking out gives me vertigo and I shift my eyes to the dots moving around my feet, which doesn't help.

Perhaps realising it's too much for me, he gives my elbow a squeeze. I relax a little, moving into his space, and his arm skims my waist through the thin dress. I lean in a bit more, seeking reassurance. When his hand tightens around me I let myself breathe, scrunching and releasing my toes as he quietens the crowd with a single word.

'So . . .'

The hush is immediate, and they hang, like me, on his full lips. 'I look around today and see clusters of new light all around me. Aly, our latest signing, has been shining quietly on Instagram for two or three years but I guarantee the combination of her brilliance and our care will soon take her stratospheric.' As Rick's voice caresses the microphone, it feels like he's whispering into my ear alone. A dot of glitter lands on his bottom lip and becomes an emerald streak as my vision blurs.

'Some of you may recognise the AlyCat Instagram feed,' Rick says as some of my better images flash up on the screens. 'Aly's satirical, contemporary cat is always on the mark. Earlier in the week her milk post was picked up and shared by the Leader of the Opposition and led to a question in the House of Commons. And in a complete contrast, yesterday her Westwood image celebrated Great Britain at its finest. That's Vivienne Westwood to the non boomers here. Google it, folks!'

They don't need to. An image of the fashion designer flashes up onto the walls and ceiling, and a crash of Sex Pistols accompanies some more of my images. He turns to me and touches my arm again. 'Aly, will you please fill us in on how you come up with the ideas for those adorable outfits. And how in golden hell do you get the cat to agree to wear something like that?'

Rick holds out his hand and one of the stage crew comes forward with a microphone and a programme, like he ordered them by telepathy. He holds the mic up to me, but sensing I've lost the power of speech, he then unfolds his programme to the centrespread. Molly is dressed as a pirate to protest against EU rules on vegetables, with a sword carved out of a mini cucumber. It was only fastened to her paw for half a second before she bit me. I can't help but smile at the memory.

'Hope it was OK to steal the image for promotional purposes,' Rick shouts into my ear, before chatting to the crowd again about my talent. I feel like the top layer of my skin is peeling away under the spotlight. I don't have a talent. I can't even talk coherently. The dots continue to swirl at my feet and I start to lose my sense of gravity. Is that what happens when you fly too close to the sun?

*You? On stage at a conference? You can't even hold a one-on-one conversation with an adult.*

The voice creeps in, sharp and unwelcome, finally extinguishing any oxygen I might have taken from Rick.

'I can't . . .' I say. Then, 'I'm not . . .' My words hang in the air. No one finds out what I'm not, as I spot some steps at the side of the stage and leg it into the crowd, which parts, embarrassed for me. I push through an emergency door and into a storm. The typhoon of life that Patricia predicted. I was right to turn her down. I suddenly remember Rick's words in his office that day. 'Patricia is gone.' Did I do that? Was she sacked? Because of me?

Rain barrels onto the pavement and I shield Molly with layers of flimsy dress as I make for the nearest bus stop. Hair plastered to my face, and now shivering uncontrollably, I fumble in the side of the cat-pack for my purse. There's a flash of red further along the road and I put my hand out. I'll go anywhere that's not here.

'Aly, wait!' says a male voice.

He's the last person I want to see right now.

And the only person I want to see.

He grabs my hand and places it firmly inside both of his. Like before, it is all encompassing and immediately starts to warm me. 'I'm sorry I freaked you out. You weren't ready for that, and I shouldn't have dragged you up there. These events are terrifying. They still scare me, and I speak at them all the time. I should have known better.'

I let the bus go and look him in the eyes, all six foot whatever of him. He is soaked too; the rain falling from the groomed tips of his hair and running down his face and neck.

'I'm not coming back in,' I say. 'I'm not shiny like you and all those other people in there.' I look down at his high tops, soaked and splashed with grit.

'You're not getting off on all the sparkle?' he replies, and I reluctantly smile. Then when I don't answer, he puts his arm around me and whispers in my ear, 'You know what? Neither am I.' When he touches the backpack, he turns and checks it out.

'Hey, is that a cat in the bag?'

'It's Molly!' I say, my voice wobbling. 'I need to get her

home. This was not a good day out for her. She's a hairless cat. She can't be exposed to rain or cold and I'm not sure conferences are good for her.'

He wipes rain from his lashes and nods. 'Come with me. We'll get you both dried off.'

# Chapter 7

Rick Harvard has probably seen a million hotel suites like this. Those curtains; Liberty print? I have an urge to take a pair of scissors to the hem and snip some off for an AlyCat costume. I play follow the leader, gasping as the living room leads to a huge bedroom with a raised bed. My insubstantial shoes barely make a dent in the thick carpet as the head of Glimmer strides around the bedroom grabbing accessories. 'You're freezing. Here.'

I hold the backpack towards the fluffy dressing gown in his hands. 'Molly first.'

'Don't want you catching a cold in that wet yellow handkerchief and making a mess of my complimentary suite. I'll dry the cat off if you want to jump in the shower and warm up. We'll need to be quick as I'm due on stage again soon.'

'She won't go to you.'

'I have a way with animals.'

'She still won't. And Molly's not just an animal. She was an Egyptian princess in a former life.'

When I shiver more visibly he holds out his arms for the backpack. 'Go, before I wrap you both in bath sheets like Tutankhamun and bury you under the spa.'

I hand the bag over, still a little unwilling to leave my precious baby girl with a man I hardly know. Rick deftly lifts Molly out and she meows loudly. But she doesn't struggle or spring. Instead, she moves into his fingers, nudging them with her nose. I back off, a bit put out. Stroking her pale grey, velour-smooth neck and chest, while whispering in her ear, he places her on the bed. He unzips the combat jacket I often dress her in if it's cold. Then he instinctively finds the small amount of hair she has on the top of her head before bringing his fingers around her delicate face and underneath her chin. She stretches her neck up and purrs as though she's been waiting for a chat with him all her life. He covers her body in one of the thick towels folded in a pile on the bed before searching in the bedside drawers and producing a hairdryer. He sees me rooted to the spot like a lemon. 'What else do you need?'

'Nothing.'

'It's not nothing though is it? Tell me. I'll send out for more clothes for you if you like. I can message one of the skategels.'

'The hairdryer isn't for her, is it?'

'I actually planned to use it on my shirt.' He runs his fingers down her back and looks concerned. 'Molly's skin is already quite warm.'

'That's normal. Sphynx cats regularly have a higher resting temperature than other breeds.' I clench and unclench my fists as I take a proper look at the room, leading to a bathroom with a huge bath. I haven't forgotten the joy of a soak in a proper tub and can hardly imagine what it would be like relaxing in a hotel bathroom as lux as this. But then, this situation is weird. What if he kidnaps my cat, or exposes himself to her, or to me? He covers Molly in a second towel and pops her onto his lap. She licks his fingers and purrs, trusting him. My cats are the ultimate judge of character. I bite on my bottom lip.

'I'd like to warm up in a bath please, if there's time.'

'Be my guest.'

'I'm sorry,' I say.

He raises his eyebrows. 'Why are you apologising? It's a reasonable request.'

'I dragged you out of your conference, with all those big-name influencers.'

'Don't worry, I needed a break. I'll just go in and check you have everything you need.' He gently rests Molly on a cushion and strides into the bathroom. I walk over to her, peel the towels away and run my fingers across her skin. She amps up the purring and pricks up one ear. She's curious about him. I join her on the bed, wiggling about, enjoying the springs. When I was a kid my mother would have been straight in there: 'Alyssa, we do not jump on the bed. This is a home not a playground.' It was like a mantra with her. This house is not a playground. This kitchen is not a playground. She was too busy looking after other people's kids to take me to a playground. How was I supposed to distinguish?

I peel back the edge of the duvet, longing to warm my skin beneath it but I can't now I've made a big fuss about a bath.

'The suite comes for free for the conference organiser. I wasn't planning to use it but my PA stocks it up in case I want to escape the crowds, sleep, or knock up a PowerPoint presentation.' I hear the bath running before Rick appears in the bathroom doorway, rubbing his hands through his hair, mussing it a little. 'I'm usually sorted for drinks if you want a brandy to warm up; it's not just pop stars who come with a rider. A drink's a good idea actually. I could do with one too. It was hot on stage and I'm parched.' He throws back cupboard doors and looks inside. 'Expensive hotels have clever ways of hiding the one thing you actually need after a long day at conference. It's a conspiracy. I was joking about the PowerPoint presentation by the way.'

'I expect you stay in a lot of—'

'Do you wear coloured contact lenses?' he shouts up from a fridge he's located in the wall. 'Your eyes are so green. Very unusual. Sorry, I interrupted you.'

'You didn't,' I say, even though he did. 'My eyesight is fine, though I do have a pair of Union Jack glasses from a bargain store that I wear for fun. Do you?'

'Shop in bargain stores for fun? Can't say it's my hobby.'

'What hobbies do you have?' I ask, peeling back an edge of towel and tickling Molly behind one of her ears. I'm curious about how he rolls, this man who became a CEO before most people get promoted beyond their first job. I expect him to say golf, or footie on a Sunday.

'Oh, I just have one hobby. The stars. I'd have thought you'd have picked up on that by now.' He grins.

My head snaps up. Is he for real? Celebrity watching may be a national obsession, but I'd have thought he might have more varied and worthy interests than that. His weekends must be riveting. I shiver again.

'You're really cold. Go.'

As I head into the bathroom, his phone rings. He is

friendly but firm as he handles his crew. 'I'll be back in time for the top talent. If he's going down well with the crowd then let him have another ten minutes. We can declare happy hour when they've all had enough paper-cutting poetry.' I turn the taps off as his voice takes on an edge. 'Delayed how? Didn't you send a car?' When his voice tails off into another part of the suite, I push the door closed, lock it, and shrug off my wet dress. Dancing on tiptoes to stop the water burning my soles, I notice the non-slip mat still hanging on the towel rail. No matter. I displace a fair bit of water as I sink to my shoulders to broil. Dithering over a range of luxury bath products on the shelf beside me, I settle for a mixture of body lotion, bubble bath and shower gel, chucking it all in and stirring with a figure-of-eight sweep. It foams like a science experiment and I wonder what would happen if I took a whisk to it.

And then, my favourite part of any bath, especially one that's as big and roomy as a lifeboat; I go under. I enjoy letting the bubbles of air filter out, listening for the foam popping above me. When my lungs start to burn, I come up for air. Then I take another deep breath and descend into the water again, imagining I am somewhere tropical, smelling freshly cut mango and papaya. My lungs hurt but I opt for one more minute of the big sink. Reappearing with a glorious roar, I feel like a whale re-entering the atmosphere. Pushing further up the bath than I meant to, my upper body surges into the cool air as I crash against the back of the tub. I find myself sitting upright, holding on to two handles when I hear a knock. Damn, I thought he was on the phone. I look around for a towel and notice the bathroom is full of mirrors. It's like the funhouse but in all of them I am the squat one.

'All good in there?' Caught impersonating wildlife, I'm less good than I was a moment ago. 'I found the minibar and brought you that drink,' he says. 'A whisky, and a brandy; I didn't know which you'd like. I'll leave them just outside the door. Or slide them in if it helps? I've also left some extra products I forgot to pass on when I ran the bath.'

'It's OK, you can leave them outside,' I rush to tell him even though the lock prevents exposure of actual flesh. I imagine him standing in this bathroom, examining his face in the mirror. Does he admire his genetic fortune or find blackheads and feel compelled to squeeze? If it's the latter, I could pass on some of the acne-blasting treatments that have been sitting in a Jiffy bag in my front room for several years.

*That sweet tooth of yours will pile on the weight. You don't want to go around looking like you have measles as well.*

I run my tongue around my teeth and nip out of the bath, grabbing the drinks and a purple gauze bag. I down one of the drinks and open the bag. Inside it is a small pink ball and an aerosol spray. The scent reminds me of the tightly arranged boxes of bath cosmetics under my bed, making my bedroom smell like a church bric-a-brac stall. I remove the oval. It's shrink-wrapped in plastic and comes with a paper tag that opens out into a long list of instructions. I then take out the small spray can and squirt it into the air. I read the label. It's not a hair product. Not that kind of hair anyway.

When I got up this morning, I definitely did not envision myself sitting in a hotel bath, holding a glitter spray in one hand and a vaginal glitter bomb in the other. I am human scales and both hands feel weighted with expectation. What's going on here? You don't lob a v. bomb someone's way unless you are interested in the results. Perhaps the products were in the conference goodie bags? Influencers are given all kinds of tat. But I didn't see him with a bag. Or maybe he does fancy me, and this is his idea of foreplay. When I think about his light touch on Molly's chin and imagine it on mine, I shiver, and it's not just because I'm naked.

*Cover yourself up. No one wants to see cellulite as lumpy as a school dinner.*

I take a quick glance in the mirror to see if my body has any similarities with semolina before giving myself a talking-to. 'Aly, you are looking to reinvent your life. Awarding yourself a man is not being grabby or presumptuous. He is gorgeous, kind to cats and standing in the next room waiting for you. He must like you if he's giving you this sort of gift, and he clearly believes you are sexually adventurous enough to try it.' I grimace as I read the instructions. 'Hold the can at least 20 cm from the area and immediately stop in the event of irritation.'

I'm irritated just reading it. I am not the kind of girl who vajazzles.

But maybe I could be?

I knock back the second drink and the alcohol burns my throat. I haven't kissed a man in a gazillion years and now

I'm considering pimping my bush for one of the hottest in central London? This is all kinds of crazy.

I read the instructions again. They're easy to understand and I figure spraying some glitter down there isn't exactly agreeing to his hand in marriage. Taking a deep breath, I blast the contents of the thin can onto the neat trim of my mound. In seconds, it glitters like the Cinderella carriage in a Disney parade; at any moment Tinkerbell could whizz up on a zip wire. In a few more seconds it starts to tingle. But not in a particularly good way.

I pick up the glitter bomb. Are these even legal? The instructions come with a health warning. Tick, tock, toxic shock, whole minutes of indecision pass.

There's no way this is going up there.

No. Just no.

Wrapping myself completely in the dressing gown, I try to ignore a slight irritation beneath my belly. Exiting the bathroom, I stop to let my toes luxuriate in the carpet. And then I stop to stare. The singular reason I came to GlimmerCon is standing with his back to me with his shirt off. Rippling with light muscle, he is almost unbearably attractive. My eyes skittle down his backbone to where a scattering of hair meets the seam of his low-slung black jeans. The hint of blue and white striped boxers sitting on unblemished olive skin does nothing to calm my butterflies. I need to get out of here. Women like me do not hook up with men like him; he's made for getting sexy with skate-boarding angels, not hanging out with a hobbit. A man like this needs someone who can match his looks and confidence. Someone who will whip off their dressing gown and show him her glittery goods with abandon. I proved on stage that I am not that person. And then I proved it in the bathroom when I bottled out of v. bombing myself. So why am I still standing here? I adjust the dressing gown cord tightly as the burning sensation grows, starting to feel like I've chucked acid at my own groin.

Rick spins around. His chest is no less ripped than his back, but my body heat isn't down to being aroused. Whatever he has in mind for me, I can't go through with anyone touching me below the waist.

'Better now?' he asks.

No, much, much worse. My head starts to pulse in time with pains flashing through my core.

'How were the bath products?'

No words. I try not to look at his chest, the muscles curving like a life drawing. The burning sensation moves to the top of my thighs, and in moments, every nerve in the lower half of my body is alert and trying to defend itself against an attack of punk pink glitter. I hold my breath as he stuffs the hairdryer back into one of the bedside drawers. Is he clearing the bed for action? I need to pull the plug on this quickly.

'I'm sorry, I can't do this. I went a bit mad with the spray can and I'm totally Vivienne Westwood down there, which obviously fits in with your shimmery conference. But the thing is, I'm possibly allergic to glitter as there's some kind of burn going on. And whilst it was really kind of you to give me the v. bomb, I didn't use it. Couldn't face the idea of it exploding inside me – to be honest I'm not sure how I'd even have got it up there.' As I speak, the burning intensifies so much I'm half afraid the hotel sprinklers will sense it and drench the room with water. But then, at least it might act as a squelching agent.

'You didn't use the . . . v. bomb,' he repeats, slowly, his eyebrows pushing down into a frown.

'No, I'm sorry. It was lovely of you to gift it but as I said back in your office before you took me on, I'm not mad on presents. And well, the spray you gifted me seems to be giving me a rash. It's absolute Muffmageddon down there.'

I can't say any more as I can't keep the pink gubbins on a moment longer. I run back into the bathroom and try – unsuccessfully – to scrub it off. Grabbing my dress from the floor, I find it still saturated but my sodden underwear comes as something of a relief, cooling me down with its moisture.

I walk back into the room in the dressing gown, carrying my dress. Rick has Molly in his arms and is stroking her paw while she reaches up to lick his neck. While she's now as relaxed as an Egyptian queen, he looks tense. 'Aly, I think there's been a bit of a misunderstanding. I thought I gave you a bath bomb and hairspray. The girl doing the glitter unboxing, she pushed the bag at me backstage and I popped it into my pocket. She called me Raa Raa Rick. You said a v. bomb and I assume "v" stands for . . .'

I will him not to say it out loud.

He shakes his head. 'Why would a kids' YouTuber give me something like that?'

I know exactly why she gave him something like that. Molly moves closer to him and licks his ear as he looks hopelessly at me. I think we're both relieved when his phone rings again. He walks towards the living room, and I randomly tug at drawers looking for the hairdryer. In the top drawer is a Bible, similar to the one they used to drone on with in assembly. They didn't teach us about the contents of the second drawer in RE lessons. It's my turn to look wide eyed. The draw is full of condoms, of all types, in unopened boxes. And I remember his words; it's not just pop stars who come with a rider. His PA brings all this stuff in for him? She clearly has to go further than Ryman. How many women was he planning to sleep with? All these props add up to one thing – this guy is a player.

I push my arms into a wet dress. And as Rick is briefed about a missing car for a headline guest, I cram my cat back into the backpack. After a small tussle and a couple of scratches, we are good to go. I deposit the lanyard onto the bed. I really don't need another souvenir of today.

# Chapter 8

Fumbling with my keys to the warehouse, I almost drop Molly. She slept all the way through our journey, and I had to carry her swaddled like a newborn in my arms as we walked the last few hundred metres. 'I suspect you loved and hated your day out in equal measures. Please don't tell Milly too much about it; she'll freak at the idea of all those people,' I whisper as I nuzzle her face.

I am weak with hunger and there's no space between my thoughts as I continually spool through the rushes of the last few hours in my head. Did I really paint my private parts pink and say the word 'Muffmageddon' in front of the head of a talent agency? And then follow it up with leaving abruptly when I concluded he was trying to seduce me? I idly wonder if all posh hotel rooms come with condoms. Either way, the idea of Rick Harvard fancying me is laughable. Well, it would be if I hadn't left my sense of humour in that bathroom.

As we reach the flat door, I can hear Milly mewling angrily. I buy myself some time by fiddling with the keys as a wave of panic washes over me. I can't stay here, but I've nowhere to go. Career-wise, today's events may have burned my boats with Glimmer. And it's not the only thing I've torched. All the way home it felt like Guy Fawkes was going down on me with a sparkler in his teeth.

When I finally open the door, Milly springs, almost knocking me down. Her claws dig into me as punishment for leaving her alone. I take her on my knee and rub her all over with my hands. Then I tickle all the places she loves best and tell her I missed her. While I built her a cubbyhole between boxes and stuffed it with one of my jumpers so she could smell my scent, it's clear she missed me too. 'Next time I'll ask Henry to come and look after you,' I reassure her, although I'm pretty sure there won't be a next time. When I pop her back onto the floor, she meows a gracious acceptance – no big deal, she's over it already. The sticky pink mess, however, *is* a big deal. I grab soap and a flannel and reach into the kitchen cupboard for extra reinforcement, stopping short at grabbing the bleach.

In our shared bathroom, I lock the door, scrunch up a towel, push it into the plughole and step into the shower. Water hits my shoulders as I revolve around the weak flow, trying to distribute some warmth across my body. Every time I look down, I'm confronted by unicorn sparkle, and I let tears mingle with the weak pressure as I try to scrub it off. By the time the shower starts to run cold, the soap bubbles around my feet are studded with glitter but my groin still has a luminous pink tinge. I reach out and grab one of my razors from the window shelf and search for telltale signs that Henry the Hairy Ceramicist has been trying to defoliate. When I don't find any chest hair, I run the tip of my finger along the blade and discover it's still sharp enough to nick me.

*Was this afternoon's exercise in losing your modesty not shameful enough?*

Her criticism spurs me on as I peel away the embarrassment of the day with the blade.

I peer down, finding I quite like the short runway I have created; the remaining glitter resembling guide lights. My work here is done. I wrap myself in a familiar towel and make my way through the steam back to my kitties. If I load their dishes with food, I can bag myself some unconditional love.

# Chapter 9

I'm on a long weekend from Turtle Dove Care and I make the most of it as Monday morning tips into afternoon, keeping my phone turned off for a change and sleeping in. But when the events of Saturday come flooding back, I throw a pillow across the room. Have I royally blown the only proper earning potential in months? Years even? Why did I take a cat to the most rock and roll conference in London? Why did I run out into the street in the rain? Molly licks my thumb and I try to banish the memory of her tongue on Rick's clean-shaven chin. Milly comes to sniff out my failure, her tail curling around us. Molly miaows at me to turn on one of the plug-in radiators.

'Not today, pretty kitty. I know you'd hog the sun on an August bank holiday, but I can't afford to heat the place to Spanish temperatures all year round.' She replies with an expletive. 'Hey, don't forget I speak fluent cat! You'll be on the naughty stair if you carry on like that.' I make myself schlepp over to the fridge. There's nothing in it apart from a cabbage. And the interior light's gone off. Has the electricity cut out?

If so, it hasn't affected the doorbell. As usual none of the Oddities bother to answer it. Because I live closest to the entrance, they have a habit of treating me like I'm in service. My grey slouchy PJs can be mistaken for leisurewear if you don't look too closely at the small bunny logo with the ZZZs coming out of his ears, so I stamp off down the hall without dressing.

I jump slightly as a man dressed entirely in black lunges forward with ID before snatching it back.

'Are you Aly Meadows?'

'No. I'm her neighbour.' Just in case he's here for money. 'Why?'

'I want to ask her some questions. I've been ringing all morning.'

Ah. A fan. I relax slightly. 'She does try and answer comments and emails ASAP although it's taking a bit more time at the moment. You should get a reply within a couple of days.' The amount of questions I'm getting lately has massively increased. In fact, I can't keep up with the comments, from people interested in how to care for their cat, to geeks wanting to know which lens I've used.

'I'm a reporter from the local paper – the *Hillingdon Star*. Glimmer put out a press release last week. As professional social media influencers don't tend to live in Hillingdon, I'd like to chat with her about her job and lifestyle.'

I look down at my PJs and envision his response to my flat.

'Can you DM her some questions? Her contacts are on her Instagram profile.'

'Are you sure she wouldn't like a chat now?'

'Thanks for dropping by. I'll tell her you called. How did you get the address by the way?'

'Google Maps. She shouldn't put a pin on her business if she doesn't want to be found.'

As I attempt to slam the door on its rusted hinges the guy holds up his iPhone. I sense rather than see his thumb hit the button.

'No. You can't do that. Not without her consent. And she won't give you it. Delete that photograph now please.' When he lunges for another, I retaliate and the phone falls onto the pavement, bouncing in its black rubber case. He kicks it towards him, picks it up and runs off through the car park, taking a piece of me with him.

# Chapter 10

The revolving door at Glimmer hasn't sped up any since my last visit. As I'm no closer to being able to afford any of the local coffee shops, and I've missed the morning bacon butty freebies at Glimmer, I kill time by going round it a few times.

When Sam asked me in to discuss his plans for me and get to know me a little better, I concluded Rick kept bathroom-gate to himself and was relieved to think he might not hold it against me professionally, at the same time as being mortified that it happened at all.

I'm half an hour early and whilst the receptionist points me towards the helter-skelter seats to hang out, I decide to head up to the second floor early to avoid running into Rick, deciding to plead excessive punctuality disorder if called out on it.

The newsreader drops his predictable bombshell as I vacate the lift. 'We have reached the second floor.'

The whole of this level seems to be one big room. I step into a hangar-size expanse lined with books on thin wooden shelves, halogen bulbs hanging from the ceiling on coils of wire, and shared tables in pale mahogany. There are neat piles of newspapers and magazines in the centre of every table making it feel like a cross between Wagamama and a library. Most people are locked into headphones and beavering away on laptops and other devices, while a few are chatting. A meeting is happening at the other end of the room, and I spot Sam in one of the seats. I follow the smell of coffee to a Nespresso machine in the corner, with a neat line of designer tea bags crying out to be dunked. Picking one now and one for later, I pinch two twirly sticks of sugar and snaffle an individually wrapped organic honey flapjack. I'm gobsmacked at how many are left; if I worked here, I'd have one every hour, on the hour.

A dozen or so people are gathered around the long table, which takes up a good chunk of the room. Rick's there and his dad is too. Between father and son there's a line of women with long blonde hair. No one gives me a second glance as I sit at a small table behind a bookshelf, far enough away to avoid being spotted. I plug in my USB cable and pull out my laptop, figuring I might as well claim some of the freebie leccy. Then I pretend to work while listening in to the Glimmer goss.

Rick is going round the table asking people to report on what they've achieved for their clients this week. He looks like a top boss today, in a black suit with a dark purple shirt. No tie or socks, as per. I cringe as I remember how I stood in front of him in my dressing gown burning up, while he looked footballer fit.

Rick chews on the end of a pen, even though he has no paper and someone else is taking minutes. A sneaky prop to draw attention to his rather lush lips? But no one else seems to care about them; instead, they're chewing over interviews on breakfast TV, profiles in the tabloids and the book pages of the weekend newspapers. Loads of gossip columns are talked about, and editors are approved to be approached for articles in exchange for publicity. I don't recognise a lot of the YouTube and TikTok chat but Rick's all over it. I can't take my eyes off him even though I'm still mortified about GlimmerCon.

When it's Sam's turn, he whizzes through three of his clients, all of whom sound like Blisters, and then he clears his throat to do a quick 'and finally'.

'The cat lady.' I adjust some books on the shelf to give me a bigger gap to peek through. 'She's relatively unknown at the moment, and I'm due to have a proper conversation with her about our plans for her after this meeting. But I believe there's genuine talent there we can exploit, and the whole world is mad for cats. According to some back of the envelope research, something like a quarter of UK adults own one – even more in the US, and don't even get me started on Russia. The interest spans all age groups too, giving us a portal into younger demographics. You should check out the AlyCat Instagram account if you haven't already; I know loads of you lot go gaga about fluffy things.' There's a ripple around the table as they admit their addictions to cat memes before he continues.

'We've put out some initial feelers and I'm having a conversation with a household pet food manufacturer; the marketing team is interested in a series of three advertorials in a weekend broadsheet supplement. We're looking into a studio and photographer if Aly is game to loosen her creative control and there's a decent budget. She doesn't seem precious about her images, but you know what influencers are like. I think there's a lot of potential for matches like this. Obviously as a lone wolf up to now (excuse the animal pun), Aly is cheap as chips and even if we whack her rate up, anyone we match with her will still get a great ROI. Her stats are climbing nicely too thanks to Mel and the social team and there are plenty of opps for sponsorship on Instagram. We all know how many pet products are out there, but we can also look way beyond that niche, especially as AlyCat makes a feature of the cats being like humans. There's no reason a dressed-up cat can't front an advert for fast food or trainers or even luxury cars. And as you all know, petfluencers are increasingly attractive to film companies.'

'Wasn't there a hairless cat in an Austin Powers film once?' someone asks.

'Could they make Bigglesworth, the sequel,' someone else laughs. 'And of course there's Q's Sphynxes in the Bond franchise.'

Sam's looking at a campaign for me? Why haven't I been told about this? A commercial shoot is both exciting and horrifying. While I want the work, I get the best results out of my pets because there are two of them, they look very similar, and I can swap them in and out when they start to complain. One of them won't cut the mustard and I haven't yet confessed to two. Also, Sphynx cats aren't into going out. Molly may have tolerated a couple of hours in a backpack, but I'd never get them to settle or work in a studio. They hate their environment being changed.

Rick picks up from Sam, breaking into my thoughts. 'Aly is quite unique. I agree we should do more with her as she's relatively anonymous at the moment, even amongst her superfans. Might benefit from some coaching perhaps? Hair's mad, clothes are home-made. She'll come across as gauche or beguiling in an interview. But either way, she's definitely eye-catching. And so is her cat. I had the pleasure of spending time with her at GlimmerCon. Such beautiful skin and entrancing eyes.'

For a moment I think he's talking about me and my heart breaks into a WAP dance routine, before I remember how he dried and cuddled Molly at GlimmerCon. He thinks Molly is entrancing while I am 'gauche'. Seeking to familiarise myself with the word, I google it. 'Unsophisticated and socially awkward'.

*No wonder. You go to a professional meeting wearing a gaming costume?*

I look down at my dress as people start to shuffle papers and stand. Rick takes longer than others to move on as a couple of colleagues want his ear. His dad moves to one side for a chat with a woman who wafts on about stats and targets. I close the gap on the books to prevent being spotted but leave enough space to carry on observing. The marketing bod moves off, but the two men stick around.

'Can I ask how the hot-desking is going?'

'Fine. Great.' Rick's tone is dismissive, and I'm not surprised. Must be really annoying having your decisions questioned by someone who once changed your nappy.

'Not all that great for client confidentiality though is it? Hosting meetings like this in a public space? Pretty much everyone will have heard about the cat lady, her pet food campaign and her questionable taste in clothes,' says his dad, carrying his coat in one arm and a newspaper in the other. Looking down again at my Tetris dress, with multicoloured squares, T- and L-shaped blocks suspended against a black background, I reluctantly admit it was more appropriate in my bedroom than in an office.

'Good. It'll spread the word. And I didn't say her clothes were awful, just different. Different is good. It's marketable.' This gets my goat. He can't take a bad thing back and turn it into a good thing five minutes later! Or maybe that's what they do in agencies.

Rick's dad is right though. Even their conversation about confidentiality isn't confidential. They might as well have a megaphone. 'We're all family here; you know that, William,' says Rick. Imagine calling your dad by his first name? But I guess he can't call him Mr Harvard as he'd look like he was talking to himself. And 'Dad' is a bit on the cosy side for a business meeting. 'Information is freely shared internally at Glimmer, even more so in the last few weeks. I'm open to any member of staff listening in or chipping in with ideas if it benefits the clients. They come at things in a different way to the marketing teams. My own PA recently fixed junior admin staff up with external "empowermentors" to help give them agency.' Rick is uncharacteristically loud, clearly enjoying getting one over on his father.

'Maybe we should continue this conversation somewhere else,' his dad says. But Rick doesn't budge.

'The hot-desking is all about widening horizons. We can book a meeting room for more confidential business.'

Rick's dad starts to walk, taking control again. 'This reorganisation of space is a disaster in my opinion. Everyone is carting all their stuff around with them and how is anyone going to find the accountants if they're anywhere from the basement to the top floor?' God, why would anyone want to find an accountant?

On a back foot now, Rick catches up with his dad. 'It'll take time to bed in, but in the long term it'll help the firm be more creative and less hierarchical.'

'Did you discuss it with Juliet?'

As he leans into his father and lowers his voice, I remove my headphones to hear him properly. 'I still don't know why you felt it necessary to bring her in. I thought we'd agreed you'd stay out of the operational stuff.' I stab at my laptop keys with the fervour of someone writing their life story. I should really make myself known to Sam, who has wandered out of my eyeline, but this family row is so exciting. 'Shall we continue this conversation over lunch in town?' Rick and his dad are now walking through the gap between tables and bookshelves, heading straight for me.

'Sorry, I'm due on the golf course in a couple of hours. You may as well have held your meeting in a café. Anyone could have listened in; it's a GDPR disaster waiting to happen.'

'Why would anyone want to tune into a marketing meeting they weren't invited to?' Rick asks as his dad's coat brushes the edge of my table. I close my eyes and pray they trot on. When I open them again, Rick casts a glance behind him. Unless you were looking for the slight raise of his eyebrows and the almost imperceptible shake of his head, you wouldn't know he'd clocked me. But I'm looking for it. And my heart sinks.

* * *

Sam is sweeter than I remember. I think he might be growing on me. He is super-excited about the cat food commercial. 'KittiFresh gets you. Their whole team really gets you. The MD wants you for a series of advertorials in one of the nationals. Do you know the brand?'

'Yes, it's very . . .'

'. . . high quality.' Sam finishes my sentence.

I was going to say 'expensive'. When I've googled quality cat food in the past, I've been served up links to KittiFresh. The contents of their upmarket packages use pretty much the same ingredients as the food in Milly and Molly's bowls, but they're mushed up by machines and sealed in shiny foil bags before being delivered to your door. They're also into trends like chicken katsu curry with broccoli, whereas my cats live on quite a plain raw food diet.

I zone back into Sam's chat.

'Tabloid exposure on a Sunday will get loads of eyeballs on the page. Believe it or not, most people can't tell advertorial from feature content and they digest it all. You might find you genuinely capture people's attention if the campaign is fresh and eye-catching enough and grab a new demographic of follower as well as a fat fee.' Sam's not like Patricia. He doesn't promise the world, he just wants to make you excited about it and what I took to be arrogance and a desire to impress in the first meeting I can now see is eagerness to do the best job. 'We need to book a shoot and come up with a concept. There's a studio we use on Berwick Street—'

I quickly interrupt. 'That won't work.'

'Why not?'

'AlyCat is different to normal cats. She doesn't have any fur and isn't used to going out of the house.'

He stares at me. 'Isn't used to it?' he repeats.

'Won't do it.' I say it slowly. There's no way I'm putting my cats back into that backpack for a long while.

He sighs, as though he's won the bath salts at the church raffle. 'Well, maybe we'll need to bring a photographer to you. Where do you take the shots? Do you have a studio?'

I can hardly tell him I live in a communal ex-warehouse shared by Oddities who make crafts out of yak hair and clay. Or that I am a special type of human who built a wall of boxes in my flat and have to work around them on a daily basis. And if he comes to my home, he'll notice immediately that AlyCat is not one pet but two. I missed the moment to tell Sam or Rick about the double trouble; and now it's become an accidental secret. I can't risk my fans knowing I've been deceiving them, but surely my own management is a different matter? I decide it's time to spill.

'Sam, there's something I need to tell you . . .'

'Morning, Aly.' Rick strolls in. 'You got here early today I see?'

'Ah that's because I am Percy Punctual,' I reply. Percy Punctual? What am I saying?

While he has a quick word with Sam about a meeting later, I take the opportunity to study the face that launched a thousand YouTube subscribers. Who am I kidding? He probably had a million at his peak. He definitely has a face for the screen and his body is gym honed without being overcooked. Today his upper lip and jawline have the light smattering of stubble that Premier League players opt for; the kind that springs up on handsome men just by looking in the mirror. His laughter lines give him humanity, while his clothes tell you he's rich. I feel a pang for an indecent moment that didn't happen between us, and then shake myself awake.

When he finishes speaking to Sam, I open my mouth to apologise for crashing his marketing meeting earlier. The words form on my lips. But where does the apologising stop? I am sorry for turning up in your DNA-frothed coffee bar? For being gauche and hopeless and soon to be homeless? Where does it end?

'I should go.'

'Actually, I wanted to talk about your image,' he says. Here we go. He wants to sack me off for making my own clothes, not controlling my hair, and being the worst hotel guest in infinity.

'You need to be more visible.' Not what I was expecting. 'We need to get you in front of the camera. People need to see the Aly behind the AlyCat. They love the cat, that's obvious, but they will identify with you because you are like them. Witty, young, intelligent, quirky.' He ticks the qualities off on the fingers of his left hand and my insides become Camembert left out in the sun. 'Sam, can you sort some pieces to camera and an interview with Aly when you have the crew on the day? Aly can then chop them up and use them on Facebook, Snapchat, etc. to bring people across to her Insta account. Is that OK, Aly?'

'I don't have those.'

He nods at Sam, who swipes at his phone and shows

me new accounts with my name on. I already have quite a few Facebook followers. 'Our social media team were on it this week,' Sam reports. 'Facebook appeals to a different demographic. They won't have seen the AlyCat images on Instagram so we've lifted some pics off your back catalogue. We'll make you an admin.'

I can't keep the horror off my face as I contemplate being in front of the camera. 'I prefer to be invisible,' I stutter.

Rick's eyes wander from the blocky dress to the gold boots and his lips curl into a smile. 'I think you might be fighting a losing battle there. But on the upside, you seem to be winning at Tetris.'

# Chapter 11

*Mirror, mirror on the wall, do you ever brush your hair at all?*

My mother once told me nice girls don't have the devil's hair and it's taken me twenty-five years to do something about it. But here I am, in a super-fancy salon in Soho because I figure now I have a glitzy life I need a 'do' that reflects it. OK, that's a lie. I'm here because Rick said I was gauche, and that's not a look I want stamped on my Instagram profile, let alone my life.

I shotgun the seat at the back of the salon and order an espresso martini from the cocktail menu. The guy with the Soho topknot and a pocket full of scissors doesn't seem alarmed about my choice of breakfast drink and as I could have necked back the porn-star variety of martini or a sex on the beach, I'm feeling fairly comfortable about it too. The free confidence-boosting cocktails aren't why I chose this place, but they didn't put me off either. He disappears to get the drink. Meanwhile, his brother, with the best-groomed goatee beard that's never seen a farmyard, picks up a comb with long prongs. He lifts small quantities of my hair up to his face and examines them carefully. He enquires about my grooming regime, patiently pumping me for info about how often I wash it (most days), the amount of shampoo and conditioner I use (a ton), and what my hairbrush is made of (pretty much barbed wire sadly). I confess over the years I've tried to mirror the beauty routines of every celeb who professed to taming their frizz, but in recent months gave up and used whatever conditioner Kav and Manolis stocked.

'You won't need to come to the sink after all,' he says, leaving me in my chair, puzzled. He massages my scalp for an age. At first it feels weird, but I soon relax into it while he briefs me about cuticles, how they become blocked and how frizz is created over time. Then he has a quick huddle with his brother, who places a fragile glass of martini in front of me before disappearing for ten minutes.

When he reappears with a supermarket bag, they huddle again, pouring some clear yellow liquid into a bowl. Goatee starts to paint my hair with it.

'This is the second worst case of malnourished hair I've ever seen,' he says. Bit rude? 'The first belonged to a cockapoo at my local vet's.' More than a bit! 'In future, you will not use shampoo, hairbrushes or combs, heat-styling tools, sulphates or non-water-soluble silicone.'

'I don't even know what the last two are,' I confess. 'My mother said I had horrible hair and should straighten the life out it, so I pretty much ironed it for most of my teenage years. I also have an elaborate range of Tangle Teezers, de-matting combs and detangling nylon bristle brushes. Oh, and I think there's a stock of potentially game-changing paddle brushes in boxes in the bathroom. The shopping channels are very good at flogging things that destroy hair in the name of making it better.'

'Trust me, you don't need any of it,' he says, as my frizz

becomes coated with the liquid. 'Restoring your hair to its natural beauty relies on you being kinder to it.'

'Not ever?'

He smiles. 'If you cannot keep your hands off it, I suggest you use your fingers or a long-toothed pick.'

'What's that you're putting on it?' I finally pluck up the courage to ask, expecting him to say dragon sperm or something equally exotic.

'Olive oil.'

'You're chucking olive oil on my head?' I could have got the Tesco checkout assistant to do that, for less than a fiver.

I sit for half an hour marinating like a salad before he rinses it in cold water. He rubs some conditioner in and leaves it on. Then he pats my hair dry with a towel before trimming it a little.

'That's it, you're done.'

That's the big makeover? I must look unimpressed. But when he holds a mirror up to the back of my head I gasp. For the first time in my life, I don't have frizz. Instead, rows of tight brunette curls hang down my shoulders. They might look a little greasy with the conditioner on, but they are still amazing.

'I know you were expecting something more polished, but more products will only make it worse. Think of yourself like a plant that needs hydration over time. Use shea butter, olive oil or an aloe vera moisturiser twice a week. It'll take a while, but you can repair the damage without spending very much. In a few weeks it'll settle into this kind of curl on its own. You should also check out the Curly Girl method. Lots of women are following it.'

I sit immobile, staring into the hand mirror, before taking a deep breath and letting it out slowly. 'I thought I'd always have a head of snakes. My mum stopped me eating bread once as she said it would spiral into the abyss.' Goatee raises an eyebrow. 'The crusts?' I confirm.

'Urban myth.'

*A sensible girl always listens to her mother.*

'I stopped listening to my mother when I was about twelve,' he says firmly, as though he hears her too, putting the mirror back onto his styling trolley and pulling off my gown. I open my wallet.

*A hundred pounds for someone to paint you like a roast chicken?*

As if aware of my financials, Goatee pushes the bag with the remaining olive oil into my hands and tells me he will give me a student discount as it was a quick and easy job. I already feel like hugging him and am in danger of taking him home with me on the Tube. If the frizz shows signs of being fixable, then, surely, so is my life?

In the morning, I realise I've got that wrong. My hair is untamed and greasy and a brown envelope forced under my door is stuffed with a sixty-day notice to leave.

TCP knocks on the door moments after I open the letter.

'Sixty days isn't a thing. You don't need to panic until you get the thirty-day notice.'

'You want to gather the Oddities for a chat? See if there's anything we can do?'

'Yeh, 'K, see you in an hour? I'll knock up the rest of the guys and bring them on down.'

'Wait . . .' I call, but she's gone.

The flat is a tip as I'm up to my eyes in costumes for the KittiFresh shoot. I always run up two versions of each outfit, as well as a spare, in case tiny claws rip delicate seams. I gather my sewing machine and the material together and bung it all in the bedroom. Standing back, I wonder whether the Oddities are so odd they won't even question a flat crammed with boxed-up stuff and discarded cat toys. As the cats skitter around I notice how alike they are. The only differences are Milly has a slightly lighter patch on her chest, which in some lights makes her look like she's wearing a tux, and Molly has two patches of pink on her back paws that resemble socks. This pulls me back to the question of what I should do with my double trouble? Could I rehouse one for the day and try to do the shoot with the other? Or do I brazen it out with two of them and hope Sam will go along with it? I'm not comfortable with lying to him again and not even sure how the big lie happened.

I span my hands across the folds of silver around Molly's middle, and then kiss her round belly. It's smooth to my lips and her skin is cooler than normal. I find her combat jacket and put it on her. She is vocal in her thanks and butts me slightly with her head. Later on, this closeness will be shattered when I force her paws into a suit jacket to check it fits. She wriggles out of my grip, and pads over to her bowl, noisily lapping up the value brand sparkling water I bought to soften her up for her dress fitting. And then I realise I have no snacks for the tenants' meeting.

At Kav's Kozy Korner, I wander the aisles indecisively knowing the Oddities will arrive in less than half an hour. I pick up three blocks of Turkish delight as they are on offer and I need the sugar hit. I pop some tuna into my basket for the cats and as I hand over the pink wax-wrapped confectionery, Manolis glances at his giant tray of baklava, eyeing me like a traitor as he mutters something under his breath about the Thirty Days' War. Kav bustles in, shaking her head at her husband as she dumps a crate of mushroom soup on his foot.

'The girl did not come in for a lesson in the ancient history of the Turks and Greeks. Please be less of an arsehole to the customers, at least until they leave the shop.'

Manolis starts hopping around and I can't help laughing. Months ago, Kav would never have used that language in front of me. She was all politeness as she checked out my home-made style behind eyelashes the Instagram generation would die for. But I soon learnt there's steel to her. This woman is highly competitive and enjoys a never-ending feud with the supermarkets. She regularly puts Fray Bentos pies into the jelly section at Tesco Metro to tie up their staff with the meaningless task of re-shelving them. She drops boxes of eggs on the floor in Aldi, apologises loudly for her mistakes, and calculates any small impact on their profits.

'We are comparable if not superior to the big five,' she often tells me. 'You prefer to shop here, like all our loyal customers, because we offer the best service. The best quality goods.' Not strictly true; before I became friendly with the couple it was all about convenience. I shopped because it was on the corner of my street, and I was always running out of things.

I tell them about the eviction. Then I confide about the lie that continues to bother me. 'I still don't know what to tell Sam. Or whether to tell him at all.'

'Remind me why it's such a big deal if there's two cats?'

'My fans think AlyCat is one. And if I come out to my management team, they may force me to be honest with my followers. It won't sound like a big deal to you, but some of them have been with me since the beginning and have a huge emotional connection to AlyCat. Rick thinks I need to be more visible, but my followers only care about the cats.'

I looked down at my outfit; a bright green pinafore with bright blue linen trousers. Pretty damned visible.

*Blue and green should never be seen. You look like . . .*

'Enough,' I say. Kav looks at me inquisitively.

*. . . a slutty mermaid.*

'What age did you stop listening to your mother?' I ask my friend. She reacts with a fluster and proceeds to bag up my shopping like it's a new Olympic sport.

'Would you like to buy some baklava as well as your traitor cake?' Manolis appears in an aisle. 'It is cheap today.'

'Sorry, I can't afford both. I will need to spend my pennies on exciting food for the cats this week. We're doing a shoot for a national newspaper, and I'll have to bribe them to behave.'

'We can source it for you from the cash and carry.' Kav recovers her composure, swiping a gold sari behind her shoulder.

'I'm thinking strange body parts. Stuff like liver, kidney,

that kind of thing. My babies love raw meat. It's probably a butcher's job.'

'There is nothing my Kavita cannot source,' says Manolis.

'I found quail in Chorley,' she confirms. Then, 'I think you should fess up about the cats, Aly.' Kav wipes down the counter with disinfectant and places a half-price sign on the baklava. I'm lucky she hasn't sold me as damaged goods.

'And if I can't find the courage to do that?'

'Give one of them away for the day?'

'Maybe Henry will help. I have a meeting with the Oddities in a few minutes, about trying to delay the sale. Wish me luck.' Neither Kav nor Manolis proposes frying chips on my hair. That's a sign of true friendship.

On the way home, I pick up a message from Greg to say he's already had interest in the warehouse. Maybe our sixty-day war was wildly optimistic. 'I'll make finding you a flat my priority now,' he says.

I nibble on a corner of Turkish delight. It smells of roses and tastes of diabetes. A few days ago, when the location of the shoot was starting to become an issue, I emailed Sam and caved, suggesting we set it up here. Hosting the Oddities is a dry run for opening my home to the real world.

The motley selection of tenants is led by my graffiti artist neighbour.

'Hi, TCP!' I say and am rewarded with a scowl.

Henry the Hairy Ceramicist is last. He grabs my hands and shakes them. His hunched body, long beard and bald head make him resemble a chimp in the process of evolving into a caveman. 'I hear we are to have a rent riot. Thank you, Aly, for providing your kitchen as our terror camp.'

'I've never had so much as a speeding ticket, so this is all very exciting,' says Yakker Karen, pulling a huge knitted cardi around her midriff. As the nickname suggests, Karen's obsession is yak hair. She spins it into mittens, hats, scarves and jumpers and sells them, along with knit kits, at the local markets. I think she may also grow cannabis as the smell of weed often drifts downstairs. On my first week in the warehouse, she came to inspect my furniture to check it wasn't made by small Romanian boys and I got top marks when she discovered my coffee table was three cardboard boxes. 'Recycled loveliness!' she said. Karen says 'lovely' a lot.

Joy is next, bringing her own chair. Not much about Joy is lovely, or in fact joyous. She has thin, wispy hair, whiskers on her chin and smells of Dettol. The picnic chair is too small to reach the breakfast bar, so she perches beneath us on ample buttocks that swamp the fold-out chair. 'I've brought snacks too. I only eat rehydrated dehydrated food now,' she explains. 'This was a banana. I think there's too much water. I'm still experimenting with the dryer. Dig in, everyone. Don't be shy.'

'And I have Turkish delight,' I say, popping a plate of it onto the table and wondering why I didn't choose custard creams.

'So, this is the official committee for Project Stay,' says TCP. 'Suze the Silk sends her apologies as she didn't want to come.'

'We don't want to go,' Henry states.

Our friendly graffiti artist looks directly at me. 'Aly is an influencer. She is going to kick Insta-ass for us.'

I look at her, surprised. 'Er . . . thanks, TCP. But . . .'

'Why are you calling me TCP?'

'I thought it was your name?'

'TCP's my tag. But actually it's a pretty name. Let's roll with it.'

Prettier than Savlon. Joy looks longingly at the plate of Turkish delight, while reluctantly tucking into liquid banana and speaking with her mouth full. 'Are we being legally ditched? That's the first question.'

'They have to give us eight weeks' notice. Which they have done.'

'Not if it's sold. We'll have thirty days then if they choose to boot us out.'

'They've had interest already. Greg called me.'

'The boyfriend you allowed in to measure up?'

'Ex. And I only let him into my flat, not everyone else's.'

'I let him into mine because he was your boyfriend! A very charming young man,' says Joy.

'You could always move into one of your own houses, Joy? What are you making at the moment?'

'Castle Howard for a bunny from Amersham.'

The conversation escalates. Henry starts quoting 1950s evictions in the Bronx, where everyone hauled their furniture back into the flat after it was tipped out, and then played tambourines during a night vigil. 'I say we board ourselves in. Who amongst us actually needs to go out?'

Karen raises a hand. 'I need to get to Shepherd's Bush Market with my knit kits.'

'We could set fire to the warehouse?'

'Definitely not,' says Joy. 'My houses are all made of wood and I can't risk them going up in flames.'

'How about we have a sit-in in the car park?'

'No one is going anywhere near my courgettes.' TCP stamps her foot.

'I think we need to get serious. Hunger strike.'

'Who would care?'

'The press? Imagine the headline: "Warehouse sale forces artists to die of starvation".'

Henry looks excited by that idea but I quickly dampen it. 'Headline grabbing certainly but not great for us. We need to focus on what the community is losing out on. Half a dozen creative people who will have to give up yak weaving and making tiny toilet rolls and dressing up their cats as the parliamentary speaker!'

We wind up agreeing about nothing, except the unfairness of it all.

'It sucks.'

'It sucks big time.'

'It sucks balls.'

Henry scrapes back his chair. 'But it's been a nice morning.'

Joy folds up hers. 'Inspiring really. I'll donate the rest of the banana.' She puts her spoon back in the goop, leaving me the washing-up.

'Henry,' I say, as they pile out. 'Can I have a minute?' The hairy ceramicist turns at the front door. 'I had a boxathon this morning.' I gesture towards a couple of stacks. 'Manned the phones for hours. There were various prizes, including a voucher for a thigh massage in the car park, but no one phoned in.'

'That's a shame.' He grins. 'I'd have taken the thigh massage.'

He seems amenable so I press on. 'I have an important business meeting here in a few days, a shoot actually, for a commercial, and as you can see the room is box heavy. Any chance you could store some of this stuff in your flat for me?'

He looks around and shakes his head. 'That's a lot of boxes. And what about the Jiffy bags?'

'If you could take, say half, you'd be really helping me out. It'd be temporary.'

'That's what I said when I went to Africa.'

And then I really chance my arm. 'Could you take Milly for a few hours as well? The job can only accommodate one of them.'

He sighs. 'A temporary arrangement for the boxes OK? My flat's full of lions so the cat will need to be delivered in a cage or it'll be seriously out of its depth.'

# Chapter 12

There's a dead weight on my chest and my duvet has bunched up around my ribs. As usual, Milly's made a bed of me, and I soon discover Molly's in there too.

'Hey AlyCats, my stomach isn't a waterbed you know.'

Milly disagrees. When I try to shove her off, she meows loudly, flicks me away and dozes off again. My cats' tiny faces and elongated ears send a fuzzy-felt feeling through me. They are the most important things in my life and my priority will have to be them when looking for a new flat. I glance at my phone. Time to get up.

'Day zero, AlyCats, the day of our big shoot.' Milly yowls again and I stroke her neck. 'Hey, lazy cat, all you have to do is play nicely with Henry; Molly's doing all the work today.' The birds outside my window push their wake-up chorus our way as I swing my legs onto the floor and start tidying up – a process I began days ago without realising how big the job would be. I stand in my PJs making a mental note to get dressed after I clean the flat, power up the laptop, answer overnight comments and deliver Milly to Henry. I grab a piece of toast as I scrub the sink. Without the clutter of boxes, I notice the early morning light highlights the scuffs and stains on the walls.

I shut the cats in the bedroom and delve under the sink for the remains of some paint. Prising open the lid of a pot close to full, I patch the nastiest spots. But when I stand back all I can see is chicken pox. I widen my brush strokes, covering more of the wall. Paint splashes onto the floor and I regret not putting a sheet down. When I stand back to view the improvement, I decide to paint it all.

I'm sweating with all the exertion and need to shower. In the bedroom the AlyCats fight over a squeaky as I select a white dress covered in bright red poppies. Time is ticking on and the crew will be here soon. The cats choose this moment to fight and are full-on squealing over the annoying toy when there's a knock on my door. 'It's probably Henry, wondering where we are.'

I find two men and a pile of kit in my hall. 'Oh! You're here. How did you get in?'

'Morning. Your neighbour let us in, but she didn't look happy.' Sam dumps two cases on the floor, closely followed by a man carrying an armful of poles – the photographer I presume.

'Mitch is here; ready to crack on straightaway,' he says.

'Who's Mitch?' I look for a third techie as the guy drops a pole. Oh Lordy, there's nothing Milly hates more than a big man who makes a loud noise. I hear her yowl from the bedroom. How am I going to sneak her out to Henry without being spotted?

'This is Mitch. The ace photographer I was telling you about,' says Sam. 'He has the best portfolio this side of Shepherd's Bush. You get used to his chat.'

The photographer is talking about himself in the third person as he hauls in an arsenal of lights, camera lenses and umbrellas. The waistband on the Australian's jeans hangs low on his generous waist, giving me an eyeful of the scenery down under each time he lays a piece of equipment on the floor.

'I have a lot of kit too.' I point towards my photo corner. 'I could have saved you carting all yours here.'

'Mitch doubts that. This clobber is the real thing.'

'Too busy to get dressed?' asks Sam. You don't know the half of it, mate.

'Mitch smells paint.'

The photographer is right; the smell is overwhelming. But a more pressing issue is the extra cat. I decide to open the block of chocolate cardamom cake I bought from Kav to distract the crew with refreshment while I take care of the cats. A growl from Molly in the bedroom halts my activity. Milly answers her with a guttural yelp. From experience I know I'll need to referee, or it'll quickly descend into a full-on scrap. These sisters can rip each other apart when they're hangry, and I haven't fed them since last night, hoping Molly would be more inclined to work for her foodie rewards.

Pushing open the bedroom door, I'm caught off guard as the cats perform an ambush. Molly jumps from the bed to my shoulders and then onto my head, wailing and digging her claws into my scalp.

'Hey get off! I need to cut your claws, lady,' I cry as Milly dives for my feet. I drop the cake onto the bed, pull Molly off my head and try to kick Milly away from my calves.

'Molly, you won't get fed until you've worked. You know the drill for shoots. And, Milly, you are going for a day out to Henry's flat.' Having easily dropped from the bed to the floor, Molly rubs her velvet haunch on my legs. Ignoring her attempt to persuade me into the kitchen, I throw on the dress I'd laid out, find a furry bodywarmer, and push Milly inside. I can go barefoot for now. Henry's flat is just down the hall.

Mitch has done a good job of setting up, so they aren't quite as occupied as I'd like. I hum along with the tune he's singing as I creep to the door with the bodywarmer in my arms. When I push it open, Milly digs her claws in through the fabric, springs to the floor and races back into the living room.

'Milly, come *here*.' She flashes past me and brushes against the wall, gathering streaks as she goes.

'Er, that's not going to be great for costumes,' says Mitch.

'It's not going to be great for her skin,' I pant, as she bolts to the sofa. I sprint after her and lunge with a grunt, catching her sleek backside and painting my palms. She darts from my grip, weaves around the back of the sofa and scales the remaining box staircase, installing herself at the top. The pale skin on the inside of her ears is now complemented by streaks of cashmere white on the tips.

'Come down now. I need to clean you up.' I hold up my hands in a truce. She mewls and lies down defiantly. The time has passed for polite requests. 'Get your skinny silver backside down here, lady.' Her eyes meet mine without blinking and I swear she smirks. Her sister chooses this moment to pad into the room. Sam looks as though he's seen a ghost.

'Ah yes, there's something I should have told you. It's a bit of a secret actually; from my fans anyway, not the neighbours who have to put up with all the noise. Meet Milly, and Molly. The famous AlyCat is two cats. Double trouble!'

'I suppose it might speed up the shoot if we use both of them,' Sam concedes after I gabble more of an explanation. 'How alike are they?'

'Sometimes I can barely tell the difference between the AlyCats myself.' I cross my fingers behind my back. 'And as they're good at different things, we can sub in whichever is the best fit.' Picking a plastic ball out of a drawer, I roll it towards Molly. Although she's super cross with me, she can't resist playing, and when it lands squarely with her paws, she boots it away. 'See, they each have their own strengths and tricks. They're like kids really.' Molly confirms this with a strangulated scream. 'Sorry, all. She's annoyed because she hasn't been fed yet. We normally operate a twenty-four-hour cafeteria system. But I need to keep them hungry to make them work. I'll feed them titbits as we go along but first I need to wash the paint off Milly before it dries.'

I lift MillyCat over to the sink. She sees what's coming and scratches and fights to get away.

'Hey, you normally like a nice bath,' I say, trying to keep a hold of her and flick on the taps. As I run a bowl of hot water, Mitch does test shots. Sam and I recap the morning's schedule while I scrub my reluctant cat with a brand new sponge. In the first shoot, an office-ready AlyCat will sit at the breakfast table in a suit, with a laptop, about to tuck into a bowl of KittiFresh before heading off to work. The tag line is simple: 'KittiFresh, not for the average stockbroker'. In the next scenario, which will be shot in our communal bathroom, AlyCat will dress in overalls, and the reader will find out KittiFresh is not for the average plumber. There's a couple more involving an NHS nurse and a jeweller. And if there's time, we plan to squeeze in a humorous photo shoot in the bedroom, with Molly dressed as a window cleaner and looking through the glass pane. The strapline? 'KittiFresh, not for the average peeping Tom.'

I kiss Milly's wet nose and Sam smiles to himself at the cat chat as I continue to wipe paint from her delicate body. She's relaxing into her bath now, but the emulsion is stubborn. Thank heavens she loves the weekly bath I give them when their skin gets oily. And thank the Lord it wasn't gloss paint.

The photographer makes some last-minute adjustments to the lighting as I abandon the big clean-up and Milly scampers away. She'll have to do for now. I cast around for a tea towel to dry my hands.

'Mitch is ready. Which cat shall we bag?'

I look around for one cat, and then the second. Both gone.

I find MillyCat rolling on the bed, perhaps trying to rub off the remaining traces of paint, while her sister quietly crouches on the bedroom floor. Resting between Molly's two front paws is the mangled chocolate and cardamom cake I discarded earlier.

'No!' I grab Molly by her neck and her long thin tail lashes out like a rat's. 'You can't eat chocolate. You know that. Are you trying to ruin the shoot? This session was going to pay the rent. It was how you were going to get your chicken legs. That cake was for the men out there.' I try to stick my finger into her throat to make her vomit, as a dose of chocolate can be lethal, but she hisses and clamps down with her jaws. Her sharp teeth puncture my skin.

'Ouch!' She scampers away. 'And you, MillyCat – how dare you spread paint on my duvet.' In a rage, I pick up the remains of the cake and throw it at a tall cardboard box marked 'Assorted Dyson'. Milly scarpers as it ricochets off the box and lands with a thud, crumbling onto a floor scattered with mismatched rugs.

As I survey the damage, I hear another knock at the front door, and I realise Henry will be wondering what's happened to us. I pick up a pillow and hold it against my face. The darkness is soothing, and I stay there for a few seconds to try and escape the media scrum in the living room, and the auditions for an episode of *Embarrassing Pets* in here. When I'm feeling brave enough, I kneel to see if I can figure out how much cake Molly has eaten and how much chocolate might have been in there. I taste some crumbs. Like everything associated with Kav, it's a delicious reflection of her warmth and culture. I feel the sweetness doing its job and shove some more into my mouth. Then a bit more.

'Are you OK, Aly? I believe Milly chose this morning to get an emulsion tattoo.'

I hold my breath. Did Rick Harvard, CEO of Glimmer, just enter my bedroom and watch me eat cake from the floor? With a face so flushed I could fry an egg on it, I remain kneeling on the rug. When I've counted to three, I dare to look up, hoping he's either gone or was never there at all. But he's leaning against the door frame, looking as well put together as ever in navy trousers and a pale blue shirt.

He nods at the cats. 'I think Molly might have cloned herself since I last saw her. But on the plus side she looks good in a suit.' The tone is friendly, but his words are a reality check. He knows there are two cats and that I've lied to him. He has also seen the squalor of my home.

I gulp down air and start to unravel. 'Molly ate the cake. It was meant for Sam and Mitch to help things to go smoothly this morning. I don't think she had more than a few crumbs, but even so we might have an explosion when her bottom catches up with her stomach. And yes, Milly brushed against the fresh paint on the wall. Her skin could react badly to the toxins. I was so busy having last-minute discussions with Sam, who has been incredibly patient with me, that I haven't had a chance to properly wash it off and I'll never forgive myself if something happens to my babies while I'm milking them for money to try and get out of this dump.' By the end of my speech, I'm practically hyperventilating. Rick looks concerned at my distress. 'Do you need a paper bag to breathe into?'

'No, but I could do with one to go over my head. Your team must be finding this whole shoot in my flat very unprofessional. Sam wanted to do it somewhere in central London, but I insisted on having it here because my cats allegedly behave better at home.'

'I'd call this unconventional rather than unprofessional,

which is part of why I wanted you on our books. And why I like you.'

He likes me? Even after he caught me eating cardamom cake from the floor?

He looks down at the mess of crumbled cake. 'Is there any chance we could get hold of another of those? I always find things go more smoothly with a decent tea break in the pipeline. Your instinct for feeding the crew was spot on.'

'Kav from the corner shop made it and she does bake them in bulk. Quite often her cakes are streaky like this one; it's not a *Bake Off* disaster, so don't be put off; she often dyes the different parts with food colouring. She blends flavours too. Makes the cake more interesting. Just like her and Manolis. He's Greek and she's Indian.' I am gabbling now.

Rick reaches out to help me stand. As ever, his hand is capable and warm. 'I'll stay and help with the shoot,' he says in a voice that tells me there's no room for argument. As I look for the ground to swallow me up, he takes my chin in his hand and lifts it. 'Slow down, Aly. Take a moment. We can all wait till you're ready.'

When he disappears into the other room, I climb over three boxes to get to the dressing table mirror. 'Pull yourself together, woman,' I tell myself, picking up a hairbrush and then putting it back down. I need to pour olive oil over my head to keep up with my beauty routine, but I'm already waterboarding myself with shame.

I text Kav.

> *How much choc was in tht cake? Mol trd to eat it. Do we nd emergency trp to vet?*

I ask my community how much chocolate cake they think a cat can stomach, before hashtagging #sphynxcat on an Instastory featuring the same query. Two followers reassure me their Sphynxes eat quite a bit of cake. To be fair, mine have never had a problem digesting small amounts of sugar. Kav replies to my text, saying she uses a few squares of awesome chocolate; no more than four per cake, as her husband likes to milk every last drop of profit from the customer.

Back in the living room, Rick has refilled the sink and is giving Milly the bath she deserves. Holding her under her stomach with one hand, he caresses her silver skin with his other.

'She doesn't like it too hot,' I tell him.

'I know.'

'How?'

'She told me.'

I check that out with Milly who turns her head to one side, finds my eyes, and stares deep into them like she's looking into my soul.

Then she blinks three times.

'She's just told me she likes being held like that.'

Following the lines of her body, he works the cloth into the fat wrinkles around her legs and hips; exactly as I would have done if I'd had the time.

By the time he's finished with Milly, Molly is creating a fuss. Either she wants a bath too or more likely she's ordering breakfast. Rick towel-dries Milly on the kitchen floor, stroking the patch that makes her shiver with pleasure while I feed Molly with tiny slivers of raw rabbit I bought from the butcher's shop on the Uxbridge Road. He's rolled up the sleeves on his shirt and the dark hairs on his skin are a contrast to Milly's pale, hairless coat.

Cameraman Mitch proves to be a top pro, but also a stickler for the perfect shot. Thankfully, the cats are up to the job. We begin with the breakfast bar shoot, and I select Molly for her show-off qualities. As she sits on the high stool, she looks like she's been drama school trained for the role. In the few seconds we have before Molly bolts, Mitch ensures her face is lit properly while I readjust her costume. We knock off the first image quickly and without fuss. When we move into the shared bathroom down the corridor to do the plumber shots, I apologise for the state of it; there are dark hairs everywhere despite my efforts yesterday to de-fuzz it. 'We have a very hairy ceramicist in our garage.'

We are an efficient team. Rick entertains whichever cat isn't being used while Sam looks after continuity and helps Mitch with the photography. As the rest of us down tools, Rick engages Molly in playtime with a pompom on a string while Milly circles his ankles. Seconds later, the kiddies are fighting over a toy mouse that's appeared from nowhere. Rick pulls a Slinky out of his pocket and lets it dangle from his fingers.

'Thought bribing them might help get the job done so I went via Pets at Home,' he says, and I wonder why such a busy man has travelled across London to a relatively unimportant shoot.

He answers my unspoken question. 'I have a new client in West London. I wanted to check out her set-up, so it seemed natural to pop in and see how you were doing, as this is your first big job with us, and it wasn't far out of my way. Sam gave me your address.' He gestures to the remaining pile of boxes as Molly pounces on the Slinky. 'Have you just moved in?'

'Yep, last month. I was in the East End before that. I fancied a change of scene.' I don't really want to lie again but equally I don't want him to think I grew up in a place with no character. This part of town is an overspill of Heathrow and a corridor to Slough and there are a gazillion better places on the planet to have a front door.

'Which part of the East End?'

I only know a couple of markets and Bethnal Green's Museum of Childhood.

'Shoreditch,' I reply. Damn. He'll know it's a lie. I wouldn't be able to afford to rent a house in one of London's trendiest areas.

'I live near there.' Of course he does. Shoreditch – where all the bars have a novelty USP and all residents speak hipster. 'Bethnal Green to be exact. You might know the road; it has a famous flower market on a Sunday?'

'Columbia Road? It's awesome. Mitch lives in Fitzrovia,' the cheerful photographer butts in. 'Staying on the floor of a fellow Kiwi who got rich in the city. Out to Nando's tonight with an English bird who might just clip his wings.'

'I assumed you were Aussie?' I say.

'Never assume. It totally makes an ass out of you and me,' he replies, speaking in first person for the first time in four hours.

Molly uses her litter tray with no problem and leisurely plonks herself down on the coffee table boxes for a snooze. I sigh in relief. In contrast, Sam and Mitch move out at military speed, leaving me, Rick, and a weird electricity in the air.

'Shall we . . . ?' he starts.

'Want to . . . ?' I crash into him.

'Sorry, you first.'

'Look, I realise you are very important and need to run your company, but all the mental energy of dressing and herding cats has made me hungry. Do you want to stay a while longer and have some lunch with me? Not that I've actually got anything in unless you like raw rabbit liver or luxury cat food.'

'I texted my PA earlier to say I've been delayed for an hour or two. Let me buy you lunch. On expenses.' I fill up the AlyCats' trays with the last of the rabbit as a reward for their cooperation and give them fresh water.

We walk down the crowded street, dodging an electric scooter and a dog scavenging in a pile of cardboard outside a closed Chinese takeaway. 'I hope you don't want something fancy because it's a foodie wasteland if you don't count pizza and burger joints. Shoreditch and Hayes operate in parallel universes.'

'Sandwich? We could find a patch of grass.'

'Actually, I think I can do better. It's sushi day at my

local mini market. There are a couple of tables outside. We can pick up a decent takeout coffee too, as long as you don't want any form of dairy substitute. If you so much as mutter the words "oat milk", Manolis will cut off your ear with a Gilbert and Sullivan pirate prop.'

Kav greets our request for sushi with sadness. 'I'm afraid it's off the menu. Manolis had a bad prawn and has temporarily banned fish from the shop. Every last kipper.' She carries the regret in her shoulders as she leads us to a small wrought iron table on the pavement. Tutting, she removes sticky gum from the mosaic tabletop with a damp cloth and turns to Rick. 'Watch that nice shirt of yours. This can be a filthy street.'

He smiles, and the weak sun can't compete. 'In marketing we call it edgy.'

'This is Rick. He runs Glimmer, the talent agency I told you about.'

'I guessed. What would you and your talented friend like today, Rick?' Kav smiles.

'Anything but cat food.'

'I recommend the onion bhaji with raita. They are as big as a tennis ball, so you won't need too many. I can prepare you a mango salad to go with it.' Kav speaks loudly above the traffic. 'You must be wondering why we choose to serve food amongst belching buses on a main artery into Southall? My husband wanted to buy a corner shop because his mother ran one in Athens and his grandmother before that. I was more in favour of an upmarket café serving nice lunches to bookish people and office workers. I was overruled when they ganged up on me but insisted on the shop having my name and doing hot food. These tables are both a confirmation that women need to be heard, and the achievement of my dream. I hope you like our bhajis. They are spicy and warming.'

While I try and work out how two outdoor tables can translate into a feminist protest, Rick jumps in. 'We'll have two then, please. To start with.' He turns to me. 'Sorry, I didn't ask. You OK with that?'

'Totally OK with it. I'm so hungry I could eat a scabby . . .' My words are lost in a crunch of metal on metal further up the road. The traffic slows and I can almost hear the line of drivers sighing. Meanwhile Manolis appears with a screwdriver and wiggles it into a machine that dispenses balls of plastic toys for a pound. Rick and I watch as one falls out and clatters into the red tray beneath.

Kav reassures us he isn't stealing his own pound balls. 'Each week he removes a toy from the pile and replaces it with a tiny toothpaste and toothbrush. I am increasingly worried about the teeth of our young customers. And sometimes I back this up by slipping a tube of Colgate into the shopping bags of mothers who do not care for dentists.'

'Does anyone care for dentists?' Rick wonders out loud and we all contemplate his question.

The queue of traffic moves around the two crashed cars as the owners involved slam their doors and stand like rookie policemen in the main road.

'Do you think we should go and help?' Rick asks.

'We have an Uxbridge Road crash virgin amongst us,' I laugh with my friend. 'You never want to get caught between angry drivers on this street. We've witnessed some shocking collisions and their aftermath. How often has a crunch ended in a punch, Kav?'

'Always. They are mentalists,' she agrees, squinting into the sunlight, the piercing in her nose glinting. I squint too, and I realise I know one of the occupants. I excuse myself and take a walk.

Greg is standing in the road, squaring up to an old man.

'I'm not sure you even saw me. When was your last eye test? More than ninety per cent of people over the age of sixty-five are prone to cataracts you know?' Greg scribbles on a piece of paper, rips it in half and passes it to the pensioner to write down his details. 'Call my guys. The light will be cheap for you to replace. It is one of the benefits of having a smart car. Mine has fuel efficiency of around sixty-seven miles per gallon. They are also one of the least expensive cars to insure due to their smaller size and low running costs.' My ex has clearly missed his calling as a car salesman.

'Are you both OK? What brings you here again, Greg?'

'My office is just down there. Good morning, Aly.' He greets me like he expected me five minutes ago.

'Is it still morning? This day is going on forever.'

'It is 11.57 so yes, it is indeed. For about two and a half more minutes.'

'I can do the maths. Do you need a push?'

'It's just a broken light so should get started although it will be inconvenient to get it fixed. Wait here while I try the engine?' The other driver backs away as Greg jumps into the compact white car, revs without a problem, and nods a curt goodbye to him through the windscreen. Then he pulls onto the pavement for a moment and opens his window. 'How is your car? Did you get the work done on it?'

Natch! My car is still on the forecourt of the garage. I'm back with Turtle Dove Care again tomorrow after a few days off, and I still haven't made a decision about whether to get the car fixed. It's a drain on my funds and if I sell it, I can add the money to my flat savings and feel a bit closer to my goal as the sixty-day eviction approaches. But can I get around to my clients without it? And what about the days when I do double shifts to try and put more money in the bank? Will I collapse from exhaustion without the car to eat my butties in and recharge my phone?

'Would you like to come out to dinner with me, Aly?'

Two free meals in one day? While my stomach is totally up for that, dinner feels like a date, and at the moment I'm only into Greg for his property details. When I hesitate to answer he jumps in again. 'It's the meal between lunch and tomorrow morning's breakfast? I know a little Italian place just down there.' He vaguely points in the direction of the mini market. I follow his gaze and my stomach flips over again at the delicious man sitting at a table waiting for me. But he's the head of a company and I'm a zero hours worker with an Instagram hustle on the side. We have yet to talk about how I have deceived him about the cats, and after that awkward conversation he will be gone, back to his hot-desking and star-launching, and I'll be here alone, inhaling diesel fumes until the end of time or until I can move somewhere else. Should I go out to dinner with a man who's more my equal?

'Tonight? Seven o'clock?'

'I'm busy tonight,' I instinctively reply. Watching paint dry on my cat? I double-check my sanity.

'Too busy for pizza?' I check it a third time as my stomach rumbles and I imagine wolfing down an American while it is still boiling hot. I shake my head but he's not giving up. 'Tomorrow night then?' I shake my head again, but my resolve is weakening.

'Maybe just a drink sometime then? I'll give you a call in a few days.' He brushes his blond hair from his eyes and takes his car from zero to thirty in a not particularly impressive amount of seconds.

The traffic is flowing again as I land with a bump on one of Kav's wrought iron chairs.

'I realise how rude it was to start while you were being the sixth emergency service, but the food was hot and utterly gorgeous.' Rick scoops up some leftover sauce onto a lettuce leaf and pops it in his mouth. 'I ate both of the bhajis, and ordered a second portion, which you should rightly have, so I might order yet another for me. Everything OK back there?'

'Bust up over a broken light.'

'Nice of you to intervene.'

I open my mouth to tell him about Greg, and then close it again. There's no reason to bore him with my past. I look away before I turn a speck of raita on his lip into a fetish.

Kav returns with more bhajis. 'My husband is

experimenting with sweet potato bhajis, which is unusual as I am usually the one slaving away in the kitchen. He has sent two on a complimentary basis, which is also quite out of character as he used to cheat his own grandmother at cards. He's either sick or going soft on me. I suggest you eat them quickly before he asks for them back.'

Manolis trails behind her with fresh silver pots of chutney and raita. 'You need to give someone else a chance at enjoying our food, Aly, especially at lunchtime,' he says, scratching his beard.

'Well, I did bring a friend . . .'

'Our tables are not rationed! Stop putting off the customers, Manolis. She is discerning about her friends and food choices so doesn't want to go anywhere else. Aly is like Rose on the *Titanic*. She would go down with the ship, rather than climb into the lifeboat. And her money is as good as anyone's. In fact, I imagine her adorable friend is paying. You should be kissing her feet and not insulting her face.' Kav swats her husband away with her tea towel, before wrapping the corner of it around her index finger. She moves in on Rick, telling him to hold still, and with a firm action she wipes his mouth like a toddler. I can't hide a smile. 'Two massive coffees for our best customers, you pointless man!'

They sweep off as quickly as they arrived. 'They love each other really. I hate people shouting at each other, but the angry vibe is all part of the frisson.' In truth, my fear of conflict runs deeper than that. If I so much as hear a man's voice raised, I start to feel sick, transported back to the years of screaming matches between my parents, punctuated by days of silence where they bore a grudge with ease.

Rick gestures for me to dig in. 'You haven't eaten since when?'

'Don't worry, I'm in no danger of becoming anorexic.'

I feel his eyes on my face as I pick up a fork. 'Sorry, I'm sounding like your mother.'

'Believe me, you are nothing like my mother.' The words escape with more force than I meant. I contemplate the bhajis to try and explain myself. 'Some people go mad for the poppadoms, but the bhajis are my favourite part of curry. I always think it's amazing how they stick together, all those random strands of onion. How does it not disintegrate and fall into a heap?' I cut into one of the balls as he closes his eyes to savour my friend's cooking. Steam rises, loosening my tongue. 'My life is an onion bhaji that never properly formed.' I sigh. 'All the strands were there. Professional parents, conventional upbringing in a house within commuting distance of the city, private school, and a cat. But the picture-perfect childhood had no substance. We couldn't stick together.'

Rick picks up the raita spoon and ladles the pale green sauce onto his lunch. He looks at his bhaji thoughtfully. 'At least someone bothered to peel and chop the ingredients. My dad never realised there were layers to an onion. Never tried to get beneath my skin.' He shrugs.

Taken aback by his response, I look up, surprised. 'But aren't you the golden child? He made you head of his company. You must be quite a bit younger than a lot of CEOs?'

He shrugs again. 'I'm thirty-two. He didn't suddenly make me head of the company, I started it for him from scratch. I was good with YouTube as a teenager and understood how social media worked. I made some good decisions with my channel, and he saw I could make money. It wasn't too much of a gamble for him.' He puts down his food and sighs. 'However, it's increasingly a battle. Our values don't overlap, and his idea of marketing is very different to mine.' I throw him a sympathetic look. I get the feeling this outwardly popular man doesn't open up very often. But he goes back to eating, scooping the last of his sweet potato bhaji into his mouth.

I feel obliged to share something in return. 'I'm sorry I lied about the cat,' I launch in, looking at my plate instead of him. 'I was scared of my followers finding out. And I was worried if I told you up front, you would demand transparency and I wouldn't be robust enough to deal with the flack. When I went to see Patricia, she asked questions I wasn't ready for, so I started the ball rolling by deceiving her. And then you summoned me in, and you were top of a glittery pyramid, and the key to the profit I hoped to grab a share of. So, I didn't want to disillusion you either, or Sam, who is super nice. But now I've admitted it to you guys, I'm thinking of telling my tribe.'

'What do you want from your future, Aly?'

His curve ball stops me in my tracks. I think for a minute.

'I want to be secure. To have a mortgage on a proper flat and look after my cats without worrying about money. I'm a late starter. They said I was bright at school but didn't ever live up to my potential and that probably sums me up.

I didn't train or invest in myself. I could have monetised my channel ages ago like a lot of my fellow Instagrammers, but I didn't. My cats have more business sense than me. I often make mistakes and don't learn from them but I'm trying to change. I signed with you because I trust you and I'm hoping . . .' I don't know where to go with my sentence as I don't know what I'm hoping for anymore. The sands continually shift when he's around.

Tick-tock, shock o'clock, he rests his hand on mine and I feel the magnetic pull of him. 'I think you are capable of learning from your mistakes,' he says, 'and I think you are more than capable of being self-sufficient and successful. I believe everyone is. Being honest with yourself and others, as well as realising when you've messed up and owning it, are key to successful business and a happy life. Come clean and you'll feel clean – that's what we teach our clients at Glimmer. My father disagrees, of course. He believes marketing and advertising is all about covering up problems, spinning the truth and pulling the wool over the consumer's eyes. Honesty is not often his favoured policy in business or elsewhere. Anyway, I understand about the cats, and we'll definitely find a way of breaking the news to your followers without damaging your credibility. If we are to build a relationship . . .' he lets this hang in the air and my stomach lurches '. . . then Sam will need to have implicit trust in you too.'

He means a business relationship. I scrunch up the serviette while he pushes his hands together and interlaces his fingers as though he's about to begin a chant of 'This is the church and this is the steeple.' 'You don't trust yourself or us yet, but you will in time. But maybe I'm a hypocrite because I don't trust anyone except myself,' he says. 'On a lighter note, I have some news. You've made the shortlist for best newcomer in the Showcase awards. I nominated you when we first took you on. You get to come to a three-course corporate-sponsored dinner where an up-and-coming comedian will tell some unfunny jokes before handing out an endless amount of ugly glass trophies. It's like a graduation ceremony but longer and slightly more boring. Up for it?'

God no. Aside from the fear of sitting on my own at a party, I'd have nothing to wear. But as I open my mouth to turn him down, something else pops out instead. 'Are you going?'

'Naturally. We're up for best agency; an award my father will be fighting me to collect. William H. is all about the golf and lunches while other people run his businesses until there's an accolade being handed out.' Rick pulls out his phone and taps a couple of times. 'There, I've forwarded you the shortlist. In a few days or so, you should also get an email from the event host with a formal invite and dress code.' His smile turns full beam. 'We will cover the extortionate price of your dinner, although it's unlikely to be half as good as your friend's cooking.'

My heart quickens with the warmth of his smile, and his approval of Kav. But I'm not used to star-studded parties, as GlimmerCon proved, and I don't want to spend a fortune on a new dress. 'Sorry, I have something else on.'

'I didn't tell you the date.'

I sigh. 'You got me.'

'No, I *get* you. I understand you might feel uncomfortable at this kind of event, but I'll have your back and Sam will be buzzing around. You'll be with the same people for three courses and the chances of you winning the award are slight, so you probably won't have to go within a mile of the stage.' He stands and lifts his man-bag onto his shoulder. 'You will not die up there, Aly; we will be there to hold your hand all the way. So, what do you say?'

When I astound myself by stuttering out a yes, his face transforms like I made a difference to his day. As he says goodbye and heads off for a more glamorous part of London, I stay put in my chair. With the words of the cat lady on Instagram still in my head, I think about how Milly and Molly would go about preparing for this awards ceremony. And then I sketch out an idea. Perhaps by channelling my cats, I can show Prince Handsome how Cinderella rolls at the ball.

# Chapter 13

I spread a slab of yesterday's bread with dregs of Marmite and hope my clients offer snacks when I go about my rounds. My cats tuck into chopped-up raw chicken breast with shredded courgette while I read them an article about me in the *Hillingdon Star*.

The lazy journalist has printed whole chunks of Glimmer's press release about acquiring me as their latest stellar client, but he also went through recent Insta comments. Normally a supportive and happy little Instagram feed, I picked up some trolls when the first of the KittiFresh advertorials came out with an info box in the corner promoting me to readers. Then a few days ago, one of my new and angry followers speculated I shaved my cat's back to make her look human.

'If you guys could read, I think you'd be shocked at how much this article sucks,' I tell Molly, while Milly joins me on my knee to sniff out the Marmite.

The paper has accompanied the article with the blurred picture of my face, snatched a few weeks ago on my doorstep, and a picture of Molly at Halloween taken without permission from my feed. She is dressed as the chancellor with a painted pumpkin as his red box. These sisters are everything to me. I would rather rip out my heart than exploit them and they know it. Molly joins Milly on my knee, rasping her insistent commentary on everything. Her guttural noises are a love letter. I enjoy how much Molly communicates. I stroke her and her long thin tail curls as she meows loudly in time with my strokes. That woman who preaches about the similarities between people and cats on Instagram has got one thing right; they do like to communicate. Now following her out of curiosity after being served two or three of her ads, I check out her feed to see if she has any new words of wisdom. This morning she's defining how cats come at a problem.

'Faced with a dilemma or a puzzle, humans will rush in. A cat does not bowl into a situation rashly. It comes with a developed cerebral cortex and uses every scrap of brainpower to work out the answer to any problem from the sidelines. A cat watches, waits and washes itself. It mentally explores every issue and opportunity without doing anything. In short, it strategises the hell out of an issue and goes in fully armed and knowing what it will do. What are your strategies for dealing with a problem? Do you wait it out, or dive in on impulse? Could your inner cat show you a new way?' There's a discount code for her courses to help you access the feline you.

I look down at Milly and Molly, nestled in my lap. Maybe I should ask them for the strategy for a successful life? They've hung around on my sidelines for long enough. Checking the time, I tip them onto the floor. If I don't get a move on I'm going to be late. Molly lands with a 'yeeeeow', before scampering up the steepest tower of boxes like Mo Farrah, while Milly complains about losing her place. I squat and kiss the top of her head, and she bats me away, taking her lean body off to make friends with the spiders. I flash back to Rick Harvard's olive skin and straight spine in that hotel room, and momentarily long for the touch of a human being. Cats are all very lovely, but they can make you feel a little bit lonely at times.

As I take the bus to my first client, I'm cheered by a sponsored post enquiry from the company that brought the world the sonic toothbrush. Would I like to advertise some dental dumb-bells for a fee? Sam says he's working on some great prospects, but surely he can't expect me to live on sunlight till the money rolls in? I forward the horrid newspaper article to him while enquiring if he has firmed anything up and ask if I can accept some sponsored posts on the side. Without waiting for his reply, I take the job and tell them to send the goods ASAP. I do briefly consider taking a moment to look at the issue from all sides before rushing in, but hey, Sam can always say no and put the brakes on it.

I check myself out on my phone. The olive oil treatment must be the most boring yet radical thing I've ever put on my hair. And a good job really because tonight I'm going on my first date in years.

# Chapter 14

The smell of garlic wafts upwards from a basement trattoria packed with families chatting and laughing as they tuck into sharing dishes of pasta, salad and pizza. Monumental pepper grinders are ground, and parmesan is scattered liberally by waiters in a cliché of red waistcoats.

After we are shown to the tiniest table in the room, Greg pulls my seat out for me. We reach for the menu at the same time before I unfold my napkin and spread it across my knees. Greg opens out a menu and puts it in front of us both. 'It's a good restaurant, but one word I'm hoping you will bear in mind is *bacillus cereus*.'

'I think you'll find that's two words . . .'

'Bacteria from spores.'

'Three.'

'My first piece of advice, even in an establishment of this ilk, is never order the risotto in case it's been cooked and left sitting around. Even in a small family-run place, shortcuts and bad food hygiene can be deadly.'

Once we've ordered drinks, Greg spoils my evening by informing me the warehouse has been sold. He's excited to have a TV chef called Logan Josh on board. 'You'll know him. He has that Irish food programme, giving the world his modern take on traditional foods like colcannon and soda bread. Sometimes he upcycles junk food – he did a whole programme on how to make the best crisp sandwiches a while back.'

'How are crisp butties Irish? I think I might have invented them. How long do we have if it all goes through?'

'It depends on the paperwork but both sides want to exchange as soon as possible.' He is animated as he speaks, and his pale skin is as perfect as ever; not a blemish or freckle to be seen.

'You wanted to be an architect. What happened?'

'I couldn't face five years or more of being a student. I wanted to earn proper money.'

'I dream of earning proper money. Being honest with you here, Greg, I've been saving up for ages to buy a flat, but I'm nowhere near being able to afford more than a shoebox and the prices keep going up all the time. And now I'm going to have to start shelling out much more to rent somewhere temporarily. Do you think there's any way we can persuade him to let us stay on once it's sold? Spinning out the subsidised fee for a while longer could make a huge difference to me and the Oddities.'

Suddenly feeling very hungry, I scan the menu for the most carby option, eyeing up the tiramisu for pudding. 'If he won't work with us then we might fight it. I wondered about writing to my MP or starting a petition.'

Greg shakes his head. 'Money talks, Aly. Places like yours are being scooped up by developers all over the world. It's the norm. Your MP is probably tied up with fighting hospital closures and worrying about climate change. I've seen the warehouse. It's a crumbling mess to you and me but gold to someone with a vision and a healthy bank balance. Logan

Josh will have loads of capital and you'll end up losing big time to him or another speculator. You'll find yourself out on the street at the end of any action with your time and energy wasted. You'd be better off doing more shifts and saving up for that crucial first rung on the housing ladder.' He breaks this news quite cheerfully, and when the waiter asks for our order, he takes charge of that too. 'We might share a couple of plates of pasta. Neither of us are that—'

'I'll have a pepperoni pizza with jalapenos please,' I interrupt, unable to disguise a flash of irritation. 'And don't forget to bring the dessert menu.' Then I feel bad. Greg and I haven't been together for years and he probably ordered on my behalf back then. Plus, he looks quite sexy tonight in a white cotton cricket jumper and dark jeans.

'You always did like spicy food. I can't cope with chillies,' he says as the drinks arrive and I glug half a glass of Prosecco in one go.

'I seem to remember us getting pretty hot on your mum's sofa,' I say, with a teasing glance.

'That definitely had nothing to do with the underfloor heating,' he flirts back.

My phone pings, and I turn it upside down on the red checked cloth.

Greg chinks my almost empty glass with his bottle of Peroni while I take a slice of pizza and bite into the hot base. 'How's Mother these days?' The boiling cheese scalds. I choke on the stringy topping. His face falls. 'Oh, Aly, I'm sorry.'

I grab my phone after all and read some of the

notifications. 'Tsk, I'm being slagged off on a site that encourages influencers to monitor their peers and call them out on anything they perceive as dodgy. The thing is that dodgy is very subjective. I'm collecting trolls by the minute too on my own channels. My fans all used to be cat lovers. Now I can't keep a handle on who's following me and what their motivations are.'

'You spend too much time on that device. You were checking it all the way here.'

'I'm an influencer; it's part of the job. Did you see the article I forwarded to you? Milking my cats for profit, pfff.' I scowl.

'Well, you aren't exactly changing the world.'

'Says an estate agent!' I seek out a waiter to bring me another Prosecco as I send Rick an image of my pizza. The evening of the shoot, he'd texted me a photograph of his curry in a tandoori restaurant.

*So pleased you've decided to come to the awards. Meanwhile, I enjoyed the starter so much I've ordered the main course for dinner.*

I'd responded by ordering a takeaway and pinging him back a shot of it. Since then we've been sending each other images of our dinner, with cute little messages. As I create a line of foodie emojis to go with my pizza, and consider whether to include an aubergine, Greg asks why I'm photographing my dinner. 'You only post about cats.'

He has caught me out and I blush. 'I might start a food channel. You never know. Sam is fixing me up with all sorts of campaigns including one on socks with paws for a national fashion chain.'

'Socks with paws?'

'You know . . . like gloves have fingers . . . the paws would be the . . .'

'Socks with paws for people or cats?'

'People of course. Who dresses their cat in socks?'

'You probably . . .' He sulks.

He's right, sometimes I do. Little doll socks to keep their feet toasty. I've also been known to pop them into tiny onesies on a cold night. I've drawn the line at offering them hot water bottles.

I order another drink and change the subject. 'Do you still believe in elves?'

'Of course not,' he says.

'Sorry, it's not a loaded question or anything. In fact, I liked that about you. And how your family stood up to the developers who were going to tear down that elf church.' Greg once proudly told me half the population of Iceland believes in the fairy realm and that his grandparents joined the fight for a road to be relocated away from suspected elf territory.

'I told you that because you went on about *The Lord of the Rings* so much. If there's a site that's suitable for building on, you can't defend it for sentimental reasons. We'd all be living in hobbit holes otherwise. Anyway, elves don't go to church.'

'Except at Christmas to say thanks for the day off,' I quip. 'Anyway, you love hobbits too. You once told me I reminded you of Frodo.'

He drains his beer, reaches out and draws back the hair from behind my ears, caressing my face as he does it. 'Those are pretty cute.' He smiles, and the bubbles from my Prosecco rise from my belly to my head. An image of Legolas pops into my head with his imposing jaw, flowing white hair and bow and arrow. Why did I not see the likeness before? Maybe if I invited Greg back to mine for a top-up later, we'd both relax and enjoy each other's company a bit more. He's already seen the mess, so I don't need to worry about boxic-shocking him.

The alcohol continues to warm the conversation as we share a tiramisu although I'm tense each time my phone pings, worrying someone else is slagging me off. I check my socials properly when Greg excuses himself to take a leak. As I suspected, the row has intensified about me on Pitch 'n' Bitch. But the bad feeling is washed away by a text from Rick asking how hot my pizza was. He includes chilli and aubergine emojis and a shiver runs down my spine.

I text back that I like it sizzling.

*Send water!*

Perhaps I've had more Prosecco than I meant to, because I find myself searching up an image of a hot fireman.

Greg requests the bill and I keep quiet when he hands his credit card to the waiter.

'Would you like a lift home?' he asks as we negotiate the wonky stairs.

I laugh. 'I only live two streets down. We can walk.'

'Driving is more efficient.'

'Than walking? I don't think so.'

*He might be impressive, but I've got a bigger hose :- )*

Rick's text makes me guffaw, causing hiccups. I'm about to reply when I receive a DM from the Instagram cat lady in response to my query about how much her courses cost. I laugh even louder when I see the price.

Then I challenge Rick to attach a picture of his hose.

Greg picks at the seal of one of the three boxes that make up my coffee table. 'What's in this one?'

I glance at the box for my labelling system. '"Things beginning with 'S'. Snakeskin phone cases"...' I read from the cardboard.

'Cases plural?'

'Ha, there's a lot of different species of fake snake.' I can't say the word 'snake' without giggling about Rick's hose. 'Also, some collapsible stilts and a collection of self-warming saucepans. Oh, and a fancy dress shark costume.'

'Collapsible stilts?'

I check my phone again. 'Don't ask me, I just receive the stuff.'

From the bedroom I hear Milly objecting to their banishment, but two cats fighting for my attention isn't the most romantic welcome for Greg.

I hand him a Chardonnay, the only booze I have in.

'Sorry, I don't keep a lot of alcohol because the cats would polish it off in front of the telly every night if I let them,' I joke, glancing at my phone again and trying not to grin like a loon. But my drink doesn't make it to my mouth as Greg takes the glass from me and stands it on the cardboard box. His lips are thinner than I remember but his kiss is cool and confident. His tongue meets my lips and finds its way to my teeth, as I taste warm wine on his breath along with something else. Rosemary? It's not unpleasant and I go with it as he leans in some more, gently pushing me back onto the cushions.

He's winding his fingers around my hair and nibbling on my lower lip, when he lets out an almighty sneeze. That's followed by seven more sneezes.

'Did you know that eight sneezes are the equivalent of . . .'

'. . . an orgasm.' He finishes my sentence for me. 'Well, one thing's for sure; I won't be having one of them tonight.' He sneezes five more times.

We get him out of the flat in record time, but not before his eyes puff up like he's been crying.

I check out the new headline on the Pitch 'n' Bitch site. The haters are going for it tonight. 'Two for one fake!' I read on with a sinking feeling. 'Ruby Tuesday' has done a forensic study of my cat pictures and discovered Milly has an extra patch of fur on her head while her skin is a lighter colour than a similar lighter patch on her sister's chest. Meanwhile, Molly is slightly fatter yet inexplicably has more baggy skin around her hips as well as the appearance of socks on her back paws. Dozens of people have pitched in with the scoop that one cat is two. Even as I watch, the row spills onto my Instagram page where AlyCat is accused of being the great pretender. Isn't that the point? I dress the cats up to look like humans for goodness' sake. None of it is real! The comments flood in, as the trolls ramp up. Thank God Rick and Sam are now aware I took creative licence with the pictures. I email them a screenshot of some of the more horrible comments.

'Don't panic. Don't respond on any of your channels, and especially not that godforsaken site,' Rick advises within seconds, copying Sam in. 'We'll talk tomorrow about the best way for you to go public on your site. Sam, can you arrange for the team to introduce Milly and Molly on our social media and give Aly's reasoning behind keeping the duo a secret?'

Sam replies with a reassuring email. At the end of it he tackles my question about whether sourcing sponsored posts on my own is a problem.

'I'd rather you didn't forge ahead on your own. I've got some fun things lined up for you if you can wait a little longer for us to close on the deals. But if you do feel the need to go it alone, please keep me updated and be sure to flag it with the hashtag #ad. Influencers are being named and shamed all over the shop right now for not declaring brand partnerships up front.'

I tell him I'm surprised a Pitch 'n' Bitch enthusiast managed to identify the differences between my two cats when my regular followers had never noticed. 'Don't suppose you leaked it?'

Sam doesn't reply. If influencer management is magic, he's keeping the tricks to himself.

# Chapter 15

Three weeks later, I accidentally shoplift a packet of sour cherries from Kav's Kozy Korner. She pushes them back over the counter when I return them. 'There's no problem that can't be sorted by an injection of Tangfastic. You have a difficult life, Aly. Let me brighten it with some E numbers, salt and sugar.'

'Ah thanks. I'm trying to view flats online but not finding much. The warehouse is perfect for what we do. My photography needs a certain amount of light, and my cats take up a lot of space. I didn't realise I had it so good. Every time I pass an estate agent's window I panic and want to run. And I'm so over being hounded by the influencers I leapfrogged on Instagram that I can barely be bothered to log on. How much for the Haribos?'

'It's a gift. Oh no, I forgot. You hate presents. One pound ninety-nine.' She grins.

'For pretend cherries?'

Manolis emerges from the storeroom. 'I sent you to the wholesaler for a dozen packs of scourers. Why have you brought me trifle bases, Kavita?'

'You sent me for sponges. You did not specify whether you wanted the sweet or savoury variety, you enormous idiot.' Kav wags an index finger stacked with gold rings at her partner.

'How many of our customers come to us because they want to make a trifle, woman?' The volume grows. 'Not a single one.'

I try to calm things down by admitting I've never had a trifle.

'Do not bullshit me!' says Kav and I'm not sure whether she's talking to me or him.

'I am not. Trifle is not for the modern customer,' replies Manolis, who assumes her comment was directed at him.

I volunteer to take a packet of the trifle sponges.

Kav draws her breath in shock. 'You cannot do that on a whim, Aly. A trifle needs serious commitment.'

Manolis starts to arrange the packets on the shelf, next to a stack of tins of value custard. He disappears again and Kav chases a fly around the counter with a tea towel, chatting as she leaps.

'Fancy a coffee? Special discounted friend's rate of zero pounds?'

Kav makes them and wipes the surfaces down while I carry the coffees outside and take my usual pew. Manolis comes out to arrange his new rack of Greek postcards. 'My mother has been sending them to me in packs of a dozen for years to lure me home. I thought I would put them out. Surprisingly, they are selling well.'

I kind of understand why; any escape from the graffiti-strewn walls and potholed pavements round here is a bonus. 'Yeah, it's a nice injection of exotic. They make me want to get on a plane. Where did you take Kav for your honeymoon, Manolis?'

His eyebrows drop. 'A honeymoon, my dear AlyCat . . .

is someone else's postcard.' He retreats quickly into the shop. What did that mean?

I'm distracted from my detective work by TCP, who approaches quickly with her trademark manly stride. The graffiti artist is wearing a vest today and I notice a rose climbing up her arm. Body art gives me an idea. I have sorted my outfit for the awards ceremony; Suze the Silk has come up with an amazing design for me that she will print up and I will make into a dress. But could I go further? Really wow Rick?

'Wait! TCP! I have a favour to ask. Remember the "For Sale" signs we did together? I want you to help me with some other . . . art work. Something completely different.'

'Vague.' She slurs the vowel like she can't be bothered to finish pronouncing it.

'Yes. At this stage. I haven't quite . . .'

'I'm in.'

At home, I receive a text from Sam telling me KittiFresh have noticed a huge uptick in sales since the campaign started and would like to reward me with a surprise. And coincidentally, as I put my key in the lock, a white van pulls up.

Slashing open the huge cardboard crate with a kitchen knife, I then rip off enough plastic to take out a coral reef. I always find if I open a gift quickly, it's less painful. Inside the parcel, lines of pastel-coloured ready meals sit in neatly ordered trays. There are also four framed pictures of the artwork that went in the newspaper.

The box comes with a note. 'A month's supply of free

KittiFresh for a year. Compliments from the marketing team and thanks for a great job.'

The cats come to sniff out the gift and Milly turns up her nose. 'Ungrateful child, you haven't tried anything but raw food in ages. You might love it. And it'll save me a fortune in meat. There's biscuits in all sorts of flavours, and pâté, and lots of gourmet dinners.' But despite my words, I'm conflicted too. It's not a payment, but a present, a massive godforsaken present. It's not necessary or wanted as I got paid for the campaign and we're not worth a whole year of posh cat food on top.

I'm taken back there again. Back to the moment where the gift was handed over; the stiff, awkward moment. Her cloying, crushing remorse for being a cold, unfeeling parent, matched with my despair at being an even worse child, and sadness from both of us at not delivering for the other. If guilt came gift-wrapped we'd have each handed it to the other with a bow on it.

How do I repay today's gift I didn't ask for? Can I send it back? Would that be rude? Remembering those Insta posts inviting me to be like my cat, I decide to canvass the opinion of my besties. 'OK, cats, help me out here. Do we take the food or weasel out of it?' Milly's long triangular ears prick up at the word 'weasel', and I note they need cleaning again. She pads over to stare into my eyes in the intimate way she does, and then wanders over to the light box on the floor and tries to get inside it. What is she telling me as she chitters and whines? A social media post to say thank you? Not the worst idea? I could pick a popular hashtag and jump on the back of it? Get the brand some gratitude exposure?

I grab her and pop her on my knee. 'Just how flexible are you, MillyCat?'

She's more pliable than I thought, humouring me while I put her in the light box. I lightly bend one paw under her and take a snap. I post it quickly, before I change my mind, tagging the brand, and a movement that will possibly define the decade. I then add my own hashtag; #catlivesmatter. And feel quite pleased with myself as it's catchy and contemporary, and shows AlyCat is in touch with a world beyond Instagram.

I text Sam and ask him when he thinks the KittiFresh money will come through.

His reply is swift. *Within thirty days of your invoice.*

I put my invoice in a while back, but a top-up wouldn't hurt. I decide to go with the dumb-bell sponsored post. Followers might not have loved an expensive toothbrush but who wouldn't want their cat to have good mouth hygiene and a squeaky toy plaything at the same time, for less than a tenner! I open the box and lift one out. Then I play around with them, taping the smallest to one of Molly's paws and a bigger one to the other.

A while ago I taught this cat a couple of show-stopping tricks. First, I trained her to sit, by issuing the single command and then rewarding her with food. When this worked, I moved on to 'high five' where she held her paw in the air for my hand to nudge. I feel a little guilty as I employ it today, encouraging her to raise her front paws while taking the dumb-bells with her. I put my good camera onto burst mode and it's done in a tick.

Replying to the dental accessories company, I attach an image that's beyond cute, and tell them I will hashtag the bejesus out of it as soon as the fee is in my bank account.

My afternoon shift is crowded, and so are the buses. I ride, sprint and ride again and by the time I get to my last client my phone and charger are both low. Marie has tubes running through her house feeding her with oxygen and I'm careful not to trip over them as I race around making her a sandwich, sorting her recycling, and preparing a milky coffee for now and a flask of tea for overnight.

'Can I get dressed for bed in my chair tonight? I don't think I can make it into the bedroom,' she says, breathing shallowly and looking grey. 'I feel a bit sick actually.'

'Of course,' I reply, adding, 'I'll close the blinds, so the neighbours don't get a free show,' which makes her laugh and then cough deeply into a hanky. Her skin is cold and clammy as I take her hand to help her into her nightie. She sits unsteadily and I gently rub cream into the sores on her legs.

'Anywhere else?'

'No that's fine. Can you draw down my morphine for me?'

'Morphine?'

'The GP left it today. It's in the bedroom.' I realise the significance of this, even as I glance at the 'Do Not Resuscitate' form on the chair arm. But I hate administering drugs I don't know, and morphine is hardcore. I find the syringe by the side of her bed with the bottle and bring the paraphernalia in to check the amount with her. Putting the adapter into the bottle neck I pull the white plunger, but nothing draws up. I must look like the amateur that I am. Embarrassed, I push the plunger back in and try again. Nada.

'You need to turn the bottle upside down.'

Oh Lord, who knew?

When I get home, I can't relax as I need to fit myself for a dress. Suze, our resident silk-printer, sketched and then hand-painted my childhood cat Mardy onto a length of fabric, working from a photograph I gave her. I then shaped the material into a long thin tube of a dress with the image of the cat splayed across my body from my knees to my boobs.

I read that when Michelle Pfeiffer dressed as Catwoman for *Batman Returns*, they had to powder her down, push her inside, vacuum-pack her in and then paint the shine on. While mine is a home-made affair, and I don't have to do any of that, I think it has a similar wow factor.

TCP drops around for a second late-night makeup practice that's sure to leave my pillows smeared with the remnants of black and silver eyeliner. She begins with my eyes, using a black matt to lock in heavy pencil in the shape of a cat's eye. She dots primer on the skin around them and I have falsies for the first time in my life, stuck fast with glue and gashed with so many layers of mascara I can hardly blink. She then draws a mask freehand in gossamer silver face paint; the contours teased out in layers of grey shadow. The effect is daunting and arresting and altogether weird.

She stands back after finishing and congratulates herself. 'Better than the time I spray-painted an active sub in the Clyde.' She then tugs and gels my hair into two kitty ears. 'You look more awesome than an awesome night under an awesome moon, Aly. Let's do a photo shoot in case we don't get time tomorrow.'

'Actually, I don't want pictures. I don't feel the need to put this on Instagram, I'd just like to enjoy it, for myself, and let it be a surprise to everyone at the awards ceremony.'

'Suit yourself.' She shrugs before striding off to answer the front door. She returns with Greg.

'Your boyfriend is here for some late-night property porn. Is it not enough that he sold us out once already?'

'Sorry for the late hour. I did text though and I know you lot never seem to go to bed. I've been out for a drink with some mates, and I was feeling like some Netflix and chill if you fancy it? I brought some snacks and a couple of beers.' He holds out a four-pack, some tortilla chips and a jar of salsa. 'There's a good new film about zombie babies. I've taken some antihistamine so I shouldn't turn into one of the undead this time.' I'm tired, but I did the same to him a few nights ago at his flat, so I can't really turn him away. Also, I'm getting nervous about the ceremony tomorrow and some after-hours zombies may be just the ticket to take my mind off the impending assault of glamour.

TCP slams the door shut behind her as Greg casts about for the remote control. He doesn't mention my makeup job or ask why I'm channelling a giant kitten. Instead, he opens the chips and dip and throws himself down on my sofa. Milly eyes him from her pile of blankets on the remaining stack of boxes in my flat, while Molly strolls over to check out the menu.

I fall asleep within minutes of joining him on the sofa and wake during a particularly loud toddler gore fest. He is attempting to soothe himself, or me, by running his fingers over the back of my hand, before turning it over and stroking my palm. I drift back to sleep again only waking for the neonatal annihilation of New York. Sleepily, I smile up at Greg.

'This is nice,' he says. 'Like old times.'

I remember horror really turned him on; I'm not sure Peter Jackson intended the battle of the Pelennor Fields to make blokes super-horny but there you are. Greg might not believe in fairies but he sure doesn't mind fantasy creatures ramping up the sexual tension in the room. As the babies prepare for their final onslaught (if I'd watched the whole film I think it would have totally put me off having kids), Greg takes my hand in his again. 'I want to put a ring on this,' he says, just loud enough for me to catch over the infant slashing.

I keep my eyes tightly shut. He said this once before, in the cinema, with a jelly ring from the pick and mix; shortly before I finished with him because the chemistry wasn't there for me. This time it's not so clear cut. While he may not have the easy charisma of Rick, he's good looking, has managed to find some Icelandic cool and is a lot more in my league than the CEO of a talent agency. My stomach lurches as I peek through sleepy dust eyes. Greg's eyes are red raw, and ringed like one of the undead. He rubs them as he smiles weakly.

'I guess the antihistamine didn't work. I don't understand how your cats can be hairless and still make me itch so badly. But I suppose at least I haven't sneezed my way through the end of the world.'

I send him home with a handful of balled-up loo roll, and then tidy up the sofa. In the gap between the cushions, I find a pair of Karen's yak knit gloves. Is that what's been setting him off? Greg clearly isn't compatible with yak, but perhaps his tolerance to my pretty kitties remains untested.

# Chapter 16

'Spectacular effort,' says Sam, snorting Cava like it's a recreational drug. 'You look incredible. Coming as your brand is an inspired idea for influencer awards.'

'I'm terrified it's too much.'

'It's totally too much. I love it.'

I'd return his warmth if I wasn't paranoid about smearing or cracking TCP's makeup job. Retaining the elegance of a cat in a crowded environment is harder than I thought. And that's before we even take a step inside the ballroom. The roof garden of London's Miramar Hotel has an awesome view of the city and is stuffed with soothing greenery although the mirrors built into stone arched windows make me feel like I'm in a church. I thank the God of Freixenet for my complimentary drink as I join Sam in knocking it back.

'Did you know the Vatican has an ATM that speaks Latin?' I ask him.

'Pray you have funds?'

'"Insert your card." And did you know every person who lives in the Vatican drinks an average of over fifty litres of wine?'

'A day?'

'A year.'

'Pff . . . my mum and the Irish Catholics of Camden

drink more than that on a Sunday. How do you know all this stuff?'

'YouTube videos. You learn stuff. I feel qualified to do minor surgery and fly a plane.' My words are drowned by the entertainment, as the cast of a new musical bob in to do their thing. Bellboys push luggage trolleys piled high with suitcases, as dancers sing of the trials of their job in a New York hotel. At the climax of the song, the suitcases flip open and rapping chefs climb out and start flipping rhymes and pancakes into the night sky. It's all a bit bonkers but they end their performance to enthusiastic applause.

'Did you know the Romans invented pancakes?' I ask Sam as a gong sounds and a disembodied voice invites us to move towards the ballroom. 'My internal organs are scrambled egg tonight,' I confess as we head downstairs together.

'Nerves are natural. It's a big night. You should talk to Rick about feeling sick at awards events. He's been known to barf into his pockets before presenting.'

'I wondered if he was exaggerating about that to make me feel better about GlimmerCon. Did you hear I bolted for the exit?'

Sam laughs. 'I saw it for myself. I love awards dinners and conferences; I was born to schmooze. Mind you, I'm only invited tonight because I'm with you. Thanks for being my golden ticket.' He pulls me into an awkward half hug, and I feel his skinny bones as I half hug him back. He has shaved his head closer for the night and looks like Spud out of *Trainspotting*.

'Any tips on how to get through it?'

'If you feel overwhelmed then tell people you're up for the newbie award; they'll fall over themselves to be nice to you. And don't worry, you won't stand out in the crowd as you've dressed so conservatively,' he teases me. 'Shame you're not next to me.'

'How do you know?'

'I checked out the table plan on my way in; I always try and get my eyes on one before a dinner. If I'm sitting next to an attention guzzler, I switch the name tab for someone a bit less time-consuming. It's prime networking and I can't face being leeched by an influencer who wants me to take her selfies for her. You're next to Rick's father, William H. on table ten,' he continues, chugging back the last of his Cava and reaching for another glass from a passing waiter. 'The trick is to ask him lots of questions. He'll leave thinking you are the most interesting woman in the world because you've talked about stuff he likes all night. And you'll find our marketing department mysteriously ups your Instagram spend a fortnight later. Billy the Dad has more clout than most of our A-listers. He's a bit of an old bore though, with some very dodgy politics and opinions. Thinks the world still revolves around public school connections and handshakes.'

'Doesn't it?'

'Not in our firm. Rick recruits based on merit. And the ability to be the last man or woman standing at the summer barbecue.'

'Is he here?' I ask casually, even though I've been to the toilet twice to look for him.

'VIP drinks reception on the fifteenth floor; the sponsors

and bigwigs of Showcase's #It'sSocial invite the most important people in the room to hang out before they are all forced to be social with plebs like you and me.'

'There's somewhere even more VIP than this? How many layers has this onion?'

'Enough to make you cry. I think tonight might be a big deal for my boss. He's presenting the awards and that's a first for an industry insider. He left early yesterday to pick up a new suit and fit in a haircut. But between you and me, I think the new look might be connected to our newest senior exec, Juliet Rae. She's at the postmodern drinks party with him now and I notice they're on the same table for the dinner.'

A pang of something stabs through me but TCP's mask holds tight, and I appear to be a rather cool cat.

We filter into a holding room and Sam is swept away in a sea of well-dressed marketing bods. I hug a corner and put up with the influencers who want an image of the crazy cat lady. Some might assume a woman who turns up to a dinner in full cat makeup with her moggy depicted on her dress wants attention, but I'm wondering why I've come like this and want to shrink-wrap myself to put a layer between them and me. I need a drink.

A crack in the double doors hints at wonderland. I slip through the doorway to grab some breathing space and find wonderland was an understatement. Candelabras dangle above each table with fat candles flickering an amber welcome. White tulle covers the backs of the chairs turning them into thrones, with instructions to #sitonme decorating the material in fairy-lit tubes. The pale walls of the ballroom are splashed with neon strips shouting #followme. The butter, on little white dishes, is moulded into an invitation to #spreadme. Metallic gold pens lie next to the cutlery; with printed invitations to write our own inspirational hashtags on the white tablecloths.

There are bottles of red and white on each table. I pour myself a large chilled white wine and wander to the front of the room in search of Rick's seat. He's bang in the front, with Juliet on his left. I examine his name card and hers, wondering momentarily if I should adopt Sam's trick and swap her out.

I find my own name in cursive writing on gold card at a table towards the back of the room. I quickly pocket it as an addition to my lanyard collection. Then I down my wine and write #moreboozeplease on the tablecloth with the freebie pen to get the party started.

A man in headphones enters the room from behind the stage. Aware I shouldn't be enjoying the party yet, I crouch down behind my chair.

'You have all you need?'

'I think so.'

A familiar figure follows him in, past the podium towards the edge of the stage. A sharp dinner suit, signature shiny shoes and, yep, no socks. The back of Rick's hair has been closely clipped and his barber either dip dyed the tips in bronze, or he's been busy with one of these pens. Shifting slightly to get a better view of him, I crouch behind a sign in a champagne bucket screaming #toastme. I'm guessing it's there to oil the faces of the losers during the ceremony and I half wonder if I should nab my consolation glass now.

'Always reassuring to get my head around the autocue in advance so I don't risk cocking up in front of a hundred and fifty people with thousands of followers at their fingertips,' Rick says to the stage manager, and I can see the stress in his shoulders. 'I hate this part of the job. Thanks for helping me out.'

'No probs, Rick. Buy me a beer in the green room afterwards. I'm not going mad this year though.'

'Me neither. I can't cope with the hangovers like I used to.'

The techie grins, pulls some gaffer tape from his pocket and fixes a loose wire to the floor. 'If you pull this off, you'll probably get the gig next year too. Last year's presenter turned up drunk on a kid's scooter and fell off the stage trying to do a wheelie as he announced he was the worst in his own category. I'd say you are a safe pair of hands.'

'The old Rick would hate to hear that, but thanks.'

'No nice surprises for you tonight though?'

Rick drops easily from the stage to the floor and turns back to address his companion. 'To be honest, it's good to have advance notice. I'm pretty exposed up here and I'd hate to read out the winner's name and burst into tears when it's not one of our influencers.' I don't have to see his face to know the lines around his eyes will be crinkling. My stomach does a cartwheel at the joy and pain of watching him all night from a distance.

The technician wanders off back to the mixing desk as a woman teeters into the room wearing the thinnest, most dangerous heels I have ever seen. She is built like a triangle, with broad shoulders giving way to a pinch-thin waist. Must be Juliet. I observe how her white-blonde hair touches her bum, swishing and gleaming in the twinkly light. She has cheekbones, and good eyelashes and everything I don't. And did I mention the shoes? I try to spot the trademark sole.

'Where were you? I've had to schmooze the sponsors on my own. A whole hour of tedious.'

'I did a dry run with the autocue to chase away the nerves.'

'I thought you clocked up millions of views over the years. Hard to believe a room of marketing people would faze you,' she says.

'Geeks of the world unite.' He shrugs. 'And YouTube is all about speaking to a single person. Talking to this lot is like being a gladiator at the Colosseum. Glimmer's bombed in every category by the way; I've just seen the list of winners.'

I breathe a sigh of relief. Imagine stumbling onto the stage dressed as a cat, to mumble a speech I haven't practised? It seemed a good idea in my bedroom, but not so much now. From my spying position, I attempt to knock back a celebratory slug of wine without dribbling on the carpet.

'Ah well then, we're relying on you to be incredible up there and steal the hearts and minds of potential influencers.' Flicking an imaginary speck of dust off his lapel, she rests her hand on his shoulder. 'Presenting the awards should help establish our profile as the leading agency even if we don't win. Maybe next year we should double head it?' Maybe you should wait to be asked, pushy lady? 'Oh, and don't forget to mention the special services we offer clients in between the gags.'

'You're expecting jokes? Making friends with the right people in the right places is what you do best, Juliet. You'll hopefully cancel out the damage my father will do with a few bourbons inside him.'

'I don't make friends. I make opportunities.' Ugh, I want to vomit into my mouth. She whispers something in his ear, and I bite my bottom lip when I notice her hand creeping down his back. Despite the suspected Louboutins, she's not a Blister, she's a bunion. They should be offering chiropodist's appointments in a raffle.

The gong bongs outside the ballroom, which prompts me to rise and knock over my glass. Rick beams at me while her smile remains as fixed as a *Mona Lisa* jigsaw that's been Sellotaped from the back. 'Aly! You've shown up? I feared you'd baulk at all the gold on the invite and decide to spend the night washing your cats' hair.'

The Julietster flicks her crowning glory like she's on a yacht trying to assess the direction of the wind. 'I think you'll find it's called fur, Rick.'

'These cats don't do fur,' he contradicts her. 'They're a one-off. Like their owner.' Rick weaves around the nattily dressed ad execs and influencers now filtering into the ballroom. When he kisses me on the cheek, even my heart turns pink.

'Hey, don't spoil the makeup!' I bluster.

'Wouldn't dream of it, Catwoman. You look amazing.'

It's exactly what I want to hear. I hope Juliet heard it loud and clear too. Unable to cope with his brown eyes burning into me, I focus on #inspireme, written on the wall in white neon. Well, I am certainly dressed to impress.

'I'm trying to work out which of your cats you have come as.'

'The tiger,' I tease, holding my hands like claws and growling under my breath.

Rick laughs out loud. 'Well, you're the best advert for new talent I've seen at one of these award ceremonies and I've been to more of them than you've had hot puddings. And I suspect you've had a lot of hot puddings.' He reaches out and touches my hair. 'Is it bolted on?'

'Pretty much. My stylist is a graffiti artist. I think I'll need a bag of chisels to free it tomorrow.'

'Worth it though. Milly couldn't destroy that "do" if she jumped on your head.'

'Believe me she tried.'

I take my seat next to Rick's dad. A woman in her fifties is on his left. Raven dark hair covers her shoulders in oversized curls and her lips look thoroughly Chanel Rouged. The red feather boa slung around her black velvet dress makes me feel less over the top. When she gives me a slight smile, I realise I've seen her somewhere before. I return it and look away, and when I glance back, she's still looking at me.

'Have we met before?' I say, leaning over Rick's dad.

'I don't think so, but it's hard to tell with that makeup job, which is amazing by the way. I'm Lola.' She smiles, before turning down a bread roll from a waiter. When he comes round to my part of the table, I consider telling him she donated her roll to me.

Rick's dad talks over us all as our soup arrives in a waiter pincer movement. Despite the table being dominated by middle-aged men in dinner suits, there's no ignoring his status. As I work out how to scoop out the last remnants of carrot and coriander without pouring it down my front, he tells everyone his plans for Glimmer, particularly championing the hot-desking I heard him slate a few weeks ago. 'Information sharing is vital in developing organic talent. We are all about equality too; every minority we sign up gets an equal marketing budget, whether they are black, white, Chinese or a woman although obviously cats demand less and we would never discriminate against short people.' He gestures to me as he mentions cats before telling everyone his son inherited his height from his mother. I glance under the table and notice his shoes have a slight platform. Anxious not to miss any details about Rick's family, I pour another glass of wine and concentrate.

'How long ago was it, William?' someone asks.

'Over thirty years now. Bought two yachts since then. New one's moored off the Dalmatian Coast. I get very silly at sunset, don't I, Lola?' He slaps his hand down onto the woman's leg and she strokes her neck as though her scarf is a boa constrictor.

'Why would a cat demand less, Bill?' she asks him coolly, and I realise where I've seen her before. She's the woman who runs the classes in the countryside about being your best kitty self and puts the adverts on Instagram.

One of his chums looks at me, glances at her and then

winks at Rick's dad. 'I think we have some feisty ones here.' The waiting staff advance upon us, distributing plates of breast-fed chicken with parcels of asparagus packaged up with knicker elastic. I sneak a peek at Rick's table, noticing Juliet hangs on his every word, whereas I can only clutch at my glass. I chug back the drink, wipe off a lipstick stain and write #socialclimber on the tablecloth.

It appears I'm not the only one checking out Juliet; when someone asks about the recent changes at the top of Glimmer, Rick's dad boasts about her steely determination, ruthless decision-making and contacts book. 'She'll wrestle the wheel from Rick if he steers the ship on the wrong bearings. That boy is too idealistic for his own good sometimes with his quest for the truth. The truth, as we all know, is whatever the most important person in the room declares it to be. Until their secrets are exposed, and we all have to reassess.' He signals to a waiter at his shoulder and asks for the best single malt they have. 'Do you know the most important place in Fleet Street was always the safe in the editor's office? It's no different in advertising. My office in the glory days of WHH was rammed full of incriminating pictures and documents, keeping them safe for my own clients. These days I have to keep the evidence under the floorboards at home because of all the damned hot-desking.'

'Old school PR! Keep the bodies buried under the patio until it's time to dig them up before you retire, William,' chuckles a man in an oversized dinner suit that can barely fasten.

'I'll never retire. And Sunday lunch in the Cotswolds

has an added frisson when the truth lies beneath,' says Tosser, tapping his nose.

I doodle with the pen and end up writing #helpme.

'You still have that place in Gloucestershire?'

'I do a run out in the Merc from time to time. I have a fondness for roast beef and a Yorkshire pudding or two in a country pub. You like yours dripping with gravy don't you, Lola?'

It's a talent to bake Sunday lunch with innuendo. His black eyebrows contrast with the white of his hair. Was he rich enough to buy someone else's face?

#I'mAnInfluencerGetMeOutOfHere

In contrast, Rick is all coordinated youthfulness as he bounds onto the stage amidst a swell of rock music. He quickly warms up the crowd with a fast and funny A to Z commentary on the social media world. I am focusing so hard on taking in every detail of him that I feel like an S for stalker. I only take my eyes off him once, to find Juliet staring just as intently and laughing a little too hard at his patter.

As 'Zoom' makes an entry after 'Zeitgeist', I doodle with the gel pen on the tablecloth. #hothost makes way for #budgiesmuggler underneath my hand after Rick's dad scrapes back his chair and excuses himself, exposing us all to tight dinner suit trousers that leave little to the imagination. He lightly touches his partner on the shoulder as he moves away.

As the waiters fill our glasses with fizz, and Rick takes a break before presenting the awards, a man with a shiny head goes roving with a microphone.

'Ladies and gentlemen, we've been asking you all night to add your inspirational hashtags to the #It'sSocial conference tablecloths. I've noticed some little works of art; particularly amongst table four who have made an entire mind map of mental health hashtags. Go you!' He reads out several, all related to #bekind. I review my own hashtags and smile to myself as I rearrange my napkin and cross my arms to cover my golden but not very kind insults.

'The cool news is we are sending around some auction paddles so you can bid to win one of our designer tablecloths.' I wet my finger and try to scrub off the writing underneath my fork. 'It's all in aid of sending underprivileged youths to a new social media academy in Brixton. You see, it's not about the table linen, ladies and gents, it's about making a difference to lives. Real lives.'

The sun is setting behind tall concrete as I emerge into the London night, desperately needing a break from the razzle-dazzle of social influence. The doorman has left his spot, and I move behind a pillar, taking a deep breath and snaking my hand down my front to locate my cash. I don't want a tablecloth, but I'll probably need to be seen to bid, so I should double-check how much I have in case I accidentally win. I withdraw three crisp twenty-pound notes from my bra. Cool cats don't carry handbags and I had to put my cash somewhere.

'That's a good trick. Now can you pull a credit card from your knickers?' Rick arrives with timing as sharp as his dinner suit. He props himself against the wall beside me.

The alcohol has loosened me up. 'You're joking but actually I can. It's pretty maxed out though.'

He passes me his glass, a goldfish bowl filled with red wine. 'Help me knock this back before we get arrested.'

'For drinking on the streets?'

'For having fun at an awards ceremony.' He rifles in his inner pocket and pulls out a stash of notes. 'I left my own wallet at home to avoid a bulge in my trousers.'

'Rick Harvard, have you met your dad?'

He laughs. 'That VPL wasn't always his signature you know. His dinner suit got tighter over the years thanks to his insatiable appetite for everything including food and drink. Oh, and, Aly, I wanted to give you the heads-up in case you are looking forward to winning . . .'

'It's OK. I heard what you said in the ballroom. I'd probably have tripped up on the way to the podium. I can't wear heels like your friend.'

'Juliet? She doesn't do friends. And she's probably wise to adopt that policy. My father is playing kingmaker and she's a pawn in his game. As am I. Here . . .' He holds out a fan of banknotes and pops the rest back into his pocket. 'Keep your money and use this. My dad will probably be bidding all over the place so everyone can see how rich and generous he is. I'll be on stage giving it the old presenter schmaltz and won't be able to bid against him so call it my contribution to helping starving influencers if you see a tablecloth you fancy.'

'I can't take that.'

'I insist.' He tries to push the notes into my hands, but I refuse again. 'Then there's only one thing for it,' he says, lifting his hand to the front of my dress. Up close and looking me in the eyes, he strokes my collarbone with the paper, after deliberately lifting the fabric from my front. Slowly rolling the notes downwards, he pushes them into my bra, keeping eye contact all the time. His thumb skims the curve of my breast and my skin tingles. My throat dries up and I swallow twice. Then he drops his hand back to his side and twitches an eyebrow no more than a millimetre, inviting me to respond.

My breath hitches and I nudge his arm playfully. 'I'm grateful you didn't look down right then, or you might have got an eyeful of Spanx.' I fish out the money as elegantly as I can, holding it up in between our bodies. 'I need to give this back. You know I'm not after you for your cash, just your super-handsome looks, although I think you nicked yourself while shaving, which means you lose a point from the judges.'

I lightly touch his clean-shaven chin with my other hand, before opening his palm and returning his banknotes to him. He puts his thumb over my knuckles and I look down as he clasps the rest of his fingers over mine. With his other hand he raises my chin gently, so my eyes meet his again. I'm not expecting his kiss, his lips warm and dry against mine. I'm not expecting the smell of red wine on his breath as it mingles with mine. But when his tongue lands it's thrilling and feather light, while my whole body is now heavy with expectation. I stop breathing and listen to my heartbeat banging in my chest as he deepens the kiss. I feel his hand on the back of my neck. He slowly strokes his fingers down the ridge of my backbone until he reaches the edge of my dress and I pray he doesn't try and wrestle with the zip as I'm pretty much pinned in. Passing my fingers over the tiny bump where he cut himself, I want to heal the wound. He pushes me gently against a post, his tongue more firmly exploring my mouth as I start to relax into it.

Footsteps on the steps force us apart.

'So, I'm a bit drunk, but the sunset is gorgeous, and they are wondering where the host has got to, so I came out to find you.' Glimmer's newest executive sweeps towards us in a river of silver gown. She doesn't look very drunk, just a little bit cross. With each click of her shiny heels another guy looks her way; the doorman has now returned, and she might as well stick a lead on his neck and drag him round with her.

'You're needed, Romeo.' Juliet claims the man next to me with a single word.

The doorman asks if he can flag her a taxi. She strokes Rick's arm like he's her pet dog. 'Oh, we're not done with this evening yet.' Then she turns to me. 'How fun of you to come in fancy dress.'

It looks like fun ran out of oxygen on her lips when she turns back to Rick. 'The stage manager is going frantic looking for you. They're well into the auction and want to start the awards soon. I bought a tablecloth for a thousand pounds. You cannot have enough #MeToo hashtags over kitchen supps, can you? You'll have to come round for some bruschetta.' Casually winding her arm into his, Juliet guides him back into the hotel like her glittery stilts are Nike trainers. She is not without talent, I think, as I hobble back to the ballroom on heels that are pathetic in comparison.

'Hashtag "#shortmansyndrome". Also hashtag "#Mysogynistatmytable". Looks like someone was inspired by their dinner companions in a wholly different way,' says Baldy gleefully, ending his celebration of hashtags at our table. A shadow passes over William Harvard's face. I stay at the back of the ballroom, relieved the compère hasn't read out #TopTosser. Finding a space on the floor next to an exhibition stand with sponsor names laid out under the word #fundme, I take my shoes off. Gratefully rubbing my toes, I tune into the low hum of conversation as people walk back to their seats. Two women in cling-film dresses glide past, chatting.

'Has Harvard hit on you yet?'

'No but it's as predictable as the men awarding each other all the trophies. Avoid the full-on charm attack later.'

'It's the octopus hands I find hard to avoid.'

One laughs and the other grimaces. 'Salty as the calamari hors d'oeuvres.'

I'm pretty convinced they are talking about Harvard senior, but they didn't actually specify which one. I blush the red of my wine as I remember the touch of Rick's hand inside my bra. After knocking back my drink, I check my phone for the conference hashtag to find out what people are saying. And then I spot a wall of notifications.

The dumb-bell post was going so well they sold out of the products on the first day. But it's suddenly turned into a shouty mess. Someone going by the name of @gardenspade101 commented that I didn't declare the post was an advert or use #ad, and other influencers ploughed in. The comments get nastier, with talk about reporting me to the Advertising Standards Authority. The bitching has spilled over to the influencer gossip site and has caused a storm on there too as my sisfurs have turned into bitchers.

I suddenly recall Sam's words to me the night I was drunk after the Italian meal with Greg, telling me to let him know if I took on sponsored posts and be sure to clearly signpost the commercial partnership to followers by adding #spon or #ad at the end.

Rick reappears on stage to present the awards. I barely register the music and lights as I quickly edit the post to include #ad and #sponsored, but it feels like shutting the stable door after the horse has won the Grand National. I read the comments again and then I google ASA rules. Blinded by the word 'fine', I am suddenly convinced I will go to jail. I need to do something drastic to sort out this mess. I search around for instructions, find my way into settings, and impulsively calm down the noise that's peck, peck, pecking at my head.

'And the best newcomer's award goes to . . .' Rick stops dead and looks out to the mixing desk, lifting his hands to query what he's reading. Then he shakes his head and continues. 'Well, this was definitely not up there during the practice run! The best newcomer is in fact one of our own – the spectacularly satirical AlyCat; otherwise known as Aly Meadows.'

The YouTubers whoop even though they have no idea who I am, and the room starts to spin. When I'm called to the stage a second time, I clasp the tablecloth to try and steady myself, if not inspire myself with my own inspirational insults. Someone helps me to my feet and I slot myself back into my shoes. My dress is restrictive, and the kitten heels cut into my skin. Several people shake my hand, which lengthens my time in the limelight when all I want to do is close it down. Finding myself once more at the edge of a stage with Rick in my sightline, I gravitate towards him and reach for his steadying hand. He kisses my cheek, guides me to the podium and steps back. I stutter, and swallow hard. I am more than a little drunk and not prepared for this.

The room goes silent. They are expecting a speech. I open my mouth, but nothing comes out. I look down at my dress, and the picture of my beloved childhood cat. I have come in her image. I'm wearing a mask – not myself up here, but someone more powerful. Someone with claws and attitude. Someone who knows their own worth. I look out at the woman with Rick's dad and think back to her advert on Instagram, remembering her pep talk about adopting your cat's attitude and listening to their voice.

*Do not speak. Collect the trophy and go. No one wants to listen to what you say.*

Not that voice.

I look down again at the face on my front. Mardy, speak to me? The room is frozen. You could hear a pin drop. And then, from nowhere a soft mewl.

*I am here for you.*

I look up at my audience. Where to start? I stutter, stop, look over at Rick. His eyes connect with mine, telling me he has my back. I suddenly sober up. And begin at the beginning.

'As a child I spent a lot of time in silence.' Well, I wasn't about to thank my sodding mother, was I? I don't know what to say next, quite how to proceed in a space where I will be judged, recorded and perhaps picked over for days to come. I study the room, to see if they are with me. Everyone's eyes seem to be on me, except for Juliet's, who is focused on Rick. I throw him another glance. He flashes me that half-smile that teases out honesty and I go with it.

'There are lots of hashtags screaming inspirational messages at us tonight. From our seats, our phones and our tablecloths, we are told to love, to live, to talk the talk, to seize the day, to inspire, influence and engage.' I stop, and listen for Mardy, our family cat, miaowing gently from the past, nudging me on with her nose.

'We are here tonight to celebrate and award effective communication. But what does that mean? As a child and teenager, I was told to be quiet. To be seen and not heard. To fade into the background while my parents waged war on each other. I had no voice. Silence was only broken by the sound of the TV and of my parents arguing. I could tell you about holding my breath till my lungs burned, looking for permission to butt in or change the conversation, opinions frosting in my windpipe, like an ice pop left forgotten in the top shelf of the freezer.' I pick up a glass of water from a table beside me and sip it. 'School was worse because once you've experienced a silent disco, it's hard to take the headphones off and dance. I learnt to not stand out, to hug my opinions to myself, to keep the volume turned down. Instead, I tuned into another conversation for support and warmth. A warm nose breathing softly against my leg, a reassuring purr in my ear, non-verbal conversations that told me I was not nothing, but something.'

Glancing at Rick, I put my trust in him, in his audience, and his glittering night. And I put my trust in my cats. I point to the image on my dress. 'I turned to my cat Mardy. I talked to her and she listened. When I was at my loneliest, I had wise, and often funny, company. When Mardy was ripped away from me I pretty much died inside. But something miraculous happened. Milly and Molly came into my life to fill that lonely hole. I talked to them, and they talked back to me. More than talked – Sphynx cats are very noisy and squealy; Milly even bitches at me in her sleep. But don't get me wrong, I'm not Dr Dolittle or anything!' I say, less nervous now as the waltzer spins more slowly and I see gently evolving support in the room. 'Tonight, you have kindly confirmed that I have a voice. I have influence. I feel both heard and celebrated. I'd like to thank you for that, and also thank Rick and Sam from Glimmer who helped give me agency. But it's not my voice that's made me who I am and prompted this award tonight. I talk to the world via my cats under my brand of AlyCat. I comment on our society through them.' An archive of my most popular posts flashes up on the massive screen above me. Some shots are making them nod, others make them laugh.

'I often get grief online for dressing them as humans and I've sometimes apologised for it, but I'm not sorry for making Milly and Molly celebrities in their own right. Contrary to what you might have heard or read, I do not mistreat, exploit or imprison them. My cats enjoy the attention and the treats and in return I bring people their voices. We satirise the ridiculousness of humans and at the same time showcase their playfulness.' Although I have everyone's full attention, it feels like time to go drink champagne from a stolen bottle. 'Ladies and gentlemen, if you have a pet, try talking to them when you get home tonight and listen to what they have to say. Cats are more human than you know.'

'I didn't realise you were one of ours,' says Tosser as I brave a return to his table, and he pushes whisky breath into my face. 'I'd have made more effort to chat during dinner. Maybe we can hook up later . . . there's a late bar in the green room behind the stage.' He over-pronounces his words and whisky-sour sputum spatters into my ear.

Thankfully Sam rescues me as Rick moves on to the final category of the night. 'Well done,' he whispers, giving me a quick hug. 'We knew you could do it. Are you taking the silent disco thing literally though? I wanted to leave a comment on Instagram and couldn't find your account. Can you sort it and post the news of your award? This is the night for reposts and new followers.'

He returns to his seat for the final award and I swipe on Instagram. My face flushes and my heart pumps loud in my chest. The implications dawn on me. My passion, my livelihood, my new life.

'And the award for best agency goes to . . . Oh my word . . . the best agency . . . is Glimmer!'

The lights go down, music blares and I almost expect tickertape to fall from the ceiling. The walking Toblerone totters onto the stage and throws her arms around Rick. They're followed closely behind by his dad, with a shabbily tucked-in shirt. Sam is last, moving up the steps like a long drink of water. As they are presented with the award and gather for a photo, Rick's eyes wander the room till they find mine and he beckons me to join them. I plonk myself on Tosser's chair, grab the sugar bowl and palm three lumps. Pushing them into my mouth I crunch down. The sweetness is familiar and soothing. I swig back a glass of flat fizz and chew the end of the gold pen before scrawling #winnerwinnerthanksforthechickendinner on the tablecloth. When I look up, Juliet has wrapped herself around Rick.

I'm joined by the woman who was sitting with his dad. I'll bet she didn't deface her side of the tablecloth with #loservillesnoozerville.

'You were great up there.'

'Well, it wasn't as disastrous as it could have been.'

She passes me a business card. She's even more stunning up close. 'I run a class on how being like your cat can improve your life.'

'I know. I joined the dots a little while ago. Instagram has been serving me your ads.'

'Ah, that's good, it means our social media manager is earning her money.'

'Well, I do search up cat stuff a lot so I'm not sure she's performing rocket science.'

'Come to one of my classes,' she says.

'I can't.'

'Why not?'

'Why not?' I repeat. She wants the truth, channelled through my inner cat? Right then, lady, here's the moodiness of Mardy, the spikiness of Milly and some of Molly's in-your-face wailing. 'Because I'm about to be evicted and my rent will now go through the roof, if I manage to find a place that suits us on my budget. I have a dead-end job and a high-end Instagram account to concentrate on, if I can claw it back from the graveyard I just sent it to. My priority is not gallivanting up to the Cotswolds or wherever you operate from to play-act on a retreat . . .'

'It's not about play-acting, it's about self-help and channelling what you know to overcome what you believe you don't.'

'Can it help me buy a flat?' I drop my voice as the room has gone quiet for Rick's acceptance speech.

'In the long run, yes, I think it can.'

'I only have a short run. Even the train fare to your place would set me back a good few quid. And your course fees? It's all money that could be put to good use saving towards a property. Sorry to sound middle class but that's my reality.'

'You don't sound middle class,' she says, and I don't know whether to be offended. 'Come for free. I'll make an exception for you.' Her voice is urgent, which makes me suspicious. Everyone is a double-glazing salesman really, aren't they?

'Why?'

'Because you turned up at a media awards ceremony dressed as your pet? Takes a lot of balls, and a certain amount of belief in cats. Maybe I can interview you and work you into a case study; I'm writing several papers for different universities, researching the female psyche and place in our patriarchal society, especially since the start of the #MeToo movement. Drop me a line when you are ready to come to a class and see what we do. That's my personal email.'

As I head for the door, Glimmer staff are smiling their best smiles for photographs, while Juliet has anchored to Rick like a limpet in the Atlantic.

I whisper goodbye, as I seem to have lost my voice.

# Chapter 17

As the end of the week bleeds into the weekend and then into another week, my mood turns on a dime. Rick messaged to see how I was after the ceremony. When he began the message *Hello winner*, my heart leapt. Since then, we've been sending each other flirty messages and I scan my phone a hundred times a day for a reply to my texts.

Sam's been working hard on my behalf, telling me some of his feelers have come back with positive replies. At the beginning of the week, he rang to report he'd had a conversation with the owner of a chain of pet-friendly pubs about adverts in the local press across the UK. I bit his hand off at a job that doesn't rely on my deleted Instagram account. 'Also, remember we sent your portfolio to Smart Rail? The folks in their advertising agency are wondering if AlyCat can pull together a *Brief Encounter* shoot to help promote the new franchise. They'd be happy to pay for a series of videos and might stretch to TV in the long term if we can get the concept right. You'd need both Milly and Molly for that one and we'd have to pretend one of them was male, probably Molly I would think. Anyway, as I said, all potentially quite lucrative.' As we chatted away about who else we could entice to work with me and the cats, I crossed my fingers he wouldn't look at my Insta account until I'd worked out if I could get it back.

For now, my sewing box and machine stay unused. I piled them on top of the box marked 'collagen ++ face cream' in the bedroom before lifting them off again, opening up the face cream and dabbing some gloop onto my cheeks.

*It's soothing isn't it? Like when you moisturise the AlyCats.*

Since the awards ceremony my mother's voice seems to have morphed into something kinder. It's a welcome relief. But my cats are not quite so supportive. Picking up on my unsettled mood, they are acting like a two-cat demolition crew. Crime of all crimes, they tried to rip into my pizza when I was in the loo. I pick at some cold Welsh rarebit that I mixed with Marmite as well as Worcester sauce to make it even rarer. I offer Milly a crumb or two while she chills out on the stool next to me, but she turns her nose up at it. She's getting used to the KittiFresh gourmet dinners I now mostly serve them.

'You're right, MillyCat. Only sugar will do. Want to come and see what delicious pastries your Auntie Kav has for me this morning?'

She turns her back on me and strolls off. I smile. If there's one thing I could learn from Milly, it's refusing to roll over for food.

Kav is excited to see me. 'Have you recovered from the longest hangover in history? I know how you feel. Manolis decided he liked bacon again. So, he went mad with the order, and we've eaten so much of the leftover stock I've had bacovers. Bacon hangovers are a thing! Did you enjoy the awards ceremony? What did they think of the new you?'

I lean on her counter, defeated, as she stacks a tinned fish promotion in the aisle. She lowers her eyelashes in concern. Only Kav could carry off bright blue mascara highlighting deep brown eyes. 'Pilchards. Why?' she says sorrowfully. Some British foods Kav really can't get her head around. I give her an account of the evening, choking back tears over the lost account.

'That does sound like the cake's fallen over, but I wouldn't panic too much. Surely you can reinstall an Instagram account?'

'Only if you disable it. I had too much to drink and for some reason unknown even to me, I deleted the damn thing. I can start again but I'll have no followers or comments.'

Kav steps into the aisle and calls into the stockroom. 'Manolis, can you take over? Aly needs a treatment for her emotional wounds, and I think I have the ingredients.' She disappears into an Aladdin's cave I've never seen inside.

'How's the singing going, Manolis?' I ask him as he ambles to the counter.

'I have a ticket for you!' He beams. 'And even more exciting, we have a new line of olive oil. I saved you a bottle.' He leads me down the aisle to view his new selection of Athenian imports, raving about a new Greek wine. Then he pauses. 'Actually, Aly, I would like your help.'

'I'm always up for a wine tasting.'

'Not that. I am fifty soon.'

'I have heard talk of it,' I say, amused. 'Kav's been obsessing about what to give you.' Everything from a cookery course to an electric bike for the paper rounds.

'There is only one thing I want from her. Her hand in marriage.'

I pick up a bottle of the olive oil and recoil from the price. 'You want to renew your vows? That's sweet. Can I be a witness? I'm happy to go to Vegas at your expense.'

'Not a renewal. I want to marry her.'

'But you already did that?'

'We are not husband and wife, Aly, even though she may refer to me that way.' He sighs and his shoulders hunch. He suddenly looks older than fifty. 'We work in this shop every hour of the day and my beard is going grey and I'm not getting any younger. I love her and want to make it legal. I don't want to have to pretend to good friends like you that we are more than we are.'

'But . . .' For once I'm lost for words. 'But you are so more than you are. And so married. More married than anyone I know. She calls you "husband" ten times a day, especially when she is hitting you with a tea towel or grabbing your crotch because she wants to get you upstairs after you've finished alphabetically ordering the cheese.'

'I accidentally put Gruyère in front of Gouda last week and that's exactly what I mean. I am getting older and so is Kavita, even though you could mistake her for a woman in her early thirties. We have been together for donkey's years, but she is not my wife. I am going to wind up a sad old man with only half a corner shop to retire on.'

The ringtone sounds on my phone and I quickly silence it. 'Have you asked her?'

'Of course, many times.'

'But why . . .'

'She walked away from her family's choice of husband. And she has always said she will not walk down the aisle without their blessing.'

'Oh.' I feel sad for my two wonderful friends. 'Maybe you're not asking loudly or publicly enough?'

He strokes his beard, wondering where I'm going with this. I'm half wondering myself.

Suddenly inspired, I grab a copy of last week's *Hillingdon Star*, flick through it till I reach the small ads and push a page under his nose.

'Those are tiny. She might not read that page and even if she does, she might not see my ad,' he says. My phone rings and flashes up Sam's name. Manolis closes the paper and picks up his own phone. 'But she will if I take a whole page.'

'Aly, what's going on with your Instagram account? I still can't find it.' Sam is as direct as I feared he'd be when he cottoned on to my stupidity.

'Sorry, Sam, I've been so busy. I've been packing for a house move and helping my friend Manolis with a marriage proposal and I've come up with an idea on your *Brief Encounter* job.' For a moment I consider spilling all and asking for his help, but this man actually believes in me, and I don't want to shatter that. I ring off after reassuring Sam I will sort it out.

Back home, to suppress the gnawing sense of panic, I concentrate on uniformly covering my toast with marmalade and a layer of orange sprinkles. It's an exact science – too many sprinkles and you get instant artery clog, too few sprinkles and it's just toast and marmalade.

A more cheerful text pings in from Sam. *By the way, KittiFresh have settled up, so I hope you've invoiced accounts.*
'Yay!' I punch the air. Finally, some cash.

# Chapter 18

I hit Kav's Kozy Korner before my care shift, picking up a Mars bar and a chocolate milk. I then add a satsuma to give my breakfast nutritional balance. With the KittiFresh money now in my account, I'm still deciding whether to get my car back, put it towards a deposit or pay my massive bill here. I'm still tired from a late-night binge of online properties I can't afford. Logan Josh has been sending builders round to eye up the property and the Oddities are panicking. The clock is ticking.

When he pops out of the stockroom, Manolis greets me excitedly, thrusting the paper at me.

'Sixteen refugees sharing a "she" shed?' I read out loud.

'Turn the page!'

He's really done it. 'Marry Me, Kavita. Live with me in our Kozy Korner of London forever.'

No mixed messages there. I'm excited for them.

My morning shift stretches into infinity, but it's not the golden infinity of Glimmer, just an endless grey procession of bus stops and household chores. My clients are grumpy, and when one of them refuses her laxative solution, I pour it down the sink and leave the box unticked in the app. I can't blame her. I'd be reluctant to trigger an unexploded bowel bomb too.

By two in the afternoon, I've run over shift by half an

hour and still have a client left to visit. Thing Two calls to say the lady doesn't want me anymore as I'm so late. I tot up the hours in my head, subtract my expenses, and realise my day's salary amounts to practically nothing.

'The thing is—' I say, but she rings off.

'The thing is . . .' I say again when I get her back on the phone, 'the thing is . . . I quit.' Neither of my cats would put up with this. And from now on, neither will I.

I call Lola and let her know I've got them on loudspeaker at last.

# Chapter 19

Power Towers isn't an easy place to get to without a car. My journey to a swag building at the edge of the Cotswolds involves two trains, a cab and a whole morning of my life. I instruct the driver to drop me in front of the gates to save money. Too knackered to rush, I take a leisurely walk on the gravel, which takes ages as the drive is so long. The only way into the house is through the open patio doors so I wander through the winding rock garden complete with an opaque water feature in the shape of a Mini Milk ice lolly. As I approach the building, a curvaceous figure strides out.

'Aly, you came. That's fantastic. Cat class is at two,' Lola says, in her unmistakable silk-red voice. 'Relax and enjoy the house. Get yourself a drink from the bar or ask one of the girls to make you a chai latte or a spoothie.' A what? I wrinkle my face. 'Our best-selling range of spinach smoothies is really popular.' She winks then slips back into the building through a side door.

A young woman in a leotard, tight Lycra leggings and ballet shoes is busy replacing black mats with white velvet beanbags in a large room lined with mirrors. Another woman sprays floral mist to cover a slight pong of sweat which two large fans are doing their damnedest to clear. Following a door into a white reception area, I notice rows of *Alice in Wonderland* style keys hanging behind a desk. A tinkle of chat leads to a tiny room studded with mosaic tiles and small orange tables; someone went to Morocco lately! At one table, two women in black leotards and black fishnet stockings sit drinking green sludge. I pick up a menu; it's filled with a ton of evil-sounding smoothies. All choices involve spinach.

A young woman with high cheekbones, pale skin and a nude lipstick asks me if I'd like anything. Craving wine, I opt for a sparkling water with ice as the two women next to me chat in loud voices.

'Lucinda used to wonder how women didn't know their husbands were having an affair. Then she discovered her own was having it away with her boyfriend and her world fell apart.'

'Makes sense though, I suppose. Similar tastes in the bedroom?'

'I think she was most offended by the fact they didn't invite her to join in. She's now declared herself celibate although I know she's worried about falling off the wagon with her son's swim coach.'

'Swim coaches are very hard to resist. It's the Speedos isn't it?' Their laughter is interrupted by a whooshing sound outside. 'That's the helicopter, whisking her back to Maida Vale. She didn't want to take part in the second round of cat class. In her opinion, everything with hooves or claws should be fenced in and managed by gamekeepers.' The women then drop their voices but are still within hearing range. 'Also, she wasn't too happy about a woman with a boob job and a cat bell telling her to be sexier and more assertive in the bedroom, although she did seem excited about cracking the whip at work.' The helicopter fades away. 'I love this place. Do you think a chopper would make you happy?'

'Only if it came attached to Lucinda's swim coach.'

'We're ready for you, ladies,' says a woman with white-blonde hair swept back into a tight ponytail. Her eye makeup is a dramatic mix of blue and green stripes and she is dressed in a white body suit. As she leads us in, a cute tail bobs about on her behind.

The patio doors are closed now, with heavy white curtains drawn across. Fans continue to circulate the air as another half a dozen women wander in. Two are in silky lounge suits and another is dressed head to toe in a pink character onesie. A rabbit? Of course not; she pulls the hood over her head to reveal Hello Kitty. Another woman has silver kitten ears on a headband. Feeling out of place in my denim skirt and puff sleeved top, I pull off my sandals and wonder about painting my toenails in alternate stripes of blue and green. Then we are invited to close our eyes and reach for a beanbag as a soundtrack starts. The low noise reminds me of home; with Molly snoring and Milly contentedly purring on the bed.

I sink into a velvet beanbag, closing my eyes. It's like being in a light and airy womb. The sounds continue for a while and I open one eye to see others are also snuggled into their oversized cushions, scattered at intervals around the room. Suddenly there's a yowl and the soundtrack morphs into one cat fighting another for a mouse. On edge now, I keep an eye open for action. The door opens. Lola has changed into a tight leopard-skin bodysuit. A cat bell around her neck tinkles as she scans the room. Without the feather boa of the awards ceremony, her neck is naked and swanlike. But with the catsuit so low cut, it takes a while to notice her neck.

'This afternoon, we will continue our quest to be more like our feline friends. We're going to start as usual with a round of purring to tune in to their universe,' says Lola. The noise begins quietly but intensifies as the women gradually join in. It builds to a wall of sound, dancing around the mirrors. I freeze on my beanbag and reach for my phone. Who can I call to come and rescue me?

Lola kneels down in front of me, takes my device and places it gently on the floor. Then she holds my palm and traces the lines on it. I hate this, and immediately tense up. Sensing my discomfort, she lifts her hand to my face and strokes my left eyebrow, running two thumbs gently along my eyelids, encouraging them to close again. It's hot in here despite the fans and my hair hangs like a wavy curtain either side of my face. Lola smooths it away, stroking my chin. She pushes a second beanbag behind me, gently nudging my shoulders back. And then she's tickling behind my ears and massaging my skull. Despite my head screaming no, my chin raises, scanning for her touch. It's intimate but not sexual and I relax into it as she moves down my neck and arms. My heartbeat slows and I don't know how much time passes, but I feel the cold air when she leaves. Soon, too soon, the soundtrack of purring dims. The back wall turns into a screen and a projector powers up. Lola pulls a laser pen from a hidden pocket. The other women rub their eyes and sit up as I haul myself to an edge of the beanbag, now intrigued.

'I want to build on our work earlier. We have lost a student unfortunately, but Aly here will be joining us instead. Aly, in order to be more feline and take pride in being female, we've been defining what it is to be a cat. In this session, we will be choosing some of the qualities we identified earlier; qualities we'd personally like to mirror. As before, don't shout out your suggestions. Instead, I'd like you to raise a paw, scratch at the floor or do whatever your inner cat needs to do to get attention.'

One of the women is keen, arching her back, meowing for Lola's attention then picking some words from the whiteboard in front of us. The others follow suit and soon I'm the only one who hasn't spoken or raised a paw.

'Aly, do you have a contribution to our list or are you drawn to a particular quality?' Lola asks. I might have some thoughts but I'm not about to yowl them out or jump up into her lap for cuddles.

As the class waits expectantly, I feel forced to join in. 'Well, as a paid-up cat owner, I think there's a tiny bit of truth in all of these but really, they are clichés,' I reluctantly volunteer. 'I think cats' personalities are more multilayered and not easily nailed, even by people like me who spend a lot of time with them.'

'What would you suggest are some of their more surprising traits?'

'It depends on the cat. They're all different. For example, my bestest buddy, Milly, can be needy and insecure.

Sometimes when she's on my lap I feel like I'm carrying the One Ring and it's sucking the life out of me. You aren't going to want to draw on that either in a workshop or in life.'

'Do you have a positive way of framing that neediness?'

'Intense? Loyal? She rewards my investment in her with undying love and licks. And once she's fed on my energy she becomes playful and outgoing and regenerates me. She enjoys being groomed but gives it back too. And people mistakenly believe cats aren't empathetic. She spots when I'm down and instinctively tries to make me feel better. Yet she knows to leave alone when I'm beyond saving. And next morning she's back. Doing it all again.'

'Good.' The whole class smiles at the licks comment and Lola writes down 'empathetic' and 'loyal' on the board. One of the women licks her own hand, moving her tongue up and down each finger. Is that necessary?

I plough on while I'm on a winning streak. 'My second bestie, Molly, is quite different but still as complex. She's brave and stubborn, and willing to try new things. If she was human, she wouldn't follow rules or care about offending anyone. She's extrovert and a bit swaggery and loves to wear a hat. She knows she is beautiful and preens in the mirror. She also knows what she wants and will tell you her feelings. One of these guys mentioned selfish, but I think it's more a natural sense of entitlement that my cats have, an inner confidence. She takes warmth and love when she needs it and, like Milly, when she's had enough she buggers off. It's not personal, it's just efficient. If I wanted unconditional love, I should have chosen a puppy,

I suppose.' My comment produces a few smiles from group members.

Lola pops a few more words on the board. 'There's a lot of good stuff there. Is that all your cats covered?'

'Yes, well no, there was Mardy, my childhood pet. Mardy was an unusual cat. Probably not worth discussing here.'

'Go on.'

'Mardy was . . . well mardy basically. Didn't know how to connect or love but also didn't know how to stay away. She hated being stroked or petted but was constantly in my face, headbutting me, rubbing her body against me, marking out her territory.' I try to remember what it was about her that so intrigued me. Her fragile spirit that cried out to be nurtured, or the brittle reluctance to accept it? 'She'd pull out her own fur, pee outside of her litter tray and destroy the furniture. To be honest, I wasn't really sure why my dad took her when he left us, and I also still don't know why I missed her so much. But I did. Maybe I saw myself in her. Someone who didn't know how to be loved.'

Lola's hand pauses next to the board, as though she's considering whether to pursue something I just said. 'Mardy in a word?'

'Independent?'

'Try again?'

'Human.' The class laughs at my left-field suggestion and Lola smiles.

The list is long, maybe twenty or thirty characteristics. 'I want you to choose the quality you feel you are lacking and split into pairs to discuss how you could learn from your cat to develop that characteristic. Let's do a quick survey of the room, find out which attribute you are drawn to.'

One of the women says she needs to put herself first more. A stout middle-aged woman with a severe haircut says she'd like to work on 'charm'. 'You know a cat has entered a room. Everyone notices him. But he doesn't ask for attention. He naturally demands it. He has charisma. That's what I want.'

'You've referred to the charismatic cat using a male pronoun. Is your cat male?' Lola asks. The woman shakes her head. 'I think you need to explore that in your pair. Aly? What will you choose?'

'Tenacity?' I volunteer.

'From what I've seen of you, I don't think you need to work on that.'

'Stubbornness?'

'Why don't you start by examining that elusive quality, self-worth? How about I work with you for the rest of the session?'

Lola is relentless.

'It's not enough to deal in generalisations. You have to break down how a cat understands their own value, and then shows they have worth. Think specifics. Think physicality. Only once you've defined it can you adopt it.'

'They take up space. More than that, they invade it.'

'Go on.'

'They assume the room is theirs and spread out and let you know it's their territory. My cats do it in my flat. They take my whole bed if I let them. And if I step on their toes, sorry, paws, they let me know.'

'How do they do that?'

'They rip my new slippers to shreds and scratch the life out of my legs,' I exclaim, showing her some of my war wounds.

Lola smiles. 'So they are vocal. They stand up for themselves. To ensure you give them a wider berth next time perhaps? How do you think you can stop people stepping on your own paws?'

'Sharpen my nails maybe? Make more noise. Claim more space.' A fight with my new landlord behind the bins? Claw Rick from the jaws of Juliet?

Lola smiles. 'What other clues are there that Milly, Molly and Mardy value themselves?'

'They put themselves first. They believe they deserve happiness.'

'Do you?'

'Deserve happiness?'

'The words you used are quite interesting. You didn't say your cats deserve happiness. You told me they believe they deserve it. Whether or not they actually do. And I think you hit the nail on the head. As women we need to cultivate this belief. Tell me, do you allow anyone to pamper you like you pamper your cats?'

'Hardly!'

'Why not? You understand the value of it. Did you like it when I pushed your hair out of your eyes and stroked you behind the ears?'

'A bit, yes,' I say shyly.

'Then learn to take it. Or even better, to ask for it. Lie down on someone's lap and demand it. And if you don't have the energy, don't give it out. You know one of the telltale signs a cat values itself?'

'It licks its lady bits or balls?'

She smiles again. 'What I was aiming for is cats say no. All the time. They don't obey orders. They refuse to be judged. They spill milk but make no effort to clear it up. They turn their back on people who annoy them. And then they turn around and walk away. How often do you say no? How often do you walk away? There's power in both.'

When the class ends everyone mingles, but I head back to the bar. I'm feeling more in the mood for a spoothie now, although ideally I'd still prefer my energy top-up to come from a barrel of wine. I order from the bar and sit on my own, digesting the last hour.

Ten minutes later, Lola appears and makes a beeline for me. 'Hope you enjoyed that. Would you like to stay on for the next class? I'm happy to comp the session once more as you contribute such intelligent comments. And I want to monitor how you get on as you start to make the changes that I'm sincerely hoping you are going to tackle. We have some good parties here too. I'll send you an invite to our next kitty-ranch party. I think you'll find it fun, especially as you like dressing up.'

'I enjoyed it very much,' I reply, as a bartender brings me a tall glass filled with swamp water and a large glass of wine.

'On the house,' Lola instructs him. 'By the way, how's Rick? I tried to speak to him at the awards ceremony, but he was . . .' She trails off, uncharacteristically looking down at her feet.

'Busy being a winner?' I help her out.

I hope the spoothie isn't as vile as it smells. I can't imagine holding your nose to knock it back would be seen as polite. I taste kale and spinach. Why don't they go the whole hog and pop a radish on a stick into this Molotov cocktail of salad ingredients?

'I haven't seen Rick since the awards. I didn't realise you knew him. But, of course, you were a guest of his dad. They're pretty inseparable I guess, working in the business together.'

You'd think she'd choked on my spoothie. 'Rick and Bill? Not all that fond of each other in my experience.'

Oooh gossip.

'Really?'

She doesn't take my bait. 'Is he a good boss?'

'He's not my boss, well he is ultimately but he works in infinity full time whereas I just snuck in for ten minutes on the night of the award.'

'Yeah, infinity has always been his thing.' She smiles to herself.

She moves on to circulate with her guests. I was a bit exhausted after the cat class, but the kale is pushing through my veins. And I have an idea. I might never get my old account back but there's nothing to stop me starting a new one is there? I've been making my cats look and act like humans for so long for my Instagram images, but why should they have to imitate us? Lola is right. We'd be better off behaving like them, and I'm sure my old followers would enjoy tips on acting like them. And I don't need her to instruct me on how to be my best cat self – I live with Milly and Molly, two cats with more attitude than a *Celebrity SAS* contestant.

I need to think up a new name for my new account; I want a new direction now from AlyCat. Perhaps Lola's next class could inspire some content for it? If I call a cab for an hour's time, I could chill out on a beanbag and still make an evening train.

I find Lola at the bar and tell her I will stay on. 'My housemate Henry is feeding the cats for me so I've got plenty of time to make a day of it.'

'Great,' she says. 'It's almost power hour so I need to go and change.'

Minutes after she leaves I create a new account; @ beyourbestcat. I remember Sam's pic of me in the cat mask at the awards ceremony and copy it from his Twitter feed as my profile picture.

There's a different vibe for the next session. Jazz music is playing, and the mood is enhanced by red lights coming from lamps with filters scattered around the room. There's a scent of dark spice I can't put my finger on, and as Lola appears in school uniform, with her skirt hitched up her thighs, I feel the anticipation rise in the room. Her white short-sleeved shirt is unbuttoned, revealing a lacy bra and stockings skim the end of her pleated skirt. She has false eyelashes and hoop earrings, and bright red lipstick inexpertly smeared around her lips.

'Lolita,' someone mutters, and a smile goes round the room.

'Good afternoon, ladies.' She lights a cigarette she takes from her bra and blows smoke into the room like she's auditioning for *Cabaret*. 'This session is about owning your past, in order to become who you are. I'm not proud, but also not ashamed to say that I started out as an escort. It formed who I was and who I became and who I will become. I embraced my past in order to become more "me" and today we are going to start the process of exploring how you can become more you.' I flash back to Glimmer's DNA coffee and hope this session has a different outcome. 'We will be splitting into groups to identify how a past can successfully shape a future, no matter how unpalatable it may seem. And later on this evening we will be inviting in a selection of "empowermentors" we have specially chosen for you. They will talk you through making sustainable changes to your life.'

The session is fascinating. Lola begins by talking us through her career and she does seem to add up to far more than her distant past. She holds degrees from British uni's and a PhD from Stanford. She's all about having agency, speaking up and being more yourself in every situation. She believes in claiming the room and tells us her most popular lecture is 'The Boardroom Mistress', where she looks at life as a CEO from the point of view of a domme and then a sub.

'As you can't separate sexual politics from office politics then you should understand both and work them to your advantage.' Her advice on clawing yourself success as a woman is even more powerful than her musings on how to be your best cat.

There's no empowermentor lined up for me as I was only planning to attend cat class. On the train home, I think about Lola's sessions, and vow to figure out who I am and what agency I have. So much of my self-esteem is tied up with Rick and Glimmer that my thoughts stray back to him again. And not just my self-esteem; I've been having some seriously sexy dreams about him lately. But who is Rick? Is he a good boss? What's his relationship with women? I tap on Google. The first page delivers everything I'd expect. 'Rick Harvard sets up new agency over the pond'; 'Glimmer wins award with former YouTuber at the helm'; 'Glimmer poaches the rich and famous from traditional agencies'; 'Glimmer is the light at the end of the tunnel for falling angels'; 'Boy wonder Harvard bags a celeb before breakfast'. I tear through headlines, lapping them up as fast as Milly devours water. But I want to know what came before that. How did he make his name on YouTube? How did he get his millions of views? How did his past shape his present?

When I'm safely back on my own sofa, and have decent Wi-Fi, I start binge-watching his channel.

And I'm astonished by what I see. No comedy videos, TikTok-style dancing or anything normal for a young YouTuber. He's handsome, and charismatic, and his voice is as rich as double chocolate brownies, but young Rick was a serious geek. I scroll thorough a feed filled with tech reviews, camera rigs and equipment overviews. Deep sky astrophotography made easy. As if! But there he is, giving people ideas for how to unravel the mysteries of the stars without having to sell their family home. I start flicking through, impressed at how accessible he makes this geekery with his easy manner and animated face and yet remain totally baffled by the subject. In the early vids he's not cool, not yet, but he is incredibly prolific, populating this corner of YouTube with the best rigs for capturing images, astrophotography on a budget, and idiots' guides to nebula knowhow. He makes trackers and tripods look like something we should all have in our lives and his humour and openness shine through every video. Who on this earth, or indeed on the next, would have predicted that? The videos are sometimes punctuated with *Star Wars* pastiches or glimpses into his collectors cards. He loves Obi-Wan as much as I worship Frodo.

Suddenly, and quite passionately, I want to know more about him: where he lives, what he does, who he does it with. I'm craving him, like Coco Pops. I know he lives on Columbia Road. I google it and find out it does indeed have a famous flower market every Sunday.

Milly is unusually silent and still. Rick gave her a toy mouse on the day of the shoot and the silly kitty is waiting for it to scarper so she can chase it. She sits on one of my tatty rugs, her back legs hunched, with just a twitch of her pale ears every now and then to communicate some hidden thought. Her lemon-shaped eyes are focused and beautiful. I nip over and lie on the floor to photograph her motionless concentration. The evening light washes her coat a lighter grey, and the sag around her hips gives her a look of Bagpuss. She uses the toe-like parts of her paws like we'd use our fingers to poke and prod at it. I make a mental note to trim her long claws before I kick the mouse and wham, she's onto it, taut as a tiger, a hunter fully in charge of her catch.

And she gives me an idea. I pull up Instagram and write my first post.

*Be an observant cat. (And learn how to stalk your prey.)*

*OK, you are hungry. You want it. Whatever it is (the man, the job, the life, the mouse), you need to work for it. In lesson one of how to be your best cat self, I advise you to do nothing. Yes really. Sit down. Lie down if you like. And take a look at your goal, or your prey, from every angle. It doesn't matter if it's from afar. A cat observes for minutes, hours and whole days if need be. She works out direct and indirect routes to her end point, and she doesn't spring until she knows her road map better than she knows herself. And when you have worked out how to get to your goal, then plan your exit. Because once you have secured your prey, the last thing you want is another predator wrestling it off you. This is my new AlyCat channel, with lessons based on my experiences of living with my two besties, Milly and Molly. And I hope to put each lesson into practice myself and feed back how well I get on in the comments. Leave your thoughts below too, lovely people. After you have lain on the floor and considered things for a while.*

I add a photograph of Milly waiting for the mouse to move and post it immediately.

# Chapter 20

East London is practically another country and the schlepp across the capital by bus and Tube almost gives me jet lag. But the empty streets and cool air pump oxygen into my lungs as I follow Google Maps' directions to Columbia Road. When I set my alarm last night, I told myself it was about getting him out of my system; batting Rick out of my head like a rounders ball. But now I'm here I realise I want to catch the ball and hold it, feel the curves, drop it to the floor and see if there's any chance of it bouncing back into my hands. I don't need to bump into him, in fact I'm not sure I even want to. It's enough to immerse myself in his universe.

I step into a puddle in my beloved DMs and shiver. Summer is turning to autumn and perhaps it was inadvisable to wear velvet shorts. The sky is plaster grey and filled with moisture, but the stalls of the Sunday morning market are rainbow dipped. Wandering through the open-air greenhouse, I soak up the colours and aromas. This is one vibey London institution; everywhere I look there's scent and life and the noise is a joyful rolling soundtrack of East End accents and trading. The smell of lilies and roses fills the air, along with exotic bouquets bulked out with gypsophila and ferns. Someone argues over the price of stall rental; someone else sings along to a Stormzy song with the wrong words.

I stop occasionally to inhale the perfume and listen to the cheeky banter and barter. Life with the colour turned up. What an amazing street to live on, I'm thinking as I zigzag around. But then I stop in my tracks as a woman dressed in a sleeveless jacket and fingerless gloves accepts a brew from a figure I recognise.

'Any sales?' Rick asks.

'Slow morning. Any scones?' Her reply is quick and easy.

'The chef is on holiday. Next week maybe when he returns,' Rick laughs. If only I could bottle that smile. 'Oh, and I'll take an armful of whatever you can't sell at packing up time.'

'Wasn't I supposed to be watering your plants?' The woman sips at the white china mug printed with a Scrabble letter R.

Rick grimaces. 'While instigating a review of business travel across the firm, I've decided I should take some of my own medicine and stay at home more.'

'Talking of medicine, did I show you the photos from hubby's hernia op . . . ?'

'Enough! Leave the mug on a window ledge when you're done.'

I duck behind a large spray of physalis as Rick moves into my sightline. When I emerge from behind the orange lanterns, I'm immediately assaulted by a pot plant. Ferns smash to the floor as the casket shatters into half a dozen pieces.

'Oh, I'm sorry,' I start to apologise and then stop. TCP would say this isn't a 'me' problem; if the owner of the pot wasn't a giant-in-training, and his huge plant didn't shield his entire face while he was taking a walk, we wouldn't be staring down at mangled lumps of greenery.

'My fault,' he says. Lanky scrambles to pick up the terracotta litter. Despite it being a 'him' problem, I drop down to help him. Wet roots and claggy mud stick to my hands as I help him push soil into a plastic bag one of the stallholders provides. Rising from the tarmac, I wipe my bare, damp knees with dirty hands. Was it sensible to team green velvet hot pants with grey Doc Martens to visit an outdoor market?

I scramble up to an amused face peering into mine.

'Making mud pies?' Rick doesn't ask why I've turned up on his street on a Sunday morning and I'm glad about that, as I'm increasingly unsure, although when I last saw him he dipped a wad of notes into the valley between my breasts, and they have a vivid memory. Those hands, and the flash of desire in his eyes charged up every nerve in my body as his relaxed stance and weekend outfit is starting to do now. I've been sleepwalking and I long for him to wake me again. He lifts the coffee-stained cup into the air and asks if I'd like a cuppa.

His sturdy front door slams behind us as we stand in a small tasteful living room Farrow & Ball would be proud of, with a staircase up the left-hand side of the compact space.

'Wow. Your house is not what I imagined.'

'So, tell me, oracle, what did you predict?'

'A bigger version of your office I suppose. A city man flat. Big windows. A lot of grey and steel.'

'Yeah that wouldn't really work here.' He gestures to a sash window. 'I tried to keep the period features throughout the modernisation. I send a small child up the fireplace to clean the flues once a year in the name of tradition. I'd light the fire and show you the room at its best, but it gets hot very quickly, and I think we'd both melt.'

The matt black fireplace is tiled in cream with curls of green. Next to it is a tall basket of wood. Cream shutters and cornicing on the ceiling sit elegantly next to muted green walls, divided up by vertical panels. A battered leather trunk is stacked with coffee table books.

'Come through and I'll make some coffee. Or whatever your poison is on a Sunday morning.'

'Wow.' The large kitchen and breakfast room is very different. 'Just wow.'

'Welcome to Glimmer at Home,' he laughs. 'Not so much shooting stars into infinity as tethering them to the walls.'

LED ceiling lights give the place a bright sheen in the dull morning light. There's a small kitchen area with a wooden table and chairs. And on all four walls: planets. Or one in particular: Saturn.

I walk up to one and study it closely. It's astonishing. Almost unreal. A large, creamy snooker ball in the sky with circles of peach and grey, and in the centre the recognisable ring slicing around it, thin as a Frisbee, perfect as a wedding band.

'The sexiest planet on our cosmic doorstep. I kind of like it, as you can tell.'

'Did you take these?' He replies with a nod and the top ten tips on choosing the right telescope, tripods and cameras all make sense. 'You show others how to do it on your YouTube channel.'

'Saturn's my thing. But I share it with a lot of other geeks. Everyone should experience the wonders of deep space.'

'Why are some of them blurrier than others?'

'Sentimental value. This was my first.' He points to a grainy image on the opposite wall. 'You can capture it quite cheaply with the right camera, lens and filter. Or you can spend an absolute fortune to get this.' He sidesteps to a spectacular framed image which takes up much of the wall and talks me through using a specialist filter and taking it at the right time of year. His enthusiasm is catching.

'Why is it the only planet with a ring?'

'Most of the big guns in the solar system have rings, but they're too dark to see from Earth. Saturn's are the brightest, and hence the easiest to capture as an amateur.'

I hold my hand out and run it around its sphere, hoping he has a cleaner to remove the smudges I leave behind.

'What is it made of? The ring?'

'Pieces of comet, asteroid or moon that were ripped up when pulled into the planet's gravity. In turn they're made of dust and ice. Not very romantic. To be honest some people think Saturn's boring as it doesn't have the storms of Jupiter. But I find it fascinating because of the rings and the shadow of the rings.' He picks up a book and flicks through it, falling on a page where a pin-sharp picture of Jupiter sits in a black galaxy. 'Look at this NASA image. That's a shadow of Saturn across its own rings. Mind-blowing or what?' He tells me there's something of a rivalry between the Saturn and Jupiter geeks. 'It's

Saturn all the way for me although one of Jupiter's moons is a dead ringer for the Death Star. Coffee?' Rick pulls a selection of plastic pods from a special S-shaped holder and holds them out to me.

'Thanks. I've actually been on an astronaut's diet this week.'

'Rehydrated food?'

'Milky Ways and Mars bars.'

He laughs. 'No judgement from me. Let's do massive coffees and you can torpedo yours with sugar.' When the machine has finished doing its stuff, he drops three sugars into a cup bigger than a Starbucks trough and passes it to me. I smirk when I see Saturn sprinkled on the froth.

'Shall we blow away all those calories with some fresh air?' He opens a back door which leads onto a tiny patio. Every inch is packed with plants – hanging from the walls in enamel pots, vying for floor space, and crowding into nooks and corners. Half of the courtyard is covered with a plastic roof, pumping up the humidity.

'I hope you don't have hay fever. Traders often force the plants they can't sell onto me in return for an ear or some warmth.'

'I don't mind plants although I can't keep them alive for more than five minutes. Can you capture the stars from here?'

'Ha, you can barely see the moon from here. The light pollution in the East End is horrendous. Those pictures were all taken from our family home.'

'I don't know the East End at all. Been a Westie all my life. It's like a foreign country to me.'

'I thought you lived in Shoreditch?'

Bullshit and buttercups! I cast my mind around for another half-decent lie, but when nothing comes I go with the truth. 'I made it up. I was trying to distract you from the boxes,' I admit, before cursing myself for opening up that embarrassing topic of conversation.

'The boxes in my living room?' I sigh. 'There were boxes in every room up until the day of the shoot. I hadn't just moved. I'd never unpacked. The boxes were full of gifts . . .' I take in a deep breath, like I'm about to puff a massive dandelion clock '. . . from my mother.'

I wait for the inevitable follow-up questions, but Rick simply squeezes my hand. After a moment he says something, so quietly I don't catch it. Something about his own mother.

'Your mum . . .' I prompt him.

'Died, a long time ago. It would be a proper shock if I received a gift.' Excusing himself, he collects my cup at the same time as his front door clatters. When he reappears a few minutes later, he brings an armful of newspapers.

'That's a lot of headlines. Are they delivered by lorry?'

'It's nearly the afternoon. Paper boys today eh?'

'You've probably broken his back. The *New York Times*? The *Washington Post*? All of the broadsheets?'

'If your agency is global, you need to know what you're getting into.'

'I heard something about conquering America at the dinner.'

'My father wants to be everywhere.'

'And you don't?'

'I'd like to know what we are before we try to clone ourselves. I want to expand slowly. The US is littered with failed PR and management companies, especially on the East Coast.'

'Then why . . .'

'I don't get to make the big decisions. Sure, I have a vote but there's a board, which my father chairs. Glimmer is part of his wider portfolio of companies. Family leg-ups in business often come with a ball and chain and mine's getting heavier by the week. I was supposed to be in New York tomorrow, meeting the team Juliet has assembled. But it's been cancelled and that's not just about addressing our climate footprint. Something's not right. Juliet's . . .' He stops. Frustratingly.

'What . . .'

'Sorry . . .'

'Juliet's what?'

'Still here.'

A thought pops into my head. Does he mean she's actually here? In this house? Is that why he's ordered the *New York Times*?

'I need the loo. Mind if I . . . ?'

'Upstairs, first on the left.'

I nip up the wooden staircase and check out both the main bedroom and the spare, confirming there's no tragic heroine in any of the beds. The en suite is uncluttered, but a mattress big enough for three kings confirms he isn't one for sleeping alone. The bed is made, and the duvet looks hotel starched. Clothes rails run alongside an exposed brick wall, hung with pressed shirts arranged in colours, each shirt darker than the next. Suits follow, with tees and casual clothes folded into shelves that sit between two sash windows. I visit the loo to justify coming up. The bathroom is tidy, and there's no second toothbrush, although a large cupboard over the sink is neatly overloaded with hair products and cologne. I wash my hands with soap that smells of lavender. Outside the bathroom window, I hear the market in full swing.

Lurking at the top of the stairs for a moment, I'm drawn back into the bedroom. My experience in the hotel proved you can judge this man by his bedside table. I bend down and pull open the drawer. A spare phone cable, a camera lens cap and some deodorant. He's not a serial condom owner.

'Are you looking for something?' A voice makes me jump. Rick hasn't pimped his hair to office standards this morning and with the trademark spikes gone, a light fringe falls across his forehead.

'Er, I was looking for a tissue?'

He retreats into the bathroom and returns with a loo roll. 'What's it for?'

Aaaargh! Think, Aly. Hay fever is an option as I just came from a garden full of plants. A mystery spillage?

'Do you know there's a Guinness World record for the time it takes to wrap someone in toilet roll? An Egyptian mummy challenge.' All those sensible excuses and my mouth comes up with this?

'Really?'

'I saw it on Instagram this week so it must be true.'

'What's the record?'

'Can't remember exactly. Maybe about a minute? It was #EgyptDay you see.' I cross my fingers hoping he doesn't check. 'I'd have dressed Milly as Cleo*cat*ra if I still had my . . .' I clamp my jaws together, wondering if it's a good time to confess all about my account.

'Should we have a go?' He interrupts my thoughts.

'You serious?'

He backs into the bathroom and in seconds returns with two more rolls.

I make a snap decision to go with it. 'I'd be the obvious choice for the mummy as I'm smaller than you. I won't be able to help you though. Assistance by the subject is against the rules.'

He doesn't ask how I know the rules to a world record no one has heard of. 'How would you even start to dress someone as a mummy?'

'I'd probably begin at the temple. Maybe trap the end behind their ears.'

'Like this?' He starts at the top of my head, and in seconds he's winding tissue round my neck, wrapping and circling me in four-ply. It's erotic, especially when he holds out my lower arms, and gently but quickly covers me from my elbows down. My legs are the next erogenous zone, and I pull my tummy in as he criss-crosses my groin. I'm feeling all the flutters, and nearly topple over trying to stand on one leg as he covers my boot.

'There.' He presses the timer on his phone. 'Just over a minute. We didn't break the record but that was fun.'

He holds up his phone.

'No. You can't take a photo!'

'No one knows it's you and anyway it's not for sharing. Humour me please; a woman impersonating a dead Egyptian in toilet roll has always been a fantasy.'

'Then lucky you have good quality loo rolls, or it would never have worked. Trust me. I've bought the cheap stuff without perforations.'

'Stop it before you push me over the edge,' he laughs, his face close to mine. I stand on tiptoe to meet his eyes. 'You know the real test is how long it takes to remove the sacred garments?' he says.

I hold his gaze. 'Reset the clock.'

This time he doesn't start at my temples, but clears the tissue from my mouth, tracing his index finger along my lips. I can feel his breath on my skin. He is unwinding me at glacial pace, continuing to stare into my eyes as he smooths the paper away.

'I'm not sure you're putting your back into getting this record.'

He strips the tissue from my neck. 'No, but I'm enjoying unwrapping you.' He speeds up as he moves down my body, his fingers brushing my chest as he strips the paper from my vest top.

'What were you looking for in the drawer?' he asks as he turns his attention to unwinding my waist.

'Condoms,' I confess. 'But it's not what you think.'

'That's an interesting answer and one I'd like to explore further.' He pushes the tissue from my hips with more urgency. 'And for the record, what I think can change pretty quickly when you are around. One minute I was preparing to be immersed in the New York obituaries and the next I am creeping up the stairs to make you soft, strong and very, very . . .'

Turned.

On.

'I knew you were quiet coming up those . . .' I don't finish as his lips are on mine. The clock resets and starts to spin; he is ripping through perforations as fast as the tissues inside my body are coming alive. My heartbeat races and I clench my fingers within their soft encasing as he tears at that too. I lean towards him and hope for dear life he's got me as my feet are still bound. We fall onto the quilt and before I find time to blink, he's pulling the toilet roll from my thighs, calves, ankles. He moves to the end of the bed and pulls my boots off. Then he starts to work his way up again, this time caressing my skin with his lips. His Sunday morning stubble tickles and arouses me. And I don't care who he's slept with in the past or is sleeping with now or whether he wraps them all in Andrex and bounces onto them like a puppy, I want him to go further. I want it with every part of my being.

Apart from my brain.

'Wait!' I say.

'Too fast?'

My body is light years from my head, which is swiping through anxieties. What if I get it wrong? What if I'm not good enough at it for someone as experienced as him? He's a player. He's a company boss. I'm a random Instagrammer without an account. We are from extremely different backgrounds and have entirely different genitals. He presses his face against my stomach. Can he hear my heart? The roar of fire in my core? I touch the back of his head, trace my fingers down his neck.

The *Top Cat* theme rings out.

'That's me. I'll leave it,' I say, coming to a decision. I lift my T-shirt and quickly unhook my bra.

The phone goes again. 'Still leaving it.' He pushes a strap down my upper arm. I moan quietly as he rains soft kisses onto the skin where it was. The phone rings a third time. I pull it from under me and recognise Kav's name.

'Leave it,' he says. And I want to, God I want to, but Kav doesn't do phones unless she's being held hostage in her own stockroom. I dither. And then I answer.

'Yep. What?' I don't attempt to disguise my impatience.

'You need to come,' she says, with no preamble.

I groan softly. 'I think I'm about to.' Rick has moved to my neck, an all-time erogenous zone for me. He nibbles my ear as he unfastens the button of my hot pants, tracing a finger lightly around my belly button and then along my hip bone. It is the most exquisite feeling in the world. I squirm and wriggle and try to help him free my thighs while still holding the phone. There's an urgency now that neither of us can stop. He is breathing heavily, and I am trying not to gasp down the phone. I groan softly as he runs his fingers along the lace of my knickers before teasing them down.

'I'm coming. Oh God, I'm coming right away.'

'Good. I need you. Manolis has left me.'

In any other circumstance those words would chill my blood. But it's already at 200° F and I'm inching into a space I've never inhabited before. 'I'm coming now,' I say one final time before hitting the call end button.

'Before you rush off, I have something for you. Almost forgot.' Taking the last two stairs together Rick lands evenly on the wood and produces a heavy square of white material from the banister. 'This went for a pitiful amount of money at the Showcase awards. So I bought it from the owner and added a small donation on top.'

A reminder of an evening I won and lost within the same hour. I choose my words with care. 'Bollocks.'

He grins. 'That's hashtag #bollocks I think you'll find. Written in drunken calligraphy above #WilliamH. TosserKissMyAwardWinningBum.'

He hands the tablecloth to me, and I push it back.

'What would I do with a textile Twitter rant about my dad? It's not something we need at our dinner table in the Cotswolds,' he says, gently bundling me and the cloth out into the street. Is he talking about the family home where Tosser keeps his secrets? Or perhaps I was imagining that when I was as drunk as a skunk dressed as a pussycat.

'Sorry about your friend, but I'm glad you came,' he says, the twinkle in his eye brighter than the stars on his wall.

Kav brings a plate of warm custard tarts with a sprinkling of red on the top. She may have been dumped from a great height, but the woman is still dedicated to serving in the shop and feeding the local population. 'I've customised pastel de nata. Thought I could make them sizzle.' She places the plate on the wrought iron table, jangling a row of pink and purple bangles on her arm.

'It's all right, I need to self-harm.' I shove one in my mouth and wince as my taste buds find the chilli.

'Manolis put rose petals in our bed last week. Unfortunately, the idiot didn't clean them first and we had greenfly all over the sheet. I thought about throwing him out. Didn't imagine for a minute he'd be the one leaving me.' Kav pulls off the bangles one by one and throws them onto the table, releasing a sob as the final bracelet clatters down. 'Where were you when I phoned? You sounded odd. Breathless.'

'Bethnal Green.'

'Where Rick lives?' She narrows her eyes, scrutinising me closely. 'Your cheeks are flushed.'

I fish around on the plate for flakes of chilli so I can legitimately burn up.

'O.M.G. you've hooked up?'

I'm already doubting myself again and I voice my fears. 'He's super attractive, and runs a company, and is probably a millionaire, and even if he isn't, his dad is, so he will be one day. I can't go to bed with him again. I can't compete.'

'You were in his bed? Awesome.' Kav hugs me. 'And you're not supposed to compete, you soggy noodle. You're meant to merge.' Kav points to the traffic. 'Like that. Two lanes become one. And you're not snogging his dad. Unless you're snogging his dad as well, in which case, you need to rethink.'

'Manolis is your soggy noodle not me. Tell me what happened.'

She sits down on one of the seats balanced on her patch of rickety pavement and relates a row that went beyond any they'd ever had before. 'He's gone. Back to Greece. He left me because I won't marry him. Gave me an ultimatum.

He'll come back if I agree to it before he's fifty. After that he's putting the shop on the market unless I buy him out. It's all such a mess.' Her shoulders start to shake and when I rub one she heaves a seismic sob. My heart breaks for her. I continue to rub her back and when she looks up I wipe her eyes on a serviette.

'Aaah what are you doing? That has chilli powder on it!' She stands, an angry toddler now, and suddenly there's a customer upon us looking for feta cheese.

'It's under F for F. off, because my husband . . . I mean boyfriend . . . I mean ex-boyfriend . . . alphabetised the shit out of them,' she says, dipping the serviette in cold coffee and holding it against her eye. I offer to go and find it for the lady, and next thing I know I'm behind the counter trying to figure out how to work the till.

A few minutes later, Kav enters the shop, blowing her nose. While her sari is as gold as an Olympic postbox, her eyes are still redder than the regular version.

'He put a proposal in the paper.' She holds up the advert and I glance away. 'You knew!'

'It was kinda my idea.' I grimace. 'I thought it was a nice gesture.' She looks at me like she wants to stuff my head into the till and ring up several items on my forehead. 'You love him, I assume, so why not do what he asks?'

She picks up a box of lighters and clicks on one. When a flame pops up, she lets it die before doing it again. 'When I was younger my father curated me a selection of husbands to choose from. It was all arranged and then two days before the ceremony I fled to Greece.'

'To Manolis?'

'I'd met him on holiday and continued a long-distance relationship in secret. Papa told me never to come back. I couldn't marry without his blessing so . . .'

'How many years ago?'

'Twenty-seven.'

'You've been pretending to be married for twenty-seven years? I'm surprised you didn't have a silver "not really" party. What country do your parents live in?'

'Southall. Just off this road actually.'

'Your mum and dad live down the road and you've avoided them for almost thirty years?'

'I saw them in Tesco Metro a few Christmases ago. Mama was buying Brussels sprouts. I noticed Papa was also fully integrated into British culture as he was purchasing a copy of the *Daily Mail*.' She flicks the lighter again and sets fire to the edge of the *Hillingdon Star*, stamping it out on her tiled floor before she burns the shop down. 'Want to get drunk with me, Aly?'

'I can probably stay and keep you company tonight if that might help?'

'Please.'

I ring Henry and explain the situation, asking if he'd mind sleeping at my place for the night to take care of the cats. As he's known Kav for years, he readily agrees, sending her his love. I text Rick to let him know my friend is physically fine, if not mentally. He asks if I'm OK and I privately wonder if I am. This chock-full shop, with its volatile owners, was my rock. Kav and Manolis were proof that someone like me can sort out a decent life, and if they can't make it work, what chance do I have?

We drink white wine and talk about men. At one point, Greg texts to say he's made an appointment to view a flat later in the week. He also sends me a selfie of his naked chest in front of the mirror and Kav checks it out with interest. If I wasn't crushing on Rick then I might be equally as keen. But he's doing sterling work on the flat front, so I send a smiley face.

*Keep the whole night free. I've got some surprises in store.*

'Greg may have found me a flat I can afford. I'm going to see it with him.'

'Where?'

'Somewhere at the other end of the Tube line is my guess. Probably Morden.'

'You can't go to Mordor,' she cries. 'You can't abandon me too.'

'I said Morden, but I'd get better value for money by buying a place in Middle Earth.'

# Chapter 21

As I leave the shop, Kav presses a box of Jaffa Cakes into my hand.

'For your meeting this morning,' she says, her eyes red from lack of sleep.

I've barely time to shower and change before the Oddities amble into my flat for our second meeting on how to delay the flat sale.

'Thanks for coming,' I say when they are all assembled, some standing, some sitting. TCP, for some reason, is lying on the floor with her head on a cushion. Normally I'd wait for someone else to begin. But I think back to Lola's instructions to be like my pets, and I know my cats would take charge of a meeting in their own home.

'The last meeting was a bit inconclusive,' I say. 'Also, the problem has obviously ramped up since we got the thirty-day notice. I'm not naive, we will be evicted soon enough, and I'd love to move on to a flat with my own shower, but I don't have another place to go right now. Does anyone else?' The Oddities mumble various responses while shaking their heads and hunching together. 'So, I'm thinking we need to try and delay the move beyond a month as we've barely time to pack.'

'Aly's right. Let's balls-up his grand plan to battery farm the hell out of our building,' says TCP.

'He's going to do what to our building?'

'I did some digging and the truth is sinister,' she continues, wrestling control from me without even taking her head off the pillow. 'Logan Josh is planning to imprison emus here.'

'Emu jail? That's unspeakable!' The room breaks out into side conversations. Henry starts a conversation about the two sets of eyelids emus are born with, while Suze the Silk checks the calorie content of Logan Josh's chicken tikka masala online. 'It was nothing short of criminal; put half a stone on my thighs.'

TCP speaks over them. 'Logan Josh is gonna be making food for Go-Go Air. He's done a dirty deal with the airline. Apparently he will be moving in a team of zero-contract Polish labourers to farm the emus, quails and every other poor bird they are planning to exploit as soon as we leave, all so fat executives can have scrambled exotica for breakfast in the clouds with recipes by that arrogant TV dick-off.' She goes on for so long she runs out of breath and her statement unleashes a stream of questions.

'Do you think Logan Josh is his real name?'

'Are you sure it isn't Josh Logan?'

'Are they really going to farm emus?'

'One airline saved millions by taking an olive off every salad plate served in economy. An olive!?'

'I bet they will be serving the quail eggs with truffle toast and charging hundreds of pounds to eat it. The TV chef will probably fly with them, to hobnob with the rich.'

'I heard his real name is Mick?'

'Too Irish for TV.'

'Too economy for Go-Go?'

TCP holds two fingers to her head like a revolver and pulls the trigger, popping a bubble of gum into her own face. 'One at a time, people.'

'Let's protest. We could dress as rheas and emus and stand outside Tesco Metro with placards.'

'Good idea. I heard they are planning to farm penguins too. Keep them in a converted freezer with a pool. Anyone have a penguin outfit?' says TCP.

'It's pretty easy to get hold of one of those.'

'How do you know?'

'I often rock one on a Saturday night.' Henry giggles and makes penguin noises.

I let them all talk. And then I stand, without really knowing what I'm going to say. But a calmness has washed over me, and I'm suddenly prepared to fight. 'I will write to Logan Josh and his agent, and anyone I can think of connected to him. I'll beg them to give us some time. I'll also write to our MP. And I'll ring radio stations and regional TV; start a conversation about subsidising struggling artists in a capitalist society.'

I'm suddenly aware I've lost the crowd as their attention has switched to my cat. Molly sends a long, lazy meow into the universe, arches her back slightly and scratches the floor. She then slowly, magnetically, processes through the room, stopping momentarily at the feet of those she likes to receive strokes from. I consider what she would do if she were leading this meeting. She wouldn't take on all the jobs herself. She would delegate every last one.

'As I said, I'm going to write to our MP as he is a top

government bum licker. Henry, can you write to the *Hillingdon Star* letters page? And can someone also ring that vile journalist?' His article about me still stings. 'TCP, can you design a mural for the side of the building that gives people an idea of us as a community?'

'I can, although "mural" is a word only pensioners use,' she says.

Joy puts up her hand and says, 'I use it.' TCP withdraws the invisible pistol from her pocket again and fires it at Joy.

'Someone needs to be on it with local online sites. Also, any magazines that cover the plight of starving artists. *Big Issue*? Henry, can I give that to you? And we need a contingency plan. What if none of us have found anywhere in a month? Suze, can you phone around? Maybe we can occupy some holiday lodges for a few weeks for cheap at the end of the season. In the Chilterns or something?' I pause to gauge the mood of the room.

'It all sounds a bit legal but I suppose it's worth a try before we have to barricade ourselves in and set fire to the cats,' says TCP. Milly makes herself small as though she's heard every word and is getting defensive. Meanwhile, Molly performs a clown routine and falls on the floor to receive applause.

I suggest we do something positive to raise our profile and get some local support. 'We all work with animals in some form; TCP may not directly but most of her graffiti is about climate change and she's amazing at painting whales. How about we organise an art safari and run tours of the building over a weekend?'

We celebrate with a round of tea and the Jaffa Cakes,

which disappear in seconds. Taking charge of my life is intoxicating and I'm on a high when they've gone. Before I change my mind, I write my next post for @ beyourbestcat.

> *Be the Boss Cat.*
>
> *Your cat doesn't have the time or energy for imposter syndrome. She is too busy being the boss of you. But that doesn't mean she'll wear herself out with hard work. A cat won't catch her own mouse if she can phone for it to be delivered, as a kebab, directly to her paws. Your cat is a master at supervision and delegation. She occasionally gives, but mostly receives with a grudging amount of gratitude. In a meeting today I was struggling to keep control until I caught sight of Molly, owning the room, parading through the crowd like she was on a Disney float. Molly knows she can't please everybody, so simply pleases herself. They both make me do all the work, yet still find ways to support me. Today's challenge is to grab the reins but to delegate and let others take the strain. Comments below please.*

I make another cup of tea and sink into the sofa. Fighting talk is all very well, but at some point soon I'm going to have to pack up and leave. I also have other problems like what to do about my car, still sitting on the garage forecourt. I pick up my phone and then pause. I need to prioritise rent and a deposit. For a moment I consider what I actually need. And I look at the remaining stack of boxes opposite me. Not all that stuff for sure. And what about all the boxes in Henry's flat? I promised him they would only be there a few days. I scoop Milly up and take her with me.

Henry opens the door within seconds of my knock. 'Aly? What can I do for you?'

'Just wanted to thank you for stepping in last night. And to have a quick chat about my boxes.' I stand awkwardly on his doorstep, clutching the cat. Henry is dressed in a dark grey fisherman's jumper and plaster-coated grey jeans. He's balder than my cats yet has the best handlebar moustache in London. I wish I knew him better. Why did I wait so long to get to know a yak knitter, a graffiti artist, and a ceramicist with a passion for . . . 'What kind of ceramics do you make, Henry?'

'Come in and see if you like. Prepare yourself for the smell though. I do ventilate the room, but it's pungent most of the time.'

His flat is chock-a-block with lions. If I worship the image of small cats, this man is a disciple of the big guns. Everywhere I look. Life-size, sculpted heads. 'It's the Sahara in here.'

'Not the Sahara. The Namib. Almost twenty per cent of Namibia is desert. There's a lot of wilderness out there, and quite a few big cats. They're for an African week at a gallery in Mayfair. They'll be gone by next week.'

'The Namib.' I roll the name around my tongue.

'It literally means "an area where there's nothing". Thought to be the oldest desert in the world – fifty-five million years.'

'How come?'

'The others just formed later, I suppose.' He shrugs. The only natural light comes from a series of high windows, which are all open. His flat is basically a garage, with a camp bed, a sink, a stove and a massive kiln sitting in the middle of the room.

'I meant how come Namibia. Did you live there?'

'I ran a lodge. Took a truck out each dawn and sunset packed with tourists and cameras. When I came back here, I went to art college. Had thousands of photos of these beautiful beasts and an idea for sculpture that no one else was doing.'

'What are they made of?'

'Crushed marble, made into a paste and moulded. Then the pieces are assembled into faces. Like a 3D jigsaw. I've started focusing on the heads of endangered species, giving a percentage to World Wildlife.'

'Henry, where are my boxes?'

'Your boyfriend called in last night and took them all in his car. Said it was going to be a surprise.'

I click my tongue in irritation. When I confided in Rick about the boxes yesterday, I didn't expect him to charge in and grab them. Is he going for alpha male of the year or something? It took a lot for me to talk to him about them and with one action he's undermined that trust. Unless it was Greg? But then Greg knows the score with my mother.

'Henry was it . . .'

'What's inside the boxes? Why do you have so many of them?'

'Presents. From my mother,' I reply, shutting him down.

'She's a very generous parent. Will you go back home and live with her when we get tipped out of here?'

I purse my lips. 'My friend may have found me somewhere but he's keeping it close to his chest right now. Don't suppose there's any space in that desert of yours?'

'You wouldn't want to live there. It's thought to be one of the most inhospitable places on earth. The oryx drink from tubers growing in the ground as there's no water supply.'

'Ah, well, I probably wouldn't like it then. I've never even been abroad. Although my childhood sounds a bit like Namib. Gotta go, Henry, I have to make a phone call.'

# Chapter 22

Rick picks up my call immediately. The man has no shame.

'Aly? You've heard?'

'About the boxes? Henry just told me. Where are they?'

'About my father . . . William . . . well, you know who my father is . . . he's in intensive care.' The boxes are immediately forgotten. 'He drank a litre of Jack Daniel's and fell down the stairs at a private members club last night. The press are already on it.'

'Where are you?'

'St Thomas' Hospital. Glimmer and his advertising company WHH will be releasing a joint statement at eleven o'clock and . . .' He falters.

'What do you need?'

There's silence at the other end of the phone. 'Do you know, you're the first person to ask me that?' Silence again. 'I'd like to get out of here before it breaks. I can't stay with him in the ICU so I'm a bit of a spare part. Juliet's handling things at work for me. I need space and I'm thinking of going home.'

'To Columbia Road? Want some company?'

'I'd love it if you came along, but I'm not thinking of that home. Any chance you can ask your neighbour to look after your cats for a few hours? It's not exactly round the corner.'

Rick is later than promised, and I take the opportunity to chat to some of my new followers. There are hardly any but they are totally engaged. One woman tells me she's transformed her life based on my handful of posts. I feel properly humbled as I haven't even filled the Insta grid yet. With no luck on reinstating my old account, I've decided to tell Rick and Sam about what I've done. Maybe they can help me. Find a way to bring my old AlyCat audience to my new account. They're the digital experts, they'll know what to do.

I'm waiting beside TCP's grow bags when Rick rocks up in a BMW as sleek and navy as one of his jackets. After he doughnuts the car park, I climb into the front seat, feeling so much like a child in a grown-up's car I wonder about volunteering to sit in the back.

'Rick, I'm sorry—' I begin.

'For my loss?' he cuts in. 'He isn't dead yet, although he's pumped full of wires and drugs. He looks . . . I don't know . . .'

'UnWilliamesque?'

'Diminished.'

He bites a lip. Maybe he cares for his dad more than he lets on. Now is not the time to bring up my Instagram account. And starting a row about the boxes feels churlish. The engine purrs like Milly when she's had a big meal and I settle into its rhythm and stay silent.

'Where are we going?'

'Gloucestershire. The country seat.'

'You're aristocats?'

He laughs at my kitty wordplay. 'I was joking; he's not

been knighted . . . yet. You'd probably call our place in the Cotswolds a pile. I call it a stuffy, draughty house, which served as a lonely refuge from boarding school.'

'You're not selling it to me.'

'Wait till I start describing my childhood.' He laughs, an edge to his voice. 'I thought I could show you around and we can see if we can find some slippers or pyjamas for my father.'

'He still lives there?'

'He has a place in Chelsea but escapes a lot to the country, with random gold-diggers on his arm.' I throw him a glance. Daddy might be lying in a hospital bed but he's not going easy on him.

Rick pulls up to a petrol station. I blow the contents of my wallet on two packs of egg sandwiches, a packet of discounted sausage rolls and four cans of dodgy-looking blue liquid that promise to re-energise me, while he pays at the pump for the petrol. As I return to the car, he's resting his head on the steering wheel and I wonder if he should be driving at all.

The journey goes quicker than expected and we're soon zooming down country lanes. 'This is Gloucestershire, right? I came to a cool place here a while back.' I suddenly remember a party invite from Lola I haven't replied to as I couldn't see myself schlepping back here again on the train.

'Welcome to the Cotswolds. Home sweet home.' Rick pulls up at a gate and jumps out to open up. 'The gates weren't just for keeping burglars out – I used to regularly run away from boarding school,' he says as he climbs back in. We coast along a drive lined with trees before he parks in a gravel semicircle in front of a building with windows that could rival the White House.

'I need fresh air.' He leads the way around the building and through an archway adorned with the remains of a last burst of wisteria. The passageway spills into a garden at the back of the house, studded with bushes and trees, and a pond beyond. 'You did all your star photography here. I recognise the patio.'

'Astrophotography,' he corrects me. He walks towards the pond, lowers himself onto the lawn and removes his shoes, weaving his toes into the grass. The September air has a chill in it, and I hate the idea of winter coming. My campaign to fight Logan Josh has failed; even the *Hillingdon Star* has ghosted me and I'm gearing up to ask Kav if the cats and I can camp in her shop at night for a while. Guard the beans from burglars.

He holds out a hand and I join him on the grass. 'There are blankets in the car if you want one. The grass is a bit damp.'

'I'm OK. Why did your dad send you to boarding school if it was close enough to escape back home?' I lean back enjoying the weak sun on my face.

'No money on private education is ever wasted.' He mimics William's booming voice. 'Also, there's a lot of money in the Cotswolds. He could swan around at sports day, milking the connections and offering them his PR services. And it was convenient for him to house me elsewhere because a lot of the time he was also elsewhere. He rang occasionally and sent me socks. Quality cashmere. I gave them away. I decided back then the world is divided into two; socks on or socks off people. The latter aren't afraid of being adventurous, connecting with the earth and toughening up their feet to walk on hot coals if needed.'

'I wondered for ages why you never wore socks.'

He shrugs off his black zippered jumper, leans back and rests his head on it. Even in his emotional, tired state, he still slays me. I'm sweating slightly in swirly orange polyester; not one of my finest creations, so I close my eyes and face the sun, conserving my energy. After a few minutes I decide to tackle him.

'Rick, I visited Henry. He told me you'd come round and hijacked the boxes . . .' When I look down I see the rhythmic rise and fall of his chest. 'Great chat, thanks.'

I take the opportunity to study him. He has ridiculously long legs, and quite big feet, I'm guessing he's about a size eleven whereas I've always bought kids' shoes. I sit back and compare the length of our bodies, moving my right foot downwards and putting it on top of his left. Soon my bare feet are gently stroking his and the rest of my body is finding it unbelievably thrilling. Then I move on to his hands, touching the dark hairs scattered lightly from his wrist to his knuckles. I stroke his fingers individually, igniting a fresh spark of desire with each one.

Feeling vaguely stalkery, I heave myself up and head for the car to retrieve the stash of food and blankets. I leave my sandals on the lawn, so he will see I'm a socks off kind of person if he wakes.

When I gently drape a blanket over him, he jerks up, like he's trying not to fall asleep on a motorway. 'Hey don't panic,' I reassure him. 'Sleep for a while longer if you like. You may need to bank some energy for the hospital. You should eat too. I've brought the food. But you might not have much of an appetite if you're still in shock.'

'Not really a shock. I've been waiting for my father to kill himself for years. Booze, women, cars, it was Russian roulette. You'll be wondering why I'm here when he's there, lying in a bed stuffed with tubes . . .' he murmurs.

'Time out.'

'Time out?' he repeats as though trying to process the words. 'I'm not sure I was ever really in.'

'You really didn't get on . . .'

He sits up, shivers, and puts his sweater back on.

'As a teenager, sometimes. He was proud of what I did with YouTube. Glimmer has always been a battle; our priorities are light years apart and he tries to meddle in my decisions. But our problems go back long before that. He struggled to cope after my mum died, and made some dubious decisions and one almighty lie that we couldn't move on from.'

'I know all about not connecting with your parents. My mum and I were . . . separate.' I stare out at the lake.

'I thought you lived with her as a child?'

'I did.'

The sun goes behind a cloud. Drained of colour the pond looks like a gap in the land. Rick is still looking at me – waiting for me to elaborate and give him more of me than I want to. His eyes have that confessional effect again and, inexplicably, I want to share.

'Mum and Dad blew hot and cold all their married

life. They always had a fiery relationship. I thought that was how people spoke to each other, with a swear word just under their tongue and venom in their jabs and jibes. There was physical stuff too – not serious, but enough to have intense make-up sex. Which I heard from the next room by the way – gross. And then it stopped. Dad slept in the spare room for months. The house descended into a strange silence until one day he left for a flat in Stockley Park. Mum spent weeks accusing him of leaving her for a woman and was almost disappointed when she found out he hadn't. He'd left with our family cat, Mardy, and the two of them lived happily ever after until he died suddenly. Mardy wasn't much of a looker and Mum couldn't make head nor tail of his decision to put the cat above us in his priorities. I guess she blamed him for loving Mardy but not her. I blamed him for taking Mardy and not me. And I really, really missed Mardy. Neither of us had much contact with him after that until his heart gave up. They never divorced and she had enough money for a comfortable life; working in insurance, he'd built up an impressive range of policies, which passed on to her. But when he died, the house went from cold to glacial. All the fire of fighting him for all those years finally went out of her. She still criticised me all the time, but in a flat voice that said she didn't care. Except at school where she was vicious. Sometimes she sought me out in corridors to have a go. Can you imagine how embarrassing it is when the head of pastoral care continually bullies you in front of your peers?'

I glance up at him to see if he's dropped back off to sleep.

But his eyes are still focused on mine. 'And in periods of intense criticism, the presents came. "Guilt gifts" I called them. They stopped for a while when I moved out, before starting up again. I didn't know what to do with them, so I put them under my bed and in my wardrobe; out of sight, out of mind. Until there were too many to hide and I shifted them into the boxes. And eventually the boxes were too much too and dwarfed my flat. So much guilt.'

Rick gives me a look I can't interpret. I have a compulsion to reach out again, venturing higher than his feet. He's seen my thighs, as up close as a man can get; and I still shiver at the memory. Checking out his black jeans, my eyes wander to the creases around his crotch. Were they pre-prepared by the designer, or have they been formed by the way he sits, walks and lies? I love the way jeans become part of you as they mould around you; how even a hot wash can't erase your history. I want to stroke my fingers along his legs and see if I have any impact. He brushes his lap, and I wonder if a man can accidentally get aroused by tidying himself up.

I need to focus on something other than his lunchbox.

'Why did you take the boxes, Rick? I'm guessing it was to try and help me but really it hasn't. Where are they now? I need them back.'

He looks at me confused. 'I didn't take any boxes.'

I start to feel cross again. 'That night I stayed at Kav's after we . . .' I still can't think about what he did to me without blushing. 'Just tell me where they are and I'll recapture them and deal with them in my own way.'

'Not me,' he says, so firmly I start to doubt myself.

Then I change tack, to deflect his attention away from my pathetic problems.

'Tell me about your mum.'

'Nothing to tell. She died in a boating accident when I was a toddler.'

'Boating? Like on this pond?'

'A catamaran off the coast of Spain. It came with a crew but after a massive lunch of paella and wine, Dad bribed them to let him take the helm. Bigged up his sailing qualifications like he bigs up everything about himself. The boat turned over. My mum and I got pulled under it. He saved me and not her as I was four years old and couldn't swim. I suspect he always regretted that choice. The captain was prosecuted and Dad got away with it. But he never got away with it here.' He puts his hand on his heart and mine skips a beat in sympathy.

He presses his lips together and pulls the blanket tighter. 'Maybe while they've got him in a hospital gown they'll have a root around, see if he still has a heart.'

'You could have a human tower of Catalonians in here and still not touch the ceiling,' I say, awed by the space and the cornicing in the dining room. We've come inside for a quick tour. 'Are those carpets on the walls?' I reach out to touch an upright Axminster.

'It's a special kind of wallpaper. Useful insulation. This house is freezing in the winter. There's a reason I fill the car with blankets when I head up here. If he dies, there'll be no more Sunday dinners. No more opinions and arguments over Yorkshire pudding. That's a relief in a way.'

'He won't die,' I reassure him. My words are met with a raised eyebrow. The aim of the gesture is to show he doesn't care, but it has the opposite effect when it twitches slightly. 'Did he cook you lunch?'

'God no. In the old days he had housekeepers and latterly the local pub delivered our food, or we found a corner of the bar and talked about work. We had the last lunch a couple of weeks ago. He grilled me about the firm. Banged on about growth and expansion and overseas offices. It was draining. Having him as chair of the board means I am constantly fighting to do anything. Maybe that'll change now.' He pauses and straightens a curtain.

In the breakfast room, an oval mahogany table stands on a heavy rug, with patterns in orange and red that should clash but don't. I flash back to the awards dinner and my conversation with Rick's dad. About how he keeps compromising secrets of people under the floorboards. I decide it's best not to know sometimes.

We move upstairs and tour more rooms than Buckingham Palace could throw up.

His childhood bedroom is pale blue, generic, and filled with cardboard.

'Are you trying to out-box me?'

'You can't buy one lens, they come in packs of ten.' He grins. 'There are a lot of lenses in here. Actually, how are you doing for time? It's clear tonight. I could give you a tour of the sky if you like.' When I tell him I'd love that, I'm rewarded with a wide smile. 'The moon won't rise for quite a while, and we'll be late back to London. Can you leave the cats that long?'

As his change of mood feels good for us both, I ring Henry who offers to keep Milly and Molly for the night.

'I'm getting used to having them around and they like my lions. In fact, I'm thinking of sculpting one of them. Branching out from big cats.'

As darkness falls, Rick pulls the cover off one of two rigs on the patio and fiddles with the telescope beneath it. 'Bear with me, this'll take about ten minutes to set up and another twenty to align.' As he presses a couple of buttons on the handset, he talks me through what we might see. 'This part of the world is a four on the Bortle scale, which means you have a good chance of sighting the regular planets. The moon, Saturn, Jupiter, we should be able to look at all of them tonight. Don't expect the kind of quality of my photos though. It'll be much blurrier. But better here than in London, where trying to see the stars is like shining a torch on fog.'

'Is this a camera?'

'A telescope. The humble Celestron telescope and tracker. You don't need expensive kit to see the moon. However, you do need to spend a bit more to photograph it, which is where my other baby comes into play.' He pats the rig next to it. 'We'll get to that in a bit. For now, let's start with looking at the moon. Have you ever seen it through a telescope?' I shake my head. 'Then you are in for a treat.' He grabs my waist, which is a thrill in itself, and then guides me to the viewfinder.

'Wow. It's full.'

'Almost full. There's a filter in the eyepiece, otherwise

it would be too bright, and you wouldn't want to do this in a full moon. Too much light.'

'It's like a kid's drawing of the man in the moon but much more impressive.'

'The moon is just a dot in the sky through the naked eye, but when you get close up like this, you get an idea of how many details are within it. It reflects sunlight and is a really pretty object. See the craters at the edge?'

'They're gorgeous. Like mountains.'

'Now are you ready to have your mind blown? Because in a few minutes I'm going to show you the star of the sky – my beautiful Saturn.'

As he realigns the camera, I take in the rest of the night sky, turning my feet three hundred and sixty degrees. The sky is black, and the stars are glorious. It makes me wonder if I've ever looked up before.

Saturn and Jupiter are awesome, but not like the photographs he showed me at his house. As if tuning into my thoughts, he pulls a cover from another rig. 'This camera captures a lot of the images I talk about in my YouTube videos. It's more expensive than the telescope but still not out of reach of most budgets. You can get some great pictures by using this.'

'Can we take one now?'

'To be honest, astrophotography is not much of a spectator sport. It's too boring. If I took a single picture of the night sky through this telescope it would be little more than a smudge. To get a decent pic, I'd need to set up a long exposure and take many images over six, eight or ten hours. Very long exposures, a hundred seconds or so each, over several nights. I assume you don't want to wait up that long.'

'Why would that help?'

'These objects are very faint, which is why we can't see them through the optical telescope. But through this camera we can capture enough light to build up the image. It's like the old cameras when you had to stand still with the shutter open for ages. Here we follow the object round the sky with the shutter open for five minutes at a time. That way, if a cloud passes over or one of Elon Musk's Starlink satellites shoots across the frame, we don't ruin the whole shoot – just that one five-minute frame. Collect enough of them and you can stack them together to build up the image. When I think I have enough, I pop my memory stick into my desktop and the computer starts to process them.'

All this time he has had his hand around my waist, causing havoc in my belly. I am dreaming about spooning him here in the moonlight when he moves away. 'Want to see some crazy-big space junk now?' He grins.

Rick leads me past the pond and into another garden. When he swings away from the house and towards a glass dome, I realise this country kid was rich enough to have his own observatory. He takes out his keys and unlocks the door, then kills the alarm system.

'Welcome to my pleasure dome. Every child with an obscenely overprivileged upbringing has one. Like your mother, my father did guilt gifts big style. I'm guessing yours were never on this scale, but then, William had a lot to feel guilty about.' Dotted around the room are several rigs. 'This is how I take photos of deep space. We're talking upwards of fifty thousand pounds of guilt here. Impressed?'

I'm impressed by the images on the wall. Whilst the pictures in London were all of his beloved Saturn, there's a mix of spectacular stars here. I point to a streak that looks like blue fireworks. 'That's beautiful.'

'The Pleiades star cluster. It's a gorgeous colour, isn't it?'

'You're a collector of stars,' I say. Professionally and personally.

'I've been obsessed since I was a child. It's like twitchers spending a lifetime trying to get a picture of a rare hummingbird. The object of the exercise is to see things yourself rather than looking them up in a book.'

'What's that one?' I say, pointing to a shimmer of red in another framed picture.

'What does it look like?' he asks.

'A heart, and a dick.'

'Well, you got the first bit right. It's the Heart Nebula, near the constellation of Cassiopeia. That piece of it is called the Fish Head Nebula. But you're not the only one to imagine something more intimate,' he corrects me, failing to hide a smile. I look at the heart he has so cleverly captured and wonder if he's aware he has stolen mine. He takes my hand, so maybe he is. 'The next-door nebula is called Soul. You can't see them without all this equipment, but Heart and Soul are always shining down on us and influencing our movements, or at least they were . . .'

'. . . a long time ago . . .' I begin, turning to him.

'. . . in a galaxy far, far . . .' he continues, but we don't finish our *Star Wars* scrawl as his lips are upon mine. My heart is in my mouth, his arousal is in my hands, and our pulses are goddamn everywhere as we crash towards the wall, narrowly avoiding thousands of pounds worth of kit.

'Unconventional to start the day with a blue drink but we've no milk for tea,' Rick says, sitting on the side of the bed. He is dressed and I pull the covers up to my neck. Last night I had no trouble shedding my clothes as fast as he could rip his off his muscular frame. But I'm more inhibited in the daylight.

I take a sip of the drink he brought and wipe my mouth. I must have dribbled more than I thought as he raises a hand to my chin. But then he strokes upwards, along my lips, before planting a light kiss on them.

'I have a gift,' he says. 'While we were outside last night, I set the camera on the patio to Andromeda. You can't see it with the naked eye, but obviously I know where to look.' He opens his laptop on his knee. 'At five o'clock this morning I started stacking the images before coming back to bed and letting it run. This is for you. It's a work in progress and a bit rubbish right now, but I'll do the rest of it remotely and should be able to give you something half decent by the end of the week.' The picture he shows me is grey and grainy and I can just about pick out a blur. 'Some think Andromeda is boring as there's not a lot of colour and depth in it compared to some of the flashier galaxies. But it's seven times bigger than the moon. Its dust clouds are millions of light years long, and you'll also find supernova remnants, as well as stars the size of our sun hanging around inside it. It's one of the most photographed things in space and although I'm an Andromeda virgin and a bit embarrassed at the blur, I wanted you to have it.'

Last night he ran his hands across my body, conjuring up sensations I'd never experienced before and this morning he offers me a fuzzy galaxy. The stars have sent me a good one, although part of me wishes I'd gone to bed with a milkman as I'm gasping for a cup of tea.

# Chapter 23

'I'll drop you at home before I head back into the city. I'm planning to visit the hospital and then sort out some problems at work.' Rick revs the engine and gravel crunches under his fancy wheels. When we've passed through the gates, he nips out and closes them before selecting a tune on his phone. Rock music blasts through speakers studded around the car interior and I feel happier than I have in months.

'I keep sunglasses in the glove compartment. Can you pass them over so I can see the road?' I rummage around and produce a pair of shades and a bar of Fruit & Nut. Rick pops the glasses on just before he changes gear and pulls away from the gate.

At the same moment I rip the foil on the bar of chocolate, a car skids around us, skimming the wing mirror with a metallic scrape.

'What the . . . hey, you utter prick . . .' Rick shouts, putting his foot on the gas. In seconds we are tearing down the road after the silver car. 'I'll smash more than your wing mirror when I catch up with you,' he says under his breath, leaving me breathless with fear and lust.

The car ahead of us is fast, but we keep up. I cling on to the handle above my head, praying the airbags are working. The other car brakes about a mile and a half down the road, and veers right, down a narrow country lane. I've spotted a familiar sign and have clocked what's at the bottom of that road. I also suspect I know who is in that car. Lola is going to have her questions answered about what kind of boss Rick is. Right now, he's a pressure cooker and she's just flipped his lid.

The silver car pulls to a stop outside the gates of Power Towers. I notice a 'For Sale' sign on the gate as we screech to a stop behind it. Rick jumps out, leaving his door open like a scene from a TV cop drama and I wind down my window for a better look as he hammers on the roof of the other car.

'Too fast! Way too fast for a B road. I indicated and accelerated with enough warning for you to slow down. That was totally irresponsible driving.' He's not shouting, but his fists are clenched. 'You hardly even noticed scraping the paint off my car. Could have killed us if you'd been a second later and I'd pulled out properly. Are you on drugs or something?' He knocks on the window and pulls at the handle. I vacate the car too as I really want to see this.

As ever, Lola looks astonishingly put together. The sunlight behind her turns her white sequinned kitten ears into a silhouette as she climbs out of the Audi dressed in a white jumpsuit and the tallest heels in the land of stilt-walkers. Her extra-long eyelashes are thickly coated in kohl, and she's accessorised them with whiskers. Around her neck is her trademark silver cat bell which nestles above her half-clad mega-bust. A much shorter woman climbs out of the car with her. She's dressed like a ballerina, in a pink leotard and tights. White contact lenses make her look like an albino vampire and she's also wearing pointy ears. I wonder if she's the one who was helicoptered out of the cat class a few weeks ago; the one with the sexy swim coach. I look for signs of chlorine in her hair as Lola strolls up to Rick.

'We don't have drugs sadly, but we do have rather a lot of alcohol in the boot as we're having a party tonight. Good morning, Ricky. Nice to see you. Are you dropping Aly off for the party?' She is as cool as he is mad. I knew there was a party on the horizon! I pull out my phone and quickly search up the invite in my email.

'How do you know her name?' His eyes are full of contempt.

'Aly's one of our kittens. Are you coming to play tonight, Aly?' She holds out her hand towards me, long nails shaped into silver claws. 'I think you'll love letting your fur down at our kitty ranch party.' I finish reading the invite, which mirrors her words as she continues to bait Rick. 'Sorry, Ricky, no men are allowed. Tonight, women get to explore themselves in a non-threatening, women-only environment. And I'm not talking whiteboards and brainstorming, Aly. This night is purely about fun and games.'

Her companion meows, lifts a bottle of milk from a crate at the gate, pops the lid off and downs it in one.

'Power Towers?' says Rick, dismissing the concept on the sign with a flick of hand. 'I assume my father is bankrolling this? Well, you'd better make the most of it as he's unlikely to last the week.'

Without waiting for her to answer, he turns to me. 'Do not go near this woman again. She isn't just sour, she's toxic.'

Lola pales. 'Wait, what? What's wrong with Bill?'

'William, as he's known to everyone who isn't screwing him, is in a hospital bed right now. Excuse us if we don't hang around to make small talk.' He takes a step towards the car, and she grabs my arm. 'I said Aly is off limits,' he says through gritted teeth.

'Really?' Lola casts a glance in my direction. 'Are you sure? If Aly is listening to her inner cat right now – and congrats on the new Instagram account, it's fabulous – she might be thinking you are being a little . . . overpowering. You can stay the night if you like, Aly. Save you hiking back to London.' Her voice regains its composure, and her smile is mischievous. 'We have food and booze, and plenty of toys. The atmosphere will be relaxed and friendly and female and feline.' Rick pushes his knuckles together in front of his chest, like he's restraining himself from decking her. 'Stay with us, pretty kitty?' she begs.

Part of me really wants to. The part that could do with some fun and friends right now. And the part that channels Milly and Molly. They would not take Rick's attitude lying down. How dare he tell me who to speak to. We might have fallen into bed last night but that doesn't give him the right to bully me. Or her.

'You can put your sex toys away. Aly's not looking for a fun night out,' Rick says in a low, semi-controlled voice, turning his back on her and walking to the car. 'My garage will send you the invoice for the mirror. I'll expect it paid within thirty days.'

'How do you know I'm not looking for a fun night out? You think after last night I should just be concentrating on fun nights in with you?' I hiss as I run to catch up with him.

'Ooh, what happened last night?' Lola smirks. 'Did the cat get the cream?'

He throws her a dagger of a look, which joins mine in mid-flight. She simply purrs and smiles, putting her arm around her companion.

I can't leave my cats for another night. Rick starts the car and for a moment I wonder about walking to the station. When I remember what it cost in a taxi, I reluctantly get in.

'You're never coming here again,' he says, pretty much baring his teeth, before spinning the wheel and driving off in the other direction. I grind mine. I'm embarrassed that I let myself be humiliated in front of two strong, independent women. I'm furious that he shouted at me and tried to dictate who I should hang out with. I'm cross that I have to rely on him for this lift. And I'm annoyed that despite all this I still find him hot.

I once learnt on a YouTube vid that women have something like fifty ways of expressing how they feel on their face; telltale signs they don't even realise they are displaying. In contrast, men have about ten. Rick's ten seem to be equally divided into his eyebrows and his eyes as he conducts an internal monologue. I hate being around anger, having spent a childhood trying to avoid it. And I don't want to risk a crash if he blows up again. But hell, his behaviour needs to be challenged. I ask myself what Milly would do, and I know she'd raise her paws and sharpen her claws.

'Did you get off on talking to me like that in front of them?'

A tiny muscle twitches above his eyes.

'So, did you? Wham, bam, thank you, now I get to control what parties you go to. Is that it? And I don't believe you about the boxes. Where are they?'

He changes gear abruptly and the stick makes a crunching sound. 'As I said, she's toxic. Not someone you want to hang around with.'

'So you're my mother now? Telling me who to hang around with.'

He keeps his eyes firmly on the road. 'Lola is a liar. And a thief.'

'She seemed pretty genuine to me both times I met her. I didn't pick up any bad vibes. Maybe they were all coming from you.'

'Don't be deceived, Aly. She's a very convincing con merchant. She fancied my dad, or at least fancied his money, and cosied up to him when my mum died. She ended up living with us. I thought she wanted to be part of our family. I thought she loved him, and I believed she was fond of me when I stayed at home in the holidays. I found out in secondary school that he was paying her to be my mother.' Silence descends while I process what he said. 'The ultimate guilt gift eh? I think I just trumped your boxes, which I definitely do not have in my possession.'

'But she might have . . .'

'I don't tolerate lies. I've told you that before. And that wasn't the only time they withheld the truth. If my father dies, he'll stop bankrolling her, and we can all get on with our lives.'

# Chapter 24

I'm attempting to walk yesterday out of my system with a trip to my favourite Kozy Korner. Kav doesn't bother to say hello.

'Manolis is fifty today,' she tells me, her voice flat and her face devoid of makeup. There are few traces of her Indian heritage today; she's dressed in a black hoodie and leggings, like TCP on a night mission. 'He's not coming back, Aly.'

'Oh Kav.' My heart goes out to her.

'I've been up all night, texting and panicking.'

'You've wished him happy birthday?'

'Since midnight, on the hour. Today is his deadline. Checking my phone is giving me RSI. I hate being apart from him on his birthday and I can't run the shop on my own anymore.' She waves a hand around piles of newspapers. 'The paper boys take the piss and don't turn up till ten. And I miss him cooking omelettes using only egg whites because he once had a bad yolk.'

'He had a bad yolk and still cooks eggs?' I ask. She nods. 'And continued to sell them in the shop?' She nods again. 'And allowed the chickens of the world to go on laying them? Kav, he's more flexible than anyone knew. He'll come around.'

She smiles a little, and her cheekbones rise. 'But not

flexible enough to accommodate me. Except when we had sex in the bath, he was super-bendy then to avoid the taps on his back.'

'T.M.I. You love him.'

'Yes.'

'And you've told him?'

'Over and over.'

'Then why don't you marry him? It's not a death sentence, you know.'

She looks up from her ledger of credit granted to valued suck-ups like me. 'I have thought about marrying him every day since he left,' she admits.

'But?'

'But my family.' She bites a chunk out of her biro before throwing the rest into the bin. She then spits the bits of plastic onto the floor. 'You owe us £175.30 you know? But if you hold out, we may be bankrupt soon and you'll get away with it.'

'Said no debt collector ever. I have money. I was paid by KittiFresh and I told the garage to scrap my car rather than paying for more repairs. Today, thanks to Sam, two hundred pictures of my cat dressed as the Loch Ness Monster are being installed in the rooms of a posh hotel in the Scottish Highlands.' I give her my credit card. 'Wipe my slate and then go see your parents. I'll go with you. I'm all for continuing a long-standing familial grudge due to real or perceived injustices in childhood. But not when it's hurting you in adulthood. And this is hurting you. It has the potential to destroy you and this shop.'

My phone rings. 'Sorry, Kav, I need to take this call.'

I have been regretting downloading the wailing goose ringtone on my phone for some time and vow every day to change it to vaguely annoying Europop. When I answer, the silence is a relief for everyone, although in the background I can hear Kav also making a difficult call and I really want to listen to that.

'Aly! I'm returning your call.'

'Hey Sam, how is the Cat Ness Monster? Have you seen one in situ yet? I've been keeping an eye on their social media, but nothing has popped up.'

'I haven't I'm afraid. They're a bit behind on the installation I think.'

'Ah well, thanks anyway. I was also delighted when the KittiFresh money landed in my account, but there's something I need to tell you.' This morning I told myself it was time to grow up and face the music. Angry as I am with Rick, he's right about one thing – lies are toxic and don't benefit anyone. I launch into the story of my account annihilation and how I started a new one. 'It's healthier really as I'm not pushing the kitties to be humans. Rather suggesting we behave like them.'

'You deleted it?' He sounds like he can hardly believe his ears. 'But why? You looked amazing that night. You won an award.'

I think about that for a moment. 'I thought I didn't deserve success.'

'And you tried to get it back?'

'I think it would be easier to reach Rivendell than chat to a human from a social media platform.'

There's a short silence.

'There are certainly partnerships we can look at that don't involve your AlyCat Instagram feed, and I was expecting some of them to come to fruition this week, but your numbers on the account were huge and will be hard to follow. What are the stats like on your new one?'

'I have fifty.'

'Fifty . . . thousand?'

'Fifty followers.'

'I need to get back to you,' he says. 'Give me an hour.'

He is as good as his word, ringing me back just over an hour later. 'There may be a way of getting your account back within thirty days. Even if you deleted it. That's if you want us to. Otherwise, we might have to take another look at your contract as we can't effectively market you as an influencer if you aren't AlyCat anymore. As you know, there are many influencers out there and we have to prioritise those we feel are most commercial because there's a whole team of people involved in making someone go stellar.'

A whole team of people but the decisions come from the top down don't they? Was it only two days ago I lay with Rick on his lawn and in his bed, sharing our stories and dreaming under the stars?

He continues on, about Glimmer marketing priorities and budget squeeze and having a chat with the team to see if they can recover the @AlyCat Instagram feed. But I'm too hurt to hear it. Rick slept with me and now wants to bin me. He was a player after all, and I have been played. When I got out of the car he said he had to fix a few problems at work. Little did I know I'd turn out to be one of them.

'Thanks for everything, Sam.' Pressing the red phone icon, I help him terminate my contract.

I try not to cry into a tube of Pringles. Once you pop . . .

*You made a mistake. Take a long hard look at what happened and learn from it.*

My ears prick up like Molly's. Since the awards ceremony the voice in my head has started to grow kinder, like Mum's had a personality transplant. It's bordering on supportive. Could it be Mardy coming through again?

Kav holds out her hand for the crisps. 'Shall I ring them up or do you want to start another tab?' When I look surprised at being hurried, she shrugs. 'I've decided to close the shop for a couple of hours.'

'We're going to see your parents?'

'Not you. I have to do this on my own.'

She scans the tube and I throw her a couple of coins. 'Want to share my breakfast first?'

'I cannot eat for the rest of the day. Our culture dictates we feed people, whether we love them, hate them or are indifferent. In fact, we feed them more if we are indifferent to alleviate the guilt. Two decades ago, Mama perfected the art of sealing her samosa pastry with tears. It's the salt that makes them stand out from Auntie's inferior version. There will be a lot of those on a platter today.'

I decide not to tell her about my conversation with Sam. She has enough on her own platter.

'I'm swooping in like a golden eagle to show you a new nest,' Greg says, driving at exactly thirty miles an hour in a thirty mile an hour zone. I'm desperately waiting for news from Kav and only half listening.

A couple of miles out of the centre of Slough, we pull up at a barrier in front of a tall building. Greg taps in a code and the barrier rises. He pitches up at a visitor parking slot.

'Visitors only have twenty minutes but that doesn't apply to us.'

'What kind of place only lets visitors stay for twenty minutes?'

'An exclusive executive residency.'

'And we are here because . . . ?' He ignores my question and strides past two rows of cars. 'Nice motors,' I say, reaching out and stroking one. 'This place is out of my league and defo out of my budget.'

'Bear with me,' he says, before adding, 'The really good ones are garaged. The man in the penthouse has two Ferraris. He keeps one here in the executive garages, which have a twenty-four-hour security guard, and leaves the other at the factory as a backup.'

'How do you know?'

'I sold him the garage. I read there's a waiting list of four and a half years for a bespoke Ferrari.'

'You should have told me we were coming somewhere posh,' I plough on as he checks the driver's door is locked. 'I'd have changed.' I'm wearing ripped jeans and a rainbow top I patched together out of jumble sale finds. And my cats are in old jumpers.

Greg told me to bring them with me today.

'I know it's unusual but if you are going to be happy in a flat I imagine you need to check they like it too,' he'd said.

'OK, I have a special backpack, although I've never tried to squeeze two of them in. Or I could put them in a conventional cat cage?'

'Put them in the cage.'

Now, I lift it out of the boot. 'Let me carry it for you, Alyssa.'

'It's Aly, remember.'

'Of course. I'll have to get used to the new you.' He smiles and gives my hand a quick squeeze, before punching in a code at the front door and another in the lift. 'Only those who have a code can access our floor.'

*Our floor?* We step into the elevator. 'How do you keep track of all those codes?'

'All part of the job. Now, here we are. Valhalla. Asgard is at the top.'

'Does Loki live there?'

'I'm not sure. I haven't met the tenant.' The joke is lost on him as we find ourselves outside a white front door. 'Close your eyes for the best surprise.'

'I'm not doing that.'

He unlocks the door and moves aside. And I'm assaulted by Santa's executive flat. There are fairy lights everywhere; coloured and white, blinking on and off like Blackpool; strings of butterflies and stars. There's a huge glitter ball in the centre of the room and smaller orbs hang from exposed beams. The kitchen looks like a celebrity chef just walked out; neatly ordered with brand-new juicers and blenders. There's a line of toasters; one of them has ten slots like he's planning to open a B & B. It looks like he's been breeding lava lamps too; there are several, pushing blobs effortlessly up tubes, along with smelly candles, incense burners and an antique-looking barometer. Why would you need that if you have a phone to tell you the weather?

'Whoever lives here is addicted to sparkle. Wow. Is that Lego? It looks almost real.' I rush to the model of a ginger tabby, with outstretched white paws and a raised backside. 'Come and see this, girls.' I unlock the cage. Milly refuses to come out but Molly scampers across the room, towards a vase that looks like it might topple over with the weight of a huge bouquet.

'The vase looked a bit sad without flowers and I thought if I bought enough of them, I'd sneeze from the pollen instead of the cats,' Greg explains. We look at the Lego cat, and Milly pokes her nose out to peek at it too. 'It took me a whole day to make it. It's growing on me. Better than the parade of lava lamps. They're abysmal.'

'The Lego cat is yours?'

'No it's yours.'

'I'm confused. I've never bought a Lego set although my mum tried to foist one or two on me. Now I do like this.' I approach a mirror, decorated with shells, attached above a wood burner. As I look into it, I see a face of a teenager, hair pulled back in a misguided attempt to tame it. 'Oh! I recognise this. But why is it here, in this flat in Slough?'

'The boxes. All of this stuff came out of them.'

'The boxes? You took them? When Henry said my boyfriend, I didn't think . . .'

'I brought them here to make you feel at home. Some of the stuff is really, really bizarre and one of the garden gnomes has been talking to me through the cardboard as he was too hideous to unpack. But I knew it would make an empty flat feel like your home. I'm hoping you'll love it as much as I do. I know it's untrendy Slough and I'm only renting it on a year's lease through our executive lets department, but we can buy at the end of the year if it suits us. Living in that tiny studio flat I've saved up enough to put down a deposit and pay off a chunk of the mortgage, and you said you have some money saved too.'

I sigh, we've been here once before. I was down and couldn't cope with Mum anymore and was wondering about ditching Greg. Our relationship had dragged on past its sell-by date. Little things about him got on my nerves like the small collars and thin ties he wore, and his habit of clicking his jaw when he ate. He told me he chewed his food a dozen times before swallowing because he'd read in a self-help book it made digestion easier.

But while I plotted a separation, he had other plans. He took me to a dive in Acton. 'It smells like old lady, but the furniture is free, and we can live here quite comfortably.' I looked at the boy, about to become a man, who was offering to rescue me from a life with my mother. But all I could see was the thin tie, like he'd saved money on fabric by not going for a regular one.

This opportunity is unreal. A luxury executive home of my own, away from the grime of the Uxbridge Road. No rent problems. No more fighting to stay put. Greg and I seem compatible and he's not needy. Twice since the awards ceremony I've stayed the night with him to stave off loneliness and he didn't demand anything else from me, although I know he was hoping to get laid. He's not unattractive. He doesn't have a lot of imagination, but I'd make up for that; he might not believe in elves but I'm betting he'd get excited about other magical creatures. He likes cats. Doesn't he?

Greg sneezes three times then excuses himself to go to the 'little boys' room', returning after washing his hands for twenty seconds as anything less would be germ warfare.

'Shall we go outside before I start sneezing for Iceland?'

Together we stand, resting on the balcony, looking out over a circle of executive flats.

'So what do you say?'

'Does the invitation extend to the cats?'

'Of course,' he says, turning away to find a takeout leaflet.

The food doesn't taste as good as it smelt. Greg coats his in salt and vinegar and wolfs it down, while I chase mine around my plate. I don't even go there with the onion rings. He asks me what's wrong. 'Fish and chips and onion rings is the greatest British meal.'

'The greatest British meal is fish and chips and curry sauce,' I reply without hesitating. 'Ask Kav, if you don't believe me.'

His forehead creases but soon springs backs to a smooth brow. In contrast, Rick's face left his teen years behind; his laughter and frown lines give him character. I scold myself for comparing them but with Greg it always feels like I raised the bat signal and Robin turned up. He's enthusiastic and capable of saving the world but he's never going to do it with a kapow or a kerchung. But then, only one of them has offered to rescue me from the ledge. I push away my plate.

'Aren't you going to finish that? It's a reasonable piece of British haddock. I asked them to make it fresh, so it wasn't sitting around in the warmer.'

'Son of the salmon empire . . . you're really selling it.'

'I do have some talent.' He grins, wiping eyes that are starting to swell up from his proximity to either the cats or the flowers. 'I was recently awarded Salesman of the Quarter and I'm only getting better at the job. I got a sniff on a property in East Sussex yesterday; Grade II listed, with seven bedrooms, a swimming pool, tennis court and a hundred acres of parkland. And the main selling point; a private footpath to the train station. I'm very excited.'

Milly has been huddling close since I let her out of the cage. I think the lava lamps are freaking her out. They're spooking me too. I don't remember receiving most of them. Molly is a different matter. She's been running around like a skittish monkey, meowing loudly. A crash from the other side of the room confirms she hasn't calmed down any. The flowers topple out and she springs back, before pushing her nose into them.

'Molly . . .' I scrape back my chair, to cast my eye across the flowers and ensure there's nothing in the vase that might harm her, but Greg is there before me. He moves the vase out of her way.

'She's drinking the flower water. She must be thirsty.'

It's not like me to neglect the cats. I leap up and grab two bowls and two plates. I fill the bowls with water and pop some fish on the plates. Both cats head over with purpose.

'Here, kitty cat.' Greg lobs an onion ring onto the plate.

'Hey, they can't eat onions.'

'I thought your cats mostly ate human food.'

'They are on raw food diets but some foods, like onions, are toxic. There's a few things they can't eat.' I shoot another glance at the flowers, as Greg wanders over and bends down to the plate. 'You should consider a wee guinea pig or something more user friendly. Then we won't have a scuffed-up sofa in our new home, and I won't sneeze my way through our movie nights.' He disposes of the onion ring before wiping his fingers on a piece of kitchen roll foraged from a fancy stand.

'Cats are user friendly,' I reply, taken aback by that sentiment. 'These two are well trained and easy to look after. No bother at all.'

'That's not strictly true. They eat a lot. Cost a lot. Get sick. Get lonely. There's a pressure on you to stay at home. You can't go on holiday or work for more than a few hours at a time. No offence, but these cats are seriously attention seeking. And I thought hairless cats were supposed to be non-allergenic?' Why is it people who regularly say 'no offence' always follow it with something offensive?

'That's a myth,' I say. 'Although I don't know anyone else who sneezes when they're around.'

'I'm sending you the code to the front door,' he says, popping it into his phone and pinging it across to me. 'I've moved in already. I look forward to you joining me. We can work everything else out over time.'

I push his comments about the cats to one side as I imagine living in luxury for a while; folded PJs on my pillow, a real bath with sparkling white grouting and a sink that isn't dotted with other people's back hair. He's not the good-looking CEO of a globally successful firm, but there would be no surprises and he'd be someone to snuggle up to when Milly is being precious with her affections. So why don't I feel excited? Since my devastating call with Sam my stomach has hurt like someone is stabbing it with toothpicks. Maybe I have shingles.

Greg is waiting for a yes or no. What would my cats say? Our home is the hub of their happiness. It is their territory; they luxuriate in it and know every inch of it. They would choose the living space that best nurtures their well-being, whether or not the deal comes with expectations or a price. But they're not up for advising me right now. Milly has strolled to the window and Molly's playing with the frayed hem of my jeans. For a single moment I allow myself to contemplate the other option; the one I have pushed from my head since the eviction notice arrived. I shake the thought from my brain.

'I'm really touched by your offer. Can I think about it?' We stand, and as I awkwardly hug him, my whole body aches for someone else.

He sweeps Molly up into his arms as I hold the door of the cage. 'You're a cutie, aren't you?' he says. Even more astonishing, she accepts a cuddle, reaching up and licking his chin. He tries not to make a face. 'I need to get used to this if I'm going to be the daddy, right?' I can't help but smile and his kindness prompts a tingle at the back of my neck. She licks him again and he shakes his head and bares his teeth at her. 'No more kisses until Mummy cleans those teeth, fish breath. Back into your cage now.'

Mummy. Was there a more loaded word in the dictionary? I have always believed I was a girl made for bringing up kittens. Is it too late for chittens? The tingle spreads – are my ovaries thawing? Maybe I should stop moping for the handsome prince and grab the woodcutter and a decent cottage.

# Chapter 25

Kav turns up at my flat later on with two bottles of wine swiped from her own stock. She marches into the room, twists one of them open, find us two glasses and fills them to the brim.

'The headline? "Too little too late." Papa said Mama never got over the way I left them with no explanation and no spatulas to drain the pakoras. They didn't know what to tell our relatives or the neighbours. He told me he'd have paid for a PhD for me, or any training I wanted. He would have carefully curated a choice of husbands every year until I found one I was happy with. He made me feel wretched. And then accused me of giving him angina.'

'Did you steal their spatulas?'

'I did. They are so multi-purpose! My mum was the spatula queen. She came with me to the front door afterwards and gave me a hug and a container filled with pinwheel samosas for Manolis. I told them I wanted to marry him. To confess he'd walked out on me because I held out would have been too humiliating. There's enough samosas for two hundred.'

'You've got to sympathise with your dad really. An arranged marriage must be much more difficult in a time of Tinder.'

'Oh, my family don't do arranged marriages. He just

wanted me to get hitched to a dentist. Came up with an annual catwalk of orthodontists – I'm not even sure how he found them. I do believe in the importance of cleaning your teeth, Aly, I just never met one whose smile made me melt.'

'So where's your head at? Did you get any closure?'

'Enough I think.' She refills our glasses. 'Enough to put it behind me and move on anyway. I'll think about what to do about Manolis over another glass of wine.'

In a loo break I search out the cats as it's unusual for them not to be in our laps. Milly is scratching at a discarded Tangle Teezer in the corner of the room while Molly is buried under the quilt on my bed and doesn't respond to my touch. I leave her to her lethargy.

By the time we start on the second bottle, we have convinced each other Kav is ready to grab Manolis back. When she starts calling him a 'useless waffle brain', I know she's serious. But the alcohol gives me heartburn and I tear into Rick.

'You know how you can tell a player? Mixed signals. When they want a bit of it, they're all over you, and then when you give in and give them what they want, they lose interest. Thank you for being part of our agency but now we prefer dogfluencers.'

'Is that a thing?'

'He's a tosser like his dad. I'll tell him when he calls.'

'Do you think he will? If not, will you call him?' she asks.

*Take charge of your own happiness. Grab a fish by its tail before it swims away.*

I preferred the voice in my head when it mindlessly slagged me off.

'Your sofa is looking very squishy and snoozy. Facing up to my dad was exhausting. Can I stay here and sleep it off?' says Kav, looking half asleep already.

I find her a quilt and some pillows. 'Kav, I have to be out of here soon. Can I camp with you for a bit?'

'Yeah, course. It's not like my bed is full. How did it go with Greg?' she asks as she flings herself onto the sofa on top of the quilt.

'Fine. We had fish and chips. I came home earlier than expected and texted you.' I'm not up to sharing his proposal with her. For now, I hug it to myself. But Kav's right. Before I can make a decision I need to have it out with Rick. And I need to do it quickly as Logan Josh's eviction date is too close for comfort.

# Chapter 26

On the Glimmer front desk, the receptionist looks like she's having a conversation with several versions of herself as calls are fed directly into her ears.

'His PA is handling his emails if you would like to ping her a line and make an appointment? This is Melanie at Glimmer how can I help you? I'm afraid Rick is not here at the moment, but we are expecting him sometime soon and he will be returning calls this morning. Thanks so much. I will pass that on. It's a difficult time for everyone.'

I decide to sit and wait for Glimmer's CEO rather than trying to get past the gatekeeper. In the atrium-lit foyer, the white helter-skelter seats that lined the room last time have been replaced. I'm guessing the hot-desking is happening though as meetings are being held in the foyer by people with bottoms the perfect size for the new upturned and upcycled buckets.

I pull my backpack off and check Molly. Kav and Molly looked a similar shade of green this morning when I got up at the crack of dawn to push my friend out to open up the shop for the wayward paper boys. Molly didn't eat any breakfast and was sick all over the floor. I couldn't leave her with Kav but wanted to deal with Rick while the momentum was there. So, I popped the cat back onto my shoulders for one more journey into

London, vowing to ring the vet on the way home if she is still poorly.

As I shuffle around on a giant bucket, my eye is caught by a screen displaying Glimmer's social channels. A tweet announces the company is poised to start representing a rival influencer; the woman who rips off what I do but with bought props and a puppy. I knew it! This snippet of info has been retweeted ten times already. Then there's a pic of Juliet boarding a plane for a meeting in the US to nab herself a very important Blister. It's like I'm in a church watching women turn up to marry Rick. I put the backpack on and head for the exit, ignoring the ping of notifications that have been coming in since I left the Tube. I can't take any more bad news.

As I revolve with the help of a door that hasn't sped up any since my first visit, it's the shoes without socks I notice first. My eyes travel up Rick's legs to find him unshaven, dressed entirely in black, and looking worse than Molly. I flash back to Lola's place and cringe at our final conversation where he commanded me into the car. My emotions sink further at the thought of being ditched by his firm. My pride has taken enough of a bashing, and I've gone off the idea of a showdown in reception. There's a panel of glass between us so if I move quickly I can get away and be at the Tube in five.

'Wait, Aly!' Rick calls as I revolve outwards and head down the street. He follows me, running to try and catch up. 'This is the first time I've been back in the office. I haven't really had a chance to breathe.' I wait for the apology, or the excuse. 'I've just been briefed on what's been going on in my absence.' The excuse comes first; something about his dad. I don't fully hear it as two people come between us, and a *Big Issue* seller drowns out the end of his sentence. I walk on while he issues the follow-up apology. 'I'm sorry, Aly, but . . .' I close my eyes and hum a tune about exes, trying to drown out his words. But they pierce through anyway. 'I think your cat is sick. Milly, or it could be Molly, seems to be vomiting all over your backpack.'

I immediately pull off one strap and he helps me with the other.

'We need to get her out of that bag,' he says, taking control. 'But not here.'

Leading me back into the Glimmer building, he scans his wrist at the lift, which comes immediately. I hold Molly in my arms and the newsreader soon informs us we are on the first floor. Rick ushers me to a meeting room, followed by his PA who points to her iPad.

'I am aware of the time. Give me a moment.' He helps me lift Molly out of the backpack. Her eyes are half closed and her tail is between her legs. 'Can you bring a bowl of hot water and some towels please?' His PA scuttles off to source his request.

'I need to get her down there. On the floor. The desk is too high for me to hold her properly,' I say, sliding cross-legged onto the carpet. Molly flops into my arms and covers me in watery sick. When a towel arrives, I let Rick help me bathe her face. Then I grab another and wrap her in it. She's as slippery as a newborn.

'I didn't want to leave her. I needed to talk to you, but it was clear she wasn't very well this morning, so I decided to bring her with me. The Tube probably made her sickness worse and now it feels mad to have left the house with her. I don't know what to do.' I top off my speech by bursting into tears, snorting the conditioned air of the meeting room. He squats, grabs my shoulders and envelops us in his arms. I breathe his cologne and his kindness. And then I remember the hurt over being sacked off and pull away. 'I have to get her home.' As I attempt to stand, Molly buries her head into me. She whines like a puppy.

'Watch out, she's stuck to your lap.' Rick reaches out and steadies me.

I shake off his hand. 'I guess I should be watching my back instead,' I say, with an edge to my voice. He looks up, bemused. 'Sam rang me yesterday.'

He understands and nods. 'Juliet sent me an email. She took over the operational stuff while I was at the hospital. Our marketing department spent a whole weekend trying to firefight. But once it was out there . . .' He shrugs helplessly. 'The post was already circulating widely before they saw it, Aly. I realise you lost your account but that didn't slow it down any.'

'What post?'

He frowns. 'Look, I know you weren't deliberately trying to be controversial, but the Black Lives Matter movement is important and can't be appropriated or used flippantly on social media.'

'I have no idea what you are talking about.'

'Your Instagram post. Hashtag. Cat. Lives. Matter. You also tagged KittiFresh.'

I look down at my feet, clad in different colour hi-tops.

I vaguely remember banging something out to thank KittiFresh for the free food with my own take on Black Lives Matter weeks ago. My head was all over the place back then, and I wasn't thinking very clearly. Did I really put up a sponsored post that stated cat lives matter?

'I . . . well, I . . .'

'Coaxed your cat into taking the knee? Why didn't you go the whole hog and spray the damned creature black? That's the only way it could have looked worse. That hashtag has millions watching it around the world. Someone screenshotted it and it's doing the rounds. Pitch 'n' Bitch picked up on it in the last half an hour and dozens of influencers are up in arms. It'll get bigger today. I need to meet with Juliet and Sam to see how we can douse the flames.'

His face is serious, and I get why. Horrified at my actions, I stammer out a weak explanation. 'They sent a crate of luxury food. Every month. For a whole year. And framed pictures of the cats. I needed to repay them somehow. At the time I thought it was a nice gesture and a way of tapping into the zeitgeist. I can totally see now how offensive it was. In fact, I can't believe I did it.'

'It was pet food, Aly. They have crates of it lying around. Also, it was a thank you – you didn't have to repay it. Your actions could cost us dearly. The KittiFresh spend equates to many thousands of pounds for Glimmer over a year. Sam is working his socks off to try and persuade them not to walk. It won't just be KittiFresh either; other pet-related brands may also vote with their feet if they feel Glimmer is tainted by this.'

My insides lurch like Pooh sticks dropped from a bridge.

'But I deleted AlyCat a while back,' I tell him.

'An influencer's reach goes way beyond their account. And yours was huge.'

'But . . .'

He sweeps a hand through his spiked hair. 'But what? The moment you post an image it starts to travel. You have dedicated fans who will share anything you put out there, while competitors will be on standby waiting for you to fail. Just one person screenshots a picture and the damage is done. If you're unlucky, as you were, it has the potential to cross the globe. Sure, you can remove your account but that doesn't stop a badly judged post being shared. Social media is both instant and enduring, you know that. Once something is out there . . .' He pushes his hand through his hair in exasperation. 'How did your account get cancelled anyway? And why didn't you tell me? I could have done something about it. We spent the night together and you didn't think to mention it?'

I open my mouth to justify myself and spin back to that night, the things shared, and his touch on my skin. And I have nothing to say. He sees this and takes the reins again. 'The one value this firm promotes is honesty. I know I bang on about it all the time, but it underpins everything we say and do and all of our relationships. God, I'm a broken record, aren't I?' He stops suddenly, like he has run out of energy. He walks to the window. Looks out over his corner of London. For a moment I forget I'm angry and want to march over and ask him for another chance to be a Blister. I want to take his hands in mine and blow into them to reignite the spark we had. I want to ask if we can go out for a drink and talk about YouTubers from Hackney and Instagrammers from hell. I want to comfort him about his dad's ill health and kiss his tired eyes, the top of his head and his neck and his shoulders. But Cat Lives Matter is a now a massive elephant in the room, stopping me from reaching out. When I look to Molly for guidance about what to do, she vomits over my lap.

'I'll put you in a cab,' Rick says, as I find the number for the vet.

Molly is limp as he wraps her tightly in a towel and pops the empty bag over my shoulder. I offer him a curt thanks before descending to a reception busy with couriers. Stroking her silver coat, I keep an eye on the door, my ears pricked for the cab he ordered. Glancing at the screen above, I take a sharp intake of breath when I catch sight of the company Twitter feed.

'Glimmer is saddened to report our chairman died peacefully in the night. #RIP William H. You will be missed by all.'

# Chapter 27

Hour after hour, I binge watch TV soaps, flicking around the channels to view unhappy people screaming at each other. I constantly check my phone for a call to say Molly is OK. Pinching my hand, I wish I could start the week over again. Milly turns her back on me as if cross that I'm bringing her mood down, and slinks away to sleep under my covers.

I phone Kav for reassurance. She answers from the shop. 'It's a disaster. A living hell,' she says.

'I know.'

'How do you know?'

'Because I'm living it.'

'It's not always about you . . .'

'But in this case it is. Molly's at the vet's. They've put her on a drip. She's really poorly.'

'OK, you win. Was she sick again?'

'All over the backpack. And me and Rick.'

'You saw him then?'

'That part was a bit hellish too.' I knock back a cold coffee that's overloaded with sugar and wince. I'm still suffering from last night's hangover and I wonder if she'd deliver a flat white if I was officially pathetic enough. 'So you gave Manolis your answer. He didn't go for it?'

'He more or less said the same as my dad. Too little too late.'

'That's not a total no.'

'Sounded like it to me.' I can hear the desperation in her voice. 'I'm going to be corned beef, Aly. Left on the shelf forever.'

I glance at the phone and decide it needs a clean. 'I think you need to take a whole page.'

'A whole page of what?'

'When he asked you to marry him, he didn't take a line in the small ads. He took the whole page.' I pull a tissue out of the cardboard box on the floor. 'I'm also corned beef. Rick told me some unpleasant truths. Kav, am I thoughtless and selfish?'

'Sometimes,' she says.

'Will you call me out on it next time?'

'Will you hear it?'

'I'll try.'

'Then yes, I'll call you out.'

'I gotta go. Thanks for being my friend, Kav.'

I ring off and crumble a little.

'So sorry, Alyssa. Molly didn't make it through.' I barely listen to the vet as he talks about kidney failure and tells me he will conduct blood tests to find out what the toxin was but maybe we will never know.

I sit Milly on my knee and gently tell her about her sister, keeping my hands in contact with her skin at all times, stroking her softly and holding her paws in mine.

She looks up at me and narrows her eyes.

*Sleep now. You have done all you can.*

I crumble some more.

I sleep in fits and starts all night. Milly does my head in, trying to get so close at one point she's sitting on my face. Her skin is oily and smells and I think her ears are getting blocked again. Milly is my mini me, stuck like glue, as I sort her out. But she's quiet. I miss their jabbering and mewling. Back in the living room, she brings me toys to cheer me up. On the sofa, she tries to chew on my ear lobes, then settles for my clothes.

I grab my phone. And pick my favourite picture of Molly.

*Be a curious cat*, I type.

*Curiosity killed the cat. Literally. My cat Molly died yesterday. She was outgoing and friendly and stuck her little snub nose into everything. I could have wrapped her in cotton wool, but I felt it was important for her to be part of our glorious, vast, and sometimes disappointing world. So, I made her explore, and even took her out with me in a special cat backpack. She came with me to a conference once, but that one didn't end well so I won't go into the details. Her curiosity to try new things meant a short life, but it was a life lived.*

*As the mummy of hairless cats, it would have been easier for me to lock them away, to keep them protected from the weather, the environment, humans, other animals and any other threat to their sensitive skin. But, like me, my cats were dusted with a need to ask why. Her sister Milly will continue to seek out answers and live her best cat life. And despite everything, I challenge my small and select group of followers to stay curious. Seek out a new friend. Ask a burning question, of yourself or someone else. Explore a new avenue. Try a new food. Accept an invitation. Be a curious cat today.*

I feed Milly and then tell her I have to leave her for an hour or so. I pile all of my worn clothes onto the bed and fetch her favourite toys to make her a little comfort wigwam. I've thought all night about what could have triggered Molly's illness. I'm curious to find out why Greg killed my cat. Curious and furious.

Greg's agency doesn't go for beanbags and comfy sofas but it's a bright, airy office, filled with people being busy. When I tell them I have an appointment, they chase him up. 'He's on his way back from a viewing. He should be with you in ten minutes if you'd like a seat. Feel free to look around if you are in the market for a new property.'

There are no biscuits, but lots of screens to distract me from my loss. I hop on an information hub and browse the life I could have had if I'd bought a winning lottery ticket. When I click away from Hayes and Hillingdon I'm offered a selection of branches from urban Hanwell to the aspirational Chilterns. I type in the Cotswolds to see if Lola's Power Towers pops up with no luck.

Turning away from the screen, I watch Greg park up; a textbook example of how to squeeze a teeny car into a tiny space. He checks his face in the mirror, slides out and slams the car door as I leave the shop. He kisses me on the cheek. 'I wasn't aware we had an appointment so I'm hoping you are here on a spontaneous mission to accept?'

Anger rushes through me. He's killed my cat and he's still talking about a flat?

I think back to all the thrillers I've read. 'Psychopaths always begin their careers by torturing or killing animals,' I blurt, stepping back to prevent a woman mowing me down with a Silver Cross pram.

'Right . . .' he says.

'And your love of horror, that adds up, too.'

'Adds up to what?'

'A dead cat. You want me to share a bed with you? I'm pretty uncomfortable sharing a pavement with you right now.'

'A dead cat,' he repeats, scratching his chin.

There's a pain in my stomach that no one should have to bear and for a moment I wonder if this is what childbirth is like. 'Molly was my daughter, Greg.' I hug my midriff with both arms, as though self-soothing might chase the pain away. 'Or as close to a child as I'll ever get.'

'Was?' He puts his head on one side. 'Aly, has something happened to one of the cats?'

'She's . . .' I can't get the words out. Instead, a big fat teardrop plops onto my wrist. I push it away aware Molly would have licked it off for me. 'I think your onion ring might have caused her death.'

Greg puts his hand on mine and I snatch it away. 'Come inside and I'll make you a cup of tea.'

'You think a quick mug of Tetley will put it right? You killed my cat!'

'Aly,' he says firmly, 'I took the onion ring back and put it in the bin.' I try to choke back the hurt, but I can't, and it spews out as one of Milly's yowls. He grabs my cardigan and moves us aside to let someone leave the estate agent's. I thrash his arm away. 'Why would you think I poisoned your cat?' he asks again, more urgently this time.

'Because you are jealous that I loved her more than you.' I clutch the back of my neck. I am adrift. I realise I have spoken a truth. But it is not his truth. It's not even my truth, not directly.

I start to sob, remembering my despair at being left behind as my dad shipped out with Mardy in his arms, pulling a small suitcase behind him. 'It's OK. Aly, it's OK,' Greg whispers, lifting his hand up to mine, till we are cradling my neck together. A fog of despair flushes through me. When he pulls back and levels his face with mine, it's full of concern. And I realise he doesn't hate my cats. And didn't back then either. He just didn't particularly love them.

He fiddles with the belt of his work trousers, tucking it through a loop. 'I'm sorry, Aly, I liked Molly.'

'You put up with the cats because I liked them.'

He nods. 'My skin always itched like I touched poisoned ivy after I left your mum's house. I'm allergic to cats and dogs. That's why I don't touch or play with them. I was willing to get over it. I *am* willing to get over it, if you let me look after you. I want to look after you, and the cats. What do you want, Aly?' He steps away, as if to observe me more fully. 'What do you want?'

What do I want? Two things occur to me in quick succession.

The executive flat in Slough? That's Greg's dream; he's just filled it with my stuff.

The glittering, shimmering promise of Instagram success? Rick's life. No one is going to shoot me into infinity. If I'm going to make it out of the gutter, I will need to start from scratch. And do it my way not theirs.

'Tell me what you want, and I will make it happen for you.'

I stay silent for a moment, before letting my breath out. 'I don't think anyone else can make it happen for me. And I think I want my mum.'

# Chapter 28

In Japan there's a word for eating non-stop because your mouth is lonely. I eat to quell my sense of isolation. Starting off by dipping spoonfuls of oats in a tin of golden syrup to make my own emergency flapjack, I work my way through the cupboards and the fridge. The low point is my home-made meringue which looks like listeria. I then use the rest of the out-of-date eggs to make egg custard in a mug; my go-to cheerer upper. In a taste test of sweeteners crunched in unbrushed teeth, I decide they all taste like sugary paracetamol as I dump the leftovers into my coffee, mentally wheeling through memories of Molly. I feel her loss like a gash in my arm, and I scratch it at night, so it flares up again each morning.

The vet calls to say toxins showed up in the blood test. He thinks it's unlikely an onion ring would have killed her and asks if she may have been exposed to anything unusual like antifreeze or lilies. I kick myself for not checking the vase at Greg's properly. I couldn't see any lilies, but it doesn't mean they weren't there. She might have nibbled at one when she knocked over the vase, or maybe lapped up some of their water. I brief Milly and she speaks to me of her pain, filling my head and heart with her guttural wail. Next morning, she brings me a mouse. I try not to recoil as she drops it between us on the sofa, without losing eye contact with me. I grab my phone and focus tight on her blue eyes.

*Pain passes. Love remains.*

'It's a good thought but I don't love the remains of a mouse,' I say, pulling up Instagram.

*How to be your best cat self? Be a busy cat*, I write.

*There's a school of thinking that cats are selfish, unempathetic, that emotions and sympathy are the domain of the dog. My cat does grief. In phases. Short and sharp. And sometimes for me. A wail, a lost circle of the room, a sleepless night. But what does she do when the grief really sets in? She goes to work. She brings me gifts, of a Slinky, or a ball of wool. She explores the room, hunting for items of interest. She plays ping-pong incessantly and practises other tricks too. Milly has moved her bed twice since her sister died and is currently sleeping in the bottom of my wardrobe, making a nest on Molly's favourite combat jacket. She goes prowling at night, as though insomnia has set in, and sleeps heavily all morning, with a crazy hour at lunch. She does not mope. She works.*

*And I work too. I swap observations late into the night with you guys. I send emails. I scour the small ads. Milly and I get busy together.*

A shroud of grief dulls into a grey blanket I wear around me. Sometimes I enjoy pulling it tight, wallowing in my situation, and at other times I loosen it to give myself more breathing space. At the worst times, I feel I didn't just lose a cat, but a romance, a career, an alternative life. Milly is hardly eating and I miss her purring for food.

I'll stay with Kav for a little while until I get on my feet, but I really need that deposit now, whether it's for a house to rent or buy. I phone Thing One, although it could be Thing Two, and talk about getting my job back. I put the phone down and ache for Rick to ring without knowing what I'd say to him if he did. And then an unknown caller flashes up. I answer it in case it's work.

'Aly, it's Lola.'

'Oh hey, how are you? I've been meaning to call to apologise for that incident outside your house a while back.'

She chuckles and reassures me she didn't hold me responsible for Rick's behaviour. 'He's a big boy. Too big for his own boots sometimes.'

'He does literally have very big shoes.'

'Enormous. They were giant's feet next to mine. I can still fit into children's shoes.'

'So can I!' I exclaim.

'We have quite a lot in common,' she says. 'In fact, that's why I'm ringing. I wondered if you'd consider running my social media channels. The girl who was doing it has quit without giving me any notice. You'd rock the cat stuff and I have an intuition you'd be good at communicating my other passions too and selling them to others. I need someone straightaway.'

'Oh thanks, that's really kind of you, but I'm not sure I'll be—'

She interrupts. 'If you are about to finish that sentence

with "good enough" then you will demonstrate that I have taught you nothing and I will have to throw in the towel and open a cat café.'

'Ooh, that sounds like fun. Actually I was going to say "free". Not immediately anyway. I have to move house this week.'

'It wouldn't be full time, you can squeeze it around other things. And we could start with a couple of hours a week if you like and see how it goes?'

I pack up my flat. We are all resigned to going, but have planned a collective action before we leave – an animal art safari. Henry put himself in charge. He visited every flat to assess the space and how many people he can fit on each guided tour. We all spent days leaflet bombing the high street (with publicity designed by Suze the Silk), and Joy put an advert in the local paper and shops. TCP went on a mission to recreate a new artwork on the side of our building. At eight o'clock this morning she came banging on my door and led me out.

Her mural, on the side of the warehouse, is breathtaking. Using the Sistine Chapel fresco for inspiration, she has recreated the famous scene with God and Adam. The flowing robes are familiar but instead of the Great Creator's face, Molly's head appears, her paws reaching out to Milly. It's surreal and beautiful and instead of clawing at the Molly-shaped gash, it fuses my skin a little.

The first tour goes off on time. A family with a child in a toy car arrives in my apartment fresh from their meet-up with Suze the Silk, and before that Joy, with her miniature home of Hampton Court for a hamster, complete with adjoining maze made from strips of bonsai tree.

'She tries to source the same wallpaper and fabrics. It's so authentic,' says the mother, lifting the child out of the battery-powered car to pet Milly.

'So is the price,' laughs her husband.

I thought long and hard about what my art would be for the tour. I have hundreds of little cat costumes that might have made a display but discounted it as my USP is the cats not my sewing. I mounted the framed pictures of the KittiFresh campaign onto the walls of my flat and chuckled at how cute the cats were in their office and plumber outfits. But as I stood back and looked at them, something didn't feel quite right. Milly would never expect me to dress as a cat. So, I pulled out some pictures I'd taken of my cats way back, when I was thinking of applying for an art course at uni. They are natural, wholesome and themselves. They are cats being cats. I feel sad for Molly and then feel happy for myself and Milly as the family buys the lot. They've also bought two pairs of yak gloves from Karen and I tell them to watch out for their faces swelling up if any of them have allergies.

On his next tour, Henry leads around four pensioners and a man in a Christmas jumper. Afterwards, we all retreat outside. As the old people go on about Joy's hutches, Dodgy Jumper sidles up to me and I realise I've seen his high forehead and extra wide smile somewhere before.

'Logan Josh,' he says, holding out his hand for me to shake. 'I believe you are AlyCat. Thought I'd persuade my wife to do the Saturday morning footie run while I checked out your tours. And my investment. Anyway, thanks for your letter, or rather letters . . .'

'And emails and DMs . . .' I grimace and a smile creeps across his face.

'You were a rather enthusiastic warrior.'

'More an angry worrier.'

'It might have escalated into shouty capitals if I'd replied. I loved the tour by the way. Extremely charming, although some of the female artists could smile occasionally.'

'Joy's badly named.'

'The graffiti artist was good craic though and her mural is stunning.' His Irish accent is unmistakable.

'You don't look like a TV chef?'

'You don't look like a catstagrammer. Is that what you call yourself?'

'Catfluencer. And I'm not sure I am one anymore.'

'That's a shame. The world needs more cats to make fun of politicians.' There's an awkward silence which he fills. 'So, your letter – letters – asking me to think again on the bird farm and sublet the building to you and your colleagues as an art collective and safari? I need to put a few facts straight. You seem to be under the illusion we will be keeping live animals here? You mentioned a penguin enclosure at one point. Much as I love the fluffy things at Belfast Zoo, I don't plan to recreate it. We're all about eggs. This site will become a food-processing plant, not a battery farm. I've chosen it for its proximity to Heathrow. We'll be importing eggs, storing them, and then cooking them up and sending them into the air. Go-Go Air has provided joint funding and I'll be the face of the business, but I will have a team of people basically using this place as a kitchen. The only fully grown animal within a mile of here will be my greyhound.'

'But I heard . . .'

'You heard wrong I'm afraid. No peacocks strutting about in the car park or quails cooped up in cages. All our eggs will be free range and of the highest quality. And as for a permanent artists' collective, I'm sorry but there won't be room for any of you to work here once I take over. I will have a small office on site, but the rest of the space will be given over to cooking, packaging, storage and delivery. I could offer you a job if you want one?'

I look around for Milly to hold as a prop, as I'm feeling exposed. 'I'm not sure where the rumours came from.' I cast a glance at TCP as she swings out of the door with a sandwich in her hand.

'It's normal for stories to spread. It's perfectly natural for locals to object; that's why the world has planning committees. I hear you've all been on a cheap deal here, so I'm not surprised you're worried and inconvenienced. But having said all that, I need you out. I've been as flexible as I can. My wife follows you on Instagram by the way, has done for years. I'm more of a dog person but she shows me your posts. They're clever.'

'I started a new channel. About how we can listen to our cats to become better humans.'

He sighs. 'I prefer the company of my dog sometimes to my family, friends and entire production team. And now I'm going to take mine for a walk.'

'You do know it's not Christmas?' I shout after him, pointing at his jumper.

'I thought it might be before you lot moved out.'

The Oddities and I gather in the car park with a bottle of fizz to toast our final days and our first and last venture together.

'TCP says Logan Josh was here?'

'He's not going to be farming emus or penguins, so we have no grounds to protest about crimes to nature. We can't call him out for poaching an unusual egg on a plane,' I tell Suze.

A white van trundles into the car park and pulls up next to us.

'Boyfriend's here,' says Henry.

'He's not my boyfriend.' I say, causing TCP to raise her eyebrows as she swings back into the warehouse.

Greg steps out of the van and opens the doors at the rear. 'Loving the mural. How you all doing? I was helping with an office move, so I thought it would be a good chance to return your boxes, Aly. Sorry if they're randomly packed; I did try and keep all the blob lamps together.'

'I think Molly probably died from eating a lily,' I tell him, as we carry the boxes into my flat. 'I'm sorry for accusing you of poisoning her. Although you did buy the lilies.'

I feel sad that our friendship is over as we share a last cup of tea. I open a box marked 'trinkets' and lift out a set of small wooden carvings appropriate for a day focused on an art safari. 'Do you like elephants?'

'They're about the only animal that doesn't make me sneeze,' he says. Then he takes my hands. 'Move in with me, Aly. Take some time out to work out what you really want.'

'Greg, that ship . . .'

'. . . is only just launching. There's a cabin on it for you. Otherwise, you'll drift on until you have no other option and what then? Who will rescue you?'

'I don't need rescuing.' I take my hands back.

'You do. It's not a ship but a life raft. Grab it. Stay with me, be with me, marry me if you like.'

The 'M' word is casually dropped in. My reply is firmer. 'I'm sorry, but I can't.'

'Is it about the lilies?' He picks at some duct tape on a box we've just moved back into the room.

I go further and rip the tape away. 'We're not compatible, Greg. You were sweet. You were my friend when I had none. And you've been my friend recently. But the spark? It wasn't there, not for me.'

I pick up the carved wooden elephants and place them in his hands. 'They're lucky,' I tell him. 'Put them in the north part of your flat for career prospects. Or south for wealth. East will herald love. West brings order to chaos.'

He looks them over. 'Really?'

I smile. There's no way this man has lost his belief in elves.

When he leaves, it feels good to have given something away. I sit on the floor with Milly on my lap and unpack my life, gift by gift. And make a list of who I will re-gift each object to. Then we sit together for hours, Milly and I, observing each other. She puts her head on the rug and

I put mine next to her. Her eyes are wells of icy empathy. They hold mine for whole minutes before she blinks slowly. I blink back a butterfly kiss and we do this human-to-cat Morse code for a while. And when I find I'm blinking tears, she holds my gaze, allowing me to grieve for my companion, her sister, and tells me not to do that anymore.

*We do not let death stop us living. Life is the greatest gift.*

I turn up at Kav's with the paper boys and dump a selection of bowls onto the counter.

'We talked about a grand gesture. Why not give Manolis what he's always wanted?'

'He used to want me,' she says sadly, twiddling with the diamond in her nose, and my heart goes out to her.

'It still is you, I'm sure of it. But you've always said he wanted what he had in Athens.'

'A shrine to his mother?'

'Exactly. A Greek shop and deli on the Uxbridge Road. Something different to the norm. Not just a corner shop but a destination. Let's paint it white. Take out some of the shelves; perhaps install an island in the middle. You can cook up Greek food to sell outside. Stock the best olives, feta, honey, couscous. You can offer hampers maybe? Cook takeout meals for office workers coming home.' I am talking so fast even I'm struggling to keep up with me. Kav rests her arm on the counter as her eyes sweep the room. It's a mad plan. But sometimes you need to go big when it's all gone down. I push through her hesitation. 'Maybe when the neighbourhood is fed up with moussaka you could make it a rolling cultural feast? Kav's Kultural Kuisine? Like the Faraway Tree – a different island every year. I reckon your mother might help – it could be a way of reeling her back in.'

'Enid Blyton is a goddess.' Kav picks up one of the bowls I brought her.

'I'm re-gifting all my mum's stuff. I thought you could use them for the olives.'

She smashes it on the floor.

'OK so it was just an idea—'

'Do you know why Greek people chuck plates around at weddings?' she interrupts me. 'It signifies the couple throwing away their old life and starting a new one together. It is also a symbolic act to keep evil spirits away; making them think the couple is bickering and angry, instead of being in love and celebrating the union.' She leads me to the food preparation area and points to a shelf stuffed with bowls, plates and Tupperware. 'Look at all this. I've hardly used any and you've brought me more. Every day we will smash one of these plates or bowls until he returns. And we will destroy the final plate when he agrees to marry me, after we've transformed the shop. After that, I promise Manolis and I will never bicker again.'

'OK, but you will always bicker. And I think you'll need to separate out the Tupperware. The whole point of it is to haunt a married couple forever.'

# Chapter 29

I visit my old ladies bearing gifts. Marie is delighted with her coffee pot. Eileen loves the avocado spoons. I also re-gift a hat that doubles as an umbrella, and a pair of comfortable slippers. My phone rings as I walk purposefully up the driveway of a house I know better than any other. I recognise Rick's number but let it go.

My childhood home is an oddly located building, on the corner of two busy streets. The traffic noise is overwhelming in both the front and back garden. The house is triangle shaped, with stairs going up the centre of three floors. I used to have the sensation I was living on a ship; and dreamed the dips in traffic noise were the waves. The front garden is filled with overgrown evergreen bushes and blue ceramic pots that have faded with time. Plants gasp for water. A layer of grime coats the windows through off-white blinds that are half closed, like the house is preparing for sleep.

The front door clearly hasn't been used in a while. It still has a sign bearing my dad's name above the knocker. Or rather half of his name and half of hers: 'Jenniron'. I used to feel aggrieved they didn't include mine. Another sign says to use the back door.

I've dreamed of many barriers to entry over the years, but it's easy in the end to lift the latch, and walk in. The back porch is piled high with magazines, faded cookery books and newspapers.

'I wondered when you'd be back,' my mother says, as though I walked out yesterday. With very few words, she squashes six years into a ball and tosses it at me. I drop it. I was never good at her kind of sport. 'I suppose you want a cup of tea?'

'Shall I put the kettle on?'

'Well, I believe you know where it is.'

The kitchen floor is sticky. Used tea bags fill the sink in a large pyramid, most of them dried up like old skin. Dirty cups mingle with glasses and plates, and there are enough plastic containers to fill a skip. Tins of soup have been opened and the lids scattered along with dozens of milk bottle tops. A chicken carcass sits on the breadboard with the remains of toast and marmalade. Used tissues fill an overloaded bin.

It's much worse than when I lived here, but now I remember signs she wasn't coping. The bin that was never emptied; the dishes that were never washed. It's ironic really – she was a pastoral care head who didn't look after me, and I went on to become a carer who didn't visit my own mother.

Well, I've learnt how to do it now, sometimes for the most ungrateful people. I put on the lights and grab a black bin bag. Throwing any thoughts of recycling out of the window, I gather up the newspapers, plastic and tins. Popping into the loo, I try not to look into the bowl as I scoop up a bottle of bleach. I find gloves under the sink.

And I do what I've been trained to do.

Three times I put the kettle on before being distracted by another pile to be disposed of or another surface needing bleach. In places the counter is so engrained with grease I take a knife to it. I cannot find a single tea towel in a drawer or in the washing machine, despite the fact she's sent me enough of them for the kitchen of a stately home. I'm surprised to see there are also no fancy pans, egg poachers, timers, teacups, sieves or electronic whisks.

Once cleared of dirty dishes and rubbish, the surface is bare, like most of the cupboards. She was never one for food shopping.

'Did you go to China for the tea?' she says as I make my way back in with two freshly scrubbed mugs.

'I hope you still like it strong.' Strong enough to dye the inside of the cups brown.

She takes a sip and winces. She opens the lid of a bowl beside her which is a clog of wet sugar and spoons it in. That's your DNA coffee right there, I think, as I do the same with my own. Her nails have a smattering of scuffed polish on them whereas they used to be immaculate. Her hair is a yellowing blonde, probably a home-care kit as her roots are scrappy and uneven. She's probably not much older than Lola but looks raddled.

Her voice is the same as it was in my head, slightly sharp, with the burr of a West Country accent. 'Still biting your nails?' Now we're getting back to the mother I know.

*Watch and listen. We keep silent until we are ready to reveal ourselves.*

'So what do you want?'

She's so direct, I burst out laughing. 'Greg asked me

the same thing the other day. Remember Greg? He used to come here.'

'The boyfriend with the tight trousers.'

'That's the one.'

'And what did you tell him?'

I pause. What would Milly tell her? She'd do the same as Yoda, and Rick and all the great truth-tellers that my life is riddled with. 'I told him I want my mum.'

'Sit down,' she tells me. 'If you can find a space.' I clear a stack of *Hello!* magazines and a pile of recipe books that have never been used.

We chat about my life, my job and my impending eviction. She asks where I will go. I take a deep breath. The next moment could define whether I'll be spending winter in a sleeping bag in Uxbridge shopping centre or keeping warm in my old single bed beyond a couple of weeks at Kav's.

*You are defined by your future, not your past.*

'Oh don't worry, I'll find somewhere else,' I discover myself saying.

'You still make your own clothes I see. My fault for buying you that sewing machine.' And I remember, in a rush of nostalgia, a toy version at Christmas. A little blue plastic gadget, with a detachable lead and pedal. I can still hear the pitch of its whirr. It was her first ever gift that I remember. I never thanked her for the one that changed my life.

'Mum, I've been re-gifting some of your presents. There were too many for my small flat. And there's only so many toasters a girl can use, although I am going to officially hoard lava lamps for the rest of my life. I've given hair straighteners to a client of mine who has a longer fringe than a Highland cow and I've passed on the cappuccino maker to an old lady who used to love a good coffee but can't get out anymore.'

She looks up, surprised. 'I don't remember buying a cappuccino maker. But that's nice of you. A gift can make people happy.'

'Why don't you have a coffee maker?' I ask her. 'There are no face creams or collagen supplements in your downstairs toilet. And I'm guessing no robot hoover in your bedroom, and there definitely isn't a self-winding hose in the garden.'

'I didn't buy them for myself.'

'Then why did you buy them for me?'

'To say thank you,' she says, looking at me as though it must be obvious. 'For keeping me company. For putting up with me.' And I remember again, as I whizzed the pedal of that sewing machine, and watched the plastic needle clatter in and out of pretend material, how horrid the atmosphere was when my father lived here, before his abrupt disappearance. Perhaps she is remembering it too. 'They were also to say sorry, for being angry. I was very angry.'

'And after I'd gone?'

'I thought they might remind you I was still your mum.'

The tea is cold and it's starting to rain outside. I've been here way longer than I intended.

'I brought you this,' I say, placing a photograph of Milly and Molly in a tiny frame beside her.

She picks it up and her face lights up in a way I don't remember. 'You liked them?'

'I loved them. I still love them.' I don't tell her about Molly – that's for another time. 'I should have called you and said thank you. I don't know why I didn't. They're the best things in my life by far. They must have cost you a fortune.'

'A few hundred pounds each. If they were show cats they'd have cost thousands. But I got a good deal. I wanted you to have company. I know you were lonely when he took Mardy. I wasn't much company. I drove you away.'

'No, I was ready to move on,' I say. 'Why did you choose hairless cats, Mum? It's really unusual to own a Sphynx, let alone two of them.'

'Because I was sick to death of arguing with you about hair,' she says, standing up and hugging me tightly. 'Thank you for the photo and the frame. No one has given me a present for a very long time.'

'I'll bring another,' I say. 'Next time I visit. I have one or two things in my flat that I think you might like.'

'That would be grand. And, Aly? I was wrong about the straighteners. Your hair is glorious with a bit of curl.'

'Olive oil. Because I'm worth it.' I smile at my own joke as I softly close the door, genuinely believing I am worth something after all.

# Chapter 30

I'm living at Kav's while we convert the shop. After persuading another mini mart owner to buy some of the goods, and storing the rest upstairs for now, we strip the shop back to basics. With the help of more practical customers who have been roped in, Kav's Kozy Korner becomes quickly transformed with white panelled walls and glass shelves mounted on silver brackets.

'Manolis will need to manage the shop at first while I get my recipes straight for mezze hour,' Kav says, more confident each day that she can attract him back with our bold initiative. She confides she wrote to his mother, shared her plan, asked her not to spoil the surprise and begged for family recipes. 'You wouldn't believe her secret ingredient for Greek salad – capers! Apparently, they're big in the Dodecanese. And she says I should add some ouzo. No Greek son can resist aniseed breath apparently. Good to know.' I enjoy her chirpy conversation as she prepares savoury and sweet tray bakes in batches for freezing. She has let all the paper boys go. 'They were all hopeless anyway. The only boy who delivered them properly was my hu—my Manolis.' I help her make the invites for a grand launch. 'I will text Manolis his at the last moment so he cannot come here and sabotage our future,' she adds.

I drop in to see Thing One and Thing Two. 'I'm guessing the Cat in the Hat is either in Hull or the Caribbean,' I say.

'She's just outside actually. I can see her car,' Thing One replies, although it could be Thing Two; they've both shaved their hair off and pierced an eyebrow.

My boss is a cross between Hagrid and the Honey Monster. She has no idea who I am. I tell her I was a carer who couldn't afford to keep working for her at such a low wage.

She tuts at me. 'It's this industry. The profit margins are low. Everyone complains, but I can't put the fees up as people are already paying thirty pounds an hour for their visits. The office staff seem to eat the stationery. It's crippling,' she says as she locks the driver's door of a convertible Mercedes. 'But of course, all disgruntled carers are free to go elsewhere. As you did yourself.'

Before leaving, I reach into my handbag and re-gift Thing One a supersized pack of Post-it notes I discovered in a box a few days ago. She tosses them to Thing Two. 'She's your woman. I don't like the taste of them,' she laughs in her high-pitched tinkle. 'Would you like to join us for a bite to eat later at Nando's?'

'I'd love to.'

Lola and I have coffee in central London as the Kozy Korner is out of action. I can't stay long as Milly doesn't like being on her own, although she's enjoying Kav's company and continually finds little nooks and crannies to hide in.

'Sorry I'm late.' Lola rushes in looking as glamorous as usual. 'I had to do a Zoom "dominar" before leaving

Gloucestershire. Some of these women need a firm hand. If you agree to get on your knees in front of your boss for a basic conversation about a pay rise, you should at least have your hard limits in mind. And that includes a plan for grabbing and twisting his balls if he tries to half inch your holiday entitlement. How are you, Aly? I'm still enjoying your Instagram posts.'

'I nicked the idea off you for that whole feed.'

'Ideas are free but if you direct quote me please mention my website. How is my website going by the way?'

'The new blog is doing well. I'll show you the analytics in a moment. Instagram Stories is really taking off with those "womanars" and you'll have noticed an uptick on Twitter.'

'I've noticed it in the bookings. But I have a problem. Or I'm happy to say we have a problem. I'm being evicted too,' she says. 'I've had cheap rent on Power Towers through a friend for the last five years but he's sold up. Any chance you can come back to Gloucestershire with me today? I've an idea for a new centre for the business that might benefit us both. It involves Rick's house. Or rather Bill's house in the Cotswolds that Rick's inherited and put up for sale. I'd like you to look around it with me.'

# Chapter 31

'Are you planning to have kids? There's enough land for baseball, basketball and tennis courts.' The overconfident estate agent in an equally loud checked grey suit has assumed we are partners and is trying not to be fazed.

'I have one already,' I reply. 'She likes to sleep under the bed and chew my slippers.'

He moves quickly on. 'Take a look at the original cornicing, which of course can be removed if you want a more modern look. And the fireplace is rhyolite. The current owner had an idyllic childhood here.' I nod but am clearly not impressed enough so he takes another tack. 'Properties of this size and quality are hard to come by.' He pulls out a set of keys, unlocks the French doors and steps into a sculpted landscape I recognise. 'The gardens were designed by Capability Brown, and diligently attended to by the family.'

Tosser may have planted a lot of seeds, but I'd be willing to bet none of them were in a garden. 'Oh, I'm a big Capability Brown fan. I loved her last season on *Strictly*,' I say as we join him outside. Lola's mouth twinges as she stifles a laugh.

'Shall we wander down to the lake?' He leads the way, holding up the property details and clucking like a hen. Lola pulls a red woollen cardigan around her tight black

T-shirt. The clouds have been threatening to open since we arrived.

She steers me away from him to look at the greenery and contradicts his rosy view of Rick's past. 'It wasn't an idyllic childhood. No boy ever gets over losing his mother. Shoving him away to boarding school, Bill would have left him to fend for himself in the holidays too if it wasn't against the law. To extend his freedom from responsibility, he asked me to stand in as Rick's mother, or wicked stepmother or whatever you like to call it. Rick obviously used the latter phrase when he found out I was on a retainer for it. I was out of my depth. I was working as an escort when Bill made me his offer, and jumped at the chance of regular work and a monthly wage. I'd been a sympathetic ear and he thought Rick might bond with me too. It was fun; we made quite a good family when Bill wasn't knocking back the whisky. He became a bore as his career went on but at the time he was sharp-witted and amusing, just like his son was turning out to be. When Rick called me "Mum" now and then I didn't object. I didn't have kids of my own and it seemed a natural extension of what we'd created. But I had a mutually beneficial arrangement with the head of governors at Rick's school. We were indiscreet and his wife found out. It blew up at a rugby match with Rick rushing to defend me, shouting that his mum would never cheat on his dad. He was humiliated in front of the school and visiting sports team when it all came out about my role in that community, and then he was humiliated in private when I questioned whether he really believed I was his mum.'

'Did he?'

'Well, he said he didn't, but there were telltale signs, like his death grip on his rugby bag. I think all his life he has blamed me for lying to him and for taking his dad's money to look after him. The truth was, I did feel like his mum, and I'd probably have married Bill if he'd asked me. He never did; he settled for being wed to his career and the bottle instead. But we stayed good friends. I was gutted when he died.'

We return to the house. The dining room is exactly as it was when Rick and I toured it; still furnished and poised to collect dust. Lola admires the cornicing loudly, then lowers her voice. 'I tried to make up with Rick, many times, including the night of the Showcase awards and I've phoned him several times since Bill died. He won't hear me out. And here's the thing. When I first heard my lease on Power Towers might be under threat, Bill offered to let me use his home instead. He also backed me with some capital. I know Rick wants to sell but I have a really good idea for a business, and I want you to come in on it. I was hoping you would ask him to reconsider selling the house and let us run a rescue centre from here. A luxury cat-centred retreat for overwhelmed humans.'

'Us?'

'You and me. My cat classes are going great guns and you understand social media. I think you'd be an asset. We can run all the other stuff online. I have too many empowermentors on my books now to get them all in a room together and clients are coming from all over the world. So, I wondered if there's any chance you can talk to

Rick before he leaves? He won't accept the business plan from me.' She reaches into her bag and pulls out two files.

'Rick is leaving? Where's he going?'

'Glimmer is relocating to the US. Bill's PA told me. He left all his shares to an American. She makes the decisions now.'

The estate agent herds us into the centre of the room. 'And this is the kitchen; the hub of home and hearth.'

Reminded once again of William's words to me at the dinner, I look down at the floorboards and under the table I spot a small trap door.

'There's a time capsule in there,' says Lola, following my eyes. 'Or there was. We put it together at the millennium. Shortly before it all went pear-shaped. Let's take a look, shall we?' She crawls under the table and lifts a tiny black handle on the yellowing square. Inside there's a cheap plywood lining, and a glass tube.

'Not the dirty secrets he promised?' I murmur.

She looks up at me and smiles. 'Bill was drunk and shouting his mouth off at the Showcase dinner. He keeps the real dirt in his safe like everyone else.'

Lola fishes out the tube and explains that she used to live here, to the astonishment of the estate agent, who is all over the time capsule. She tells him we'll visit the bathroom while he reads it, then leading me into the dining room, she opens a minibar. Except it's not a bar. She taps in a code. 'Rick's birthday. It's not going to challenge an intelligent burglar.'

The safe beeps and opens, revealing a pile of pen drives and papers. She rifles through them, and pockets one with her name on. 'Bill liked to film some of our fun. I'll dispose of that. You want Rick to stick around? Your best bet is to look for files on his rival.' She stuffs the rest of the safe's contents into my yellow backpack and slams it shut. 'Let's get out of here, but think about what I said, won't you? We both want the same thing – to have a decent career and to be able to love Rick. But it wouldn't hurt to do those things from here, would it?'

# Chapter 32

At midday I rise, still tired, although aware Kav's put in the lion's share of a shift already. I feed Milly some kibble and make myself a cup of tea. She stands on my shoulder, crunching, as I slot the pen drives into my laptop, one after the other. I don't even need to ask her if she would do the same. I'm pretty sure the ghost of William H. Harvard will not be coming to ask for his past back so we might as well use it to our advantage.

By mid-afternoon I know the secrets of a whole bunch of the world's Blisters as well as a few people so low down on the Clister list I've never heard of them. There are random files containing NDAs, tax returns and other compromising stuff. I use my phone to magnify the lettering on each pen drive as it's so small, and know I've found gold when I see the word 'Succession'. His father was a kingmaker. Is it in my power to destroy the queen? I hold my breath and push the drive into my laptop.

Juliet's name heads up a number of files. There's an HR-related complaint into bullying, plus a report into meetings with a competing agency. And a voice file with a heavy conversation about stocks and promotion in exchange for favours I don't want to think about.

'William and Juliet. Ugh. Poor Rick.'

I save the content onto my laptop, and then play with

Milly for an hour or so. She's lonely without her sister and very clingy. Last night she nibbled at my ear lobe and tugged at my hair before trying to sleep on my face again. At least I'd given her a bath and cleaned out her ears the day before.

Kav rings. 'Are you coming down?'

'Soon. The party doesn't start till eight.'

'Clawing back my husband will need a lot of lippie. I need you to hold the fort while I get ready.'

Manolis is due at seven, with the rest of the invited guests coming an hour later. He turns up at a quarter to. Everything about him is trimmer, including his beard. He stands motionless at the door, eyes wide. Then he scratches his chin.

'You did this?'

'No, you fool, I don't want to marry you. I'm just here for backup. I'll text Kav and tell her you're here.'

All the tension leaves her body at the sight of him. He holds his palms out and she flies into his arms.

The opening is a triumph. Almost all the food disappears, the till rings all night and the atmosphere is so great I find myself bonding with the reporter from the *Hillingdon Star*, although I pop garlic olives into the pocket of his suit jacket for later. At midnight the stragglers smash crockery and I worry the floor might not withstand the force of hoodwinking all those evil spirits. My phone battery runs out, so I don't get to record the moment when Kavita opens my re-gift and finds a set of silicon spatulas. As I think about leaving, she is gazing into the eyes of her 'idiot husband-to-be', while feeding him defrosted samosa pinwheels blessed by her mother.

TCP turns up to the party late, wearing a head torch as she's camping in a local field.

'Amazing news,' she says, while blinding me with her flash.

'Kav's done a good job, hasn't she?'

'Not the shop. The warehouse. I met your boyfriend in the street, and he told me your other boyfriend has bought it. Can you ask him if we can get back in as I haven't had a shower in ages?' She awkwardly leans forward and hugs me, smelling of bubble gum and turps. 'You are a top influencer, Aly. I will never tell anyone your account sucks again.'

# Chapter 33

Milly is now happily settled into Kav's flat. But I need to move on again as Manolis wants to move back in. Tomorrow I have an appointment to view a tiny rental flat above a closed-down takeaway on the main road. Milly looks down at me from her new fave lounging area on the top shelf of Kav's dresser and I wonder how she will cope with more change.

'Hmm, now you're stuffed, aren't you, MillyCat?' I watch her measuring the distance, calculating the risk. Despite Milly's agile frame, it's quite a leap and I wonder if she will be brave enough to try. She sits and licks her paws. Then she stands, hind legs tense, front legs stretched, watchful, waiting. She twitches her nose as though seeking out a mouse. She shifts her weight. And fixes her eyes on mine.

'Don't do it,' I whisper. 'It's too high, you'll break a leg.' But something inside me wants her to try. Even if she fails, at least she gave it a go. What's the alternative? Sitting in a princess tower with the stairs removed?

With no warning, she jumps. She lands easily, with a thump, and strolls over to a ball of wool. Deftly tangling the red thread in her paws, she performs a comedy fall onto her back, reminding me of Molly's antics. I laugh and take a picture. Then I spool through the photographs of my cat on top of the dresser, eyes sharp, ears pricked, totally in the moment. And I realise she never planned to do anything else. She was simply calculating the best time to leap.

*Be a self-assured cat*, I instruct my followers as I share the image with them.

> *But do not confuse being self-assured for being brave. Superheroes are brave, they take risks, leap between buildings, take on impossible tasks. Cats do not take unnecessary risks. They calculate their abilities, their timing, their chances of survival. In a burning building your cat would only save itself. This is not being brave. And, more illogically, it is not being a coward. A cat knows its self-worth. And considers itself worthy of saving. If everything is on fire around you, know that you are valuable. Gather yourself, get out of there and don't look back. And then go on and save the world.*

I post it, with a touched-up picture of the moment before the leap. Then I make a late lunch and fail to eat it as thinking is taking all my concentration. I weigh up going to see Rick and talking to him about what I found in the safe or letting sleeping dogs lie. And what about Lola's suggestion? Her business plan is sound, as far as I can tell, but Rick and I are over and I have no sway over what investments he makes, even if he has come into a lot of money. Also, he's already invested in one of my former homes, even though I don't want it and don't plan to go back there. He hates Lola. And he's going to America. In fact, he may already have left.

As another afternoon threatens to steal away from me, I look in my cat's eyes. Milly places a paw on my hand and then flies into a corner and returns dragging the cat backpack.

'Where did you find that? I'm not taking you with me, pretty kitty – I learnt from my mistakes. But I think I might chance my arm.' Dropping Milly in with Kav to keep mice away from the storeroom, I tuck an envelope and two files Lola gave me into my bag and head onto the high street.

One bus sails past me and the next terminates at my stop. I hum the song about the old woman who swallowed a fly – 'She needed the bus to get to the Tube, she needed the Tube to get to his desk, she needed his desk to . . .' I stop myself imagining what we might once have done on one of his office tables – hot-desking wouldn't have begun describing it.

The sky is overcast by the time I reach the city and there's a steady flow of workers leaving Glimmer. As expected, the receptionists aren't keen to let me up without an invite. Thinking back to my last conversations with Rick, his disappointment at the #catlivesmatter hashtag fiasco and his fury at Lola, I almost lose my nerve, but then I remind myself he bought my building and has been phoning me on and off for weeks. He also gifted me something else along with the warehouse. Hope.

He answers his phone with a single word. 'Aly.'

My heart lurches. 'I'm in reception. I need to see you. I have information.' I sound like an FBI informant.

'I'm due at a drinks party and then I have a car booked. What kind of information?' He's stiff and formal too and I'm lost.

'It's not for sharing with randoms, perched on upcycled buckets. Can you please come down and collect me?'

Sam glides through the revolving doors, pass ready to flash at the lift. He breaks into a smile when he sees me. 'Aly, I was going to ring you later. I read about your new account. Well done on being featured on Pitch 'n' Bitch as their Instagrammer of the week.' The lift doors open. Rick is back to his shiny-looking self, from his clean-shaven jawline to his polished belt buckle. He walks towards us with his easy, confident stride. Sam nods to Rick and raises his hand. I follow Sam's lead and lift mine. Rick nods back and also lifts his. We look like the Lucky Cats in Chinatown windows. A raised right paw is said to bring wealth and prosperity. I reckon Rick was born with his paw in the air.

'The new feed is great, and your follower number has soared,' Sam continues.

I turn back to Sam. 'I think that's overstating it.' A thousand followers is nothing compared to what AlyCat attracted at its peak.

He turns to Rick. 'Logan Josh is Britain's hottest chef right now and he's reposting Aly regularly. Her follower count is rocketing.'

'I'm familiar with Logan Josh,' Rick says, without giving away anything more. I turn to him, ignoring the batter of my heart in my ribcage and tell him I was sorry to hear about his dad.

Sam fills the silence. 'Well, I'd best be off. It's the biggest drinks trolley in the history of Glimmer with so many people leaving. Don't want to miss it. Stay in touch, yeah?'

Leaving drinks. It's clear I have one shot at this. Greg and my mum asked what I want. Milly asks it every day with a look and a blink. I know what I want now, but it's going to take a hell of an elevator pitch. 'Can we go somewhere quieter?'

Rick accompanies me into the lift. We stand at opposite sides and our eyes meet in the mirror. 'So, how's the competitive and crowded Instaverse?' he says. I recognise the phrase I used months ago in this very lift.

'What's an Instaverse?'

'The universe of Instagram, I believe.'

It feels so long ago and yet just a moment. Like looking at a star and realising you are viewing the past. 'I was a shooting star. I crashed out of that universe pretty quickly. It was a relief to be honest. Waiting for it to happen was excruciating. I think that's why I deleted my own account.'

'Look, I overreacted. About #catlivesmatter. We kept the KittiFresh contract. Your hashtag didn't break the internet.'

'Stop. I'm mortified about that post and I fully own that terrible decision. It was crass and misjudged. I wanted to repay KittiFresh for taking a chance on me but didn't feel I was worth the crate of cat food they sent. My cats taught me that I am. And Milly has helped me reunite with my mum and start to get over my phobia of gifts.'

'We have reached the tenth floor,' the newsreader interjects.

We enter the office I reported to the day I first met Rick. The skyline is still as sexy, while the guy in the room is off the scale. I sneak a peek at his face and decide his eyebrows are not commas; they're wings.

'We changed the whole firm to a hot-desking model, but no one ever used this room,' he says. 'And most people drifted back to where they were before. It's like they were conditioned to stay in their boxes.'

'I know what that's like,' I say. 'It's comfortable to remain where you are. Change is hard.'

'I expect you're here about the warehouse. I also imagine you are furious. Hear me out for a moment?'

'It's a no to both, actually, but I'm happy to hear what you have to say.' The wings dip; I've surprised him.

'It's not a gift. It's an investment for me, and a loan for you. I'm a rich man and want to . . .' He throws up his hands, like he can't find the word.

'Blast six artists into infinity?'

'Give you all a fighting chance of staying in London and making a living. I've had a privileged life and now I've pretty much inherited a stately home. I can afford to give something back.'

'Thank you, but it would be going backwards for me. All the time I lived there I needed to open the boxes, break down the walls and take some responsibility for my own life. And now I have, or I will, as I own my past and move into my future. I had a chat with Milly earlier about how to take that leap and land on my feet.'

*Lift your head up but protect your chin with bent front legs. Rotate your tail while twisting your upper spine.*

*Lock in your hind legs while twisting the back of your body to meet the front. Stretch all four legs to absorb the impact when you hit the ground while arching your whole body to protect yourself against shock. Land. Compose yourself. Scamper on.*

I stand on the top box, focus on the goal and jump.

'I've also been talking to Lola.' His posture stiffens. 'She's sorry. For what happened all those years ago. She regrets her lack of judgement. She isn't your mum and never intended you to think she was. But at the same time, I think she enjoyed playing that role. She didn't see the question coming about payment, didn't know what to tell you. She was young and inexperienced, and her older self totally takes responsibility. You should talk to her about it.'

He prickles further. 'I've moved on too. We've both moved on.'

'Well, that's the thing actually. She hasn't. Or rather she did but wants to go back. To that house.'

'Lola's not getting her hands on my father's house.'

'I think she actually loved your dad once. And he was fond of her too, in his own weird way. I saw how he looked at her at the awards dinner. His actions didn't match his words. And you loved her – or you wouldn't have been so hurt by what happened.'

'Why are you speaking on her behalf? She's nothing to you. And the house is for sale.' Rick folds his arms and sits down on the glass desk. His watch flashes notifications.

I pause, wait, strategise and then leap again, biting at my prey.

'Don't do it for Lola. Do it for me. She's put together a

business plan and it's frankly quite awesome. She's asked me to come in with her as I've been doing her social media and we've got on really well. We'd like to run a hotel for broken humans. Offer a different kind of CBT – cat behavioural therapy. Teach people how being more like their cats can improve their lives.'

Rick shakes his head. 'The house is for sale. I already stepped in for you with the warehouse.'

'You did. You took a chance. You believed in me. You've done it several times now without me asking. Now I'm asking. Also, about Glimmer and the whole US thing, there's some stuff you should see. Your dad left an insurance policy in his safe. Lola knew the code. We were burgling you, yes, I admit it, but hopefully for a good cause. Now would probably be an ideal time to take a look at these pen drives, especially if you are about to go to America. I've brought my laptop. Can I show you?'

'Will it help you take back control of the company?' I ask, after we are done with viewing the files.

'Thanks for coming in today, Aly. But that information isn't new to me. I went through the contents of the safe just after he died and have been giving it consideration since. Juliet and I have an exit interview in a moment.' Moving to the window, his shoulders carry the weight of recent days; if Kav was here she'd ask if his man-bag is full of rocks. When he turns, his eyes drop to the patchwork miniskirt I made a few weeks ago out of a jumble sale denim haul. I'm pulling off a version of not bad today, with my hair corkscrewing olive oil curls.

A knock on the door brings Juliet. Her Calpol-coloured jacket accentuates her curves but can't soothe her personality.

'I hear you no longer have your PA. You need help packing up?' In case we are under the illusion she might lower herself to do it, she adds, 'I can divert the cleaner to this floor.'

He looks down at the cardboard box. 'Well, you see, Juliet, the thing about hot-desking is there isn't much left to pack. Most of our files are stored electronically.' He presses the space bar on my laptop to wake it. 'You remember Aly?' Juliet tries to wrinkle her brow, but her surgeon saw that action coming and blocked it months ago. 'She remembered you recently when she was going through some files of my father's.' He turns to me. 'Aly, can you wait in reception for a few minutes?'

His smile is barely there, but it's just for me.

'Now what?' I say to myself as I sit on an upturned bucket; Gnomeo, waiting for Juliet to do one. I nip to the loo where I fully enjoy the waterfall taps and Dalek hand dryer.

When I exit after brushing my teeth with my fingers, Rick's coming out of the lift. 'Sorry about the wait. I can't stay long either. I need to go to a leaving party in a few minutes. *My* leaving party.'

'It's still happening?'

'You can't stop progress.' He shrugs.

'You're not going to do anything then? About Juliet.'

'I could take your files to the board, but I can't see it achieving much. And while I didn't have a lot in common with my father, we did talk before he died. He didn't make up his sailing certificates after all; he was qualified to pilot the boat the day my mother died, and we'll never know if the accident was a freak of nature or human error but either way he took responsibility for it. And he said he has never once regretted saving me, although he never got over losing her. So I haven't the appetite for humiliating him in the grave. The New York office is Juliet's territory and she'll do a good job growing it from there. I have shares. I'll do well if the company continues to do well.'

'But she . . .'

'. . . did some morally questionable things to get ahead? My father made a career out of helping others do that so it's not exactly unheard of in this building. I've inherited property, and quite a lot of money so I have plenty of options beyond here.'

'You know most of the world still uses keys?' I say. 'Will you cope without all the swiping of doors and lifts? Oh and the world is going to be a lot less gold.'

Drawing me into a corner of reception, he fixes me with his eyes, willing me to listen. 'You brought the colour. Every time. A rainbow of it, when you came at me over and over, just being you with the crazy pink glitter spray, the dressed-up cats and the toilet roll mummifications. No one else was ever honest enough to tell me which of my ideas for Glimmer were pretentious twaddle. You called me out over and over – from the DNA coffee to the helter-skelter seats. I go on about honesty, but you blasted it like a tornado.'

'I'm actually missing the helter-skelter seats. I can't fit

my buttocks on a bucket. I was never honest though was I? I lied about everything. The twin cats, the boxes, my Instagram channel, the percentage of infinity I was really worth . . .'

'Which is more than we originally agreed. I told you we could review it after a period of time, and I'd like to offer you a house.' He takes my chin, lifts it in his steady hand and then sweeps my hair from my neck. My body is quickly overtaken by him as blood rushes to my head, and somewhere else that I'd like to gift him later. I am hyper-aware of his fingers on my skin and the diminishing space between us.

'I've rethought my attitude to presents lately. They used to give me a physical pain, here, on my neck.' I raise my hand to the back of my head.

'I can sort that.' He touches the skin lightly, in butterfly swirls.

'Now I realise gifts are about something else. They're a thank you or sometimes a please. An invitation to accept someone. And most of all they can be a gesture of love, when the words aren't there, or can't be spoken.' His eyes flash, for a fraction of a second, enough to confirm the motives for his own gift. 'Offering to buy the warehouse was putting your trust in me. You took a chance on me months ago and I let you down, but I won't again. I accept your gift. But can I be cheeky and ask to swap it? Think of it like a jumper from M&S. I love it but I'm taking it back because it's the wrong size and fit. We can run a much better cat hotel from your house in the Cotswolds. We will make it work and we will pay you rent. Or you could come in with us? Lola is going to teach and do the therapy. I'll audition the cats and do the social media. You could be the face of it. People like your face. I like your face.' I cup his jaw with my palm, taking pleasure in the smooth surface. 'Our luxury bolt-hole for broken humans and their cats will be a place to heal, take stock, listen and learn. I've learnt so much from my cats and others will too. We'll run photography courses, offer people portraits of themselves with the kitties. They can bring their own or borrow some of ours.'

A colleague walks past and touches Rick's arm. 'Good luck, sorry I can't come to the drinks party. I'm off on a gap year tomorrow.'

Leaving drinks. Of course. In a second I plunge from the hero to zero. 'Oh, I forgot. You're leaving. Going to America.' My heart stops for a moment. When it continues again, I know it'll never keep the same beat. My eyes fill and I turn away, accidentally kicking over a bucket. Those chairs are going to be hard to sell on. 'I'm sorry.' I swallow hard. 'I've been chatting batty again. You have a fab new job lined up in the States.'

'I officially resigned from Glimmer fifteen minutes ago. I'll be lucky if my watch or my pass will call the lift much beyond now. I was never going to America, although several of my colleagues are. Choose whatever property you want, and I'll gift-wrap it, but it comes with me attached, OK?'

I can barely believe it and want to punch the air, but I've already been a thousand shades of uncool. So, I slow down and put my hand on his chest. 'As I said, I've got into re-gifting lately but I'm considering keeping you.

Although I would like to examine the goods properly before I make a commitment.'

'Want to come up to my office?'

'I thought it was all about hot-desking now?'

'Then let's find a desk; after we've hijacked the drinks trolley.' He scans his watch on the blue light and flips my denim jacket open as we spill into the lift. His hands are on my waist, and under my top and there's an urgency in his eyes as he slides them upwards. When I open my eyes briefly I see several reflections of a kiss so deep and lasting it slows down time.

The newsreader is on schedule and gives us the earth-shattering news we're about to go all the way. But I'm already ahead of him, unwrapping the former CEO of Glimmer, starting with his shirt buttons, and working my way down. I only stop for a moment, to listen to the voice that reaffirms I'm no longer a catastrophe.

*Puuuuuuurrrrfect.*

# Acknowledgements

I owe a huge thanks to a small collection of people who helped bring this story to life.

Firstly, the excellent team at Embla Books, led by top-notch editor Hannah Smith who spotted its potential. I'd also like to thank my agents Caroline Michel and Laurie Robertson at Peters, Fraser & Dunlop for your enthusiasm and diligence.

The Reading Room writers in Ulverston provided me with ten years of sharing and feedback, led by the uber-creative Zosia Wand whose sharp editing skills helped me shape the narrative. Honourable mentions also go to Jilly Sumsion, Beth Broomby and David Clancy – we've surprised ourselves haven't we?

My long-time mentor Caroline Gilfillan read chapters hot off the press and was as insightful as ever. Thanks also to friends Jenny Fenhalls, Fiona Steggles, Fenella Macmillan-Clare and Sally Whittle for being early readers.

Thank you Professor Dr. G. Keith Still for the lightning education in astrophotography and Katie Steele for the veterinary advice. I am grateful to Marion Plowright for lending me your house when I needed it, and to the coffee shops of Cumbria – sorry I stayed so long!

To my RNA pals Debbie Rayner, Suzie Hull and Karen

Storey, we are more than it says on the tin, and you are a daily inspiration to me.

Thank you to Iain Pelling for making valuable introductions, Fiona Southam for years of book recommendations and my mum Mary Pelling for a lifetime of encouragement. Most of all I'd like to give my family (Stuart, Matthew, Cameron and Hannah) a big thumbs up for your endless support and offer my apologies for never being present. Oh, and Hannah, thanks for the puuuuurfect line.

A final thank you to all the cats of Instagram, and beyond, for always being yourselves.

**Kirstie Pelling** lives in South Cumbria. A professional writer and journalist, she was awarded the British Guild of Travel Writers' Travel Writer of the Year in 2016, 2018 and 2019.

Together with her husband Stuart she runs The Family Adventure Project, a twenty-year initiative and website encouraging families to enjoy the outdoors together. As part of this they have cycled more than twenty countries with their three children.

Kirstie enjoys writing poetry and was once spotted wandering the Lakeland fells dressed as Wordsworth's cloud.

# About Embla Books

Embla Books is a digital-first publisher of standout commercial adult fiction. Passionate about storytelling, the team at Embla publish books that will make you 'laugh, love, look over your shoulder and lose sleep'. Launched by Bonnier Books UK in 2021, the imprint is named after the first woman from the creation myth in Norse mythology, who was carved by the gods from a tree trunk found on the seashore – an image of the kind of creative work and crafting that writers do, and a symbol of how stories shape our lives.

Find out about some of our other books and stay in touch:

Twitter, Facebook, Instagram: @emblabooks
Newsletter: https://bit.ly/emblanewsletter

Printed in Great Britain
by Amazon

78348256R00202